Culture and Education Policy
in the American States

To our spouses:
Al, Tedi and Betty

Culture and Education Policy in the American States

Catherine Marshall
Douglas Mitchell
Frederick Wirt

 The Falmer Press

(A member of the Taylor & Francis Group)
New York • Philadelphia • London

UK   The Falmer Press, Falmer House, Barcombe, Lewes, Sussex, BN8 5DL

USA   The Falmer Press, Taylor & Francis Inc., 1900 Frost Rd, Suite 101, Bristol, PA, 19007

First published 1989

Library of Congress Cataloging-in-Publication Data

Marshall, Catherine.
    Culture and education policy in the American states/
Catherine Marshall, Douglas Mitchell, Frederick Wirt
      p.   cm.
    Includes bibliographical references.
    ISBN 1–85000–502–8. —ISBN 1–85000–503–6 (pbk.)
    1. Education and state—United States.
    2. Educational anthropology—United States.
    I. Mitchell, Douglas E.   II. Wirt, Frederick M.
    III. Title.
LC89.M227   1989
370.19′0973—dc20

British Library Cataloguing in Publication Data

Marshall, Catherine
    Culture and education policy in the American states.
    1. United States. Education. Policies of state governments
    I. Title   II. Mitchell, Douglas   III. Wirt, Frederick
    M. (Frederick Marshall), 1924–
    379.73
    ISBN 1–85000–502–8
    ISBN 1–85000–503–6 pbk

Typeset in 11/13 Bembo by
Input Typesetting Ltd, London, SW19 8DR
Printed in Great Britain by
Taylor & Francis (Printers) Ltd, Basingstoke, Hampshire

Contents

List of Tables

List of Figures

Preface

Rarely do researchers have the chance to conduct a cross-state comparative study of educational policy-making at a critical turning point. However, this book is based on such a study. In the midst of the frenetic state-level education policy-making in reaction to the crisis of confidence from *A Nation at Risk*, we were right there in six states' capitals (in Wisconsin, Illinois, California, Arizona, West Virginia, and Pennsylvania) talking with key policy-makers and devising methods for tracking the various ways in which societal values are incorporated in the policies aimed at reshaping our schools.

Rarely do scholars from different fields find ways to collaborate effectively enough to exploit the advantage of the cross-fertilization of methodologies, perspectives, audiences, literatures, personalities, and theories. However, this book is an example of such interdisciplinary work. Marshall's grounding in qualitative methodology, with perspectives from anthropology, sociology, political science, and her studies of the norms that pervade the culture of educational administration, were especially important for the analysis of policy-makers' assumptive worlds. Mitchell's early work on the stages in policy formulation and on a taxonomy of policy activity, as well as his abilities in creating instruments to elicit structured data from informal interviews, allowed us to test the theories that evolved from our first interviews. Wirt's extensive experience in linking the worlds of political scientists with education issues and structures were invaluable, especially for constructing ways to analyze the political cultures and the codes of the states. This book is, however, much more than the sum of its parts. Synthesizing a common view of the state policy system, we were challenged to go beyond merely reporting findings. We sought to bring our different perspectives to bear upon a cultural framework — to demonstrate how our methodologies and theories could document the presence of cultural pressures driving the policy world.

Team research is always both a delight and a nuisance. We were at different ends of the country; this facilitated our entry into different regions, but it exacerbated the difficulties of cross-case comparison, of comparing what works and what does not. Differences in work styles, interests, and career stages were compensated for by a shared intrigue with the policy world that energized our collective pursuit of ways to make sense of that world.

This book aims to challenge policy researchers to incorporate a cultural framework. It provides enough detail about our methods of data collection and analysis to assist future policy researchers to do just that. We hope that our instruments, methods, and our reasoning will encourage future researchers to try them in other states, at later times and even in policy areas other than education.

We are grateful to the numerous scholars who have used the frameworks and methods already — this kind of validation is reassuring. We thank the assistants, Kathleen Lynch, Peter Larsen, Elizabeth Wirt, and Paul Kavishe, who prowled the labyrinthine halls of the capitols with us to find state leaders and gather data, and we thank Sue Cato and Lynn Beck for their hard work in editing and typing the numerous drafts of this book. We wish to express gratitude to the numerous researchers whose previous work gave us a good sense of where to start and fertile concepts for data analysis. Finally, this work would have been impossible without the funds of the US Department of Education and the time of over 140 members of the policy élite of six states.

Catherine Marhall
Vanderbilt University
Nashville, TN

Douglas Mitchell
University of California
Riverside, CA

Frederick Wirt
University of Illinois
Urbana, IL

Chapter 1

A Cultural Framework for Studying State Policy

Envision West Virginia's teachers marching on the capital, pressuring the legislators to raise state-wide minimum salaries. Or watch the impassioned and the logical arguments, mixed together, in a Sacramento legislative hearing on sex education curricula. Get behind the scenes and eavesdrop on Pennsylvania's coalition of big-city lobbyists as they plot strategy for aligning the numerous senators and representatives to vote correctly to get the best funding formula for Philadelphia and Pittsburg. The activity around state-level policy formulation is dramatic, enacted through elaborate and complex interrelated processes.

How can the outsider best understand this activity in any systematic way? This book answers that question from a research project which developed methods for describing, organizing, analyzing, and predicting state education policy activity. The major focus was upon the way that values affect that policy. Energized by the heightened state activity in the 1980s, we explored the persistent questions raised about state policy by practitioners, policy-makers, reformers, scholars, and citizens, beginning with models and theories from political science, sociology, anthropology, and educational administration to frame questions. Data were drawn from six states: Wisconsin, Illinois, California, Arizona, West Virginia, and Pennsylvania.[1] They were chosen to represent ranges of political cultures and regions, fiscal stress, and a variety of formal structures, (e.g., California has an elected state superintendent of schools and a constitution that permits referenda; West Virginia's legislature meets only sixty days per year; Illinois' School Problems Commission is an atypical arm of governance). Some of the data were drawn from documents and observation, but most came from interviews with the key policy actors in each state.[2]

Originally the purposes were to develop a taxonomy of policy variables and then to demonstrate how policy choices are affected by background variables, such as different political cultures, policy systems, and power and influence structures. As researchers, we wanted to demonstrate a method for combining the strengths of comparative case studies with more focused

theory-based data collection and multivariate analysis. The results were excit-
ing, because as we sought understandings about the influence of values on
policy, we gradually realized that we were trying to understand the American
culture. We were exploring and tracking how values become forces that
influence policy; we were identifying the state policy system interactions,
disputes, and transactions which are the more explicit expressions of cultural
values (that usually are implicit). Furthermore, we were developing operational definitions and methods for tracking the cultural values that are transformed into policy action.

This chapter first outlines the historical evolution of state involvement
in education, then sets out a cultural paradigm that provides a framework
for understanding state politics. Then it identifies the persistent unanswered
questions about education policy systems. This book is our effort to use that
paradigm and to provide answers to those questions.

The State Level as the Focal Point for Education Policy

We study the states because that is where education is anchored and thrives.
The United States Constitution leaves to the states the power and responsibility to decide whether and how to set up an education system. In early US
history, schools were supported by the community, or education was private
and tutorial for the children of the wealthy (Tyack, 1967). The movement
for public education came from many forces, from those who wished to
control the problem of 'hordes' of seemingly unmanageable immigrants to
those who espoused an educated citizenry as the keystone of democracy
(Tyack, 1967; Katz, 1971). For a half-century after 1850 state policy activity
began, focused primarily on providing rules to guide localities in their public
education efforts (Katz, 1971; Tyack, 1967; Downs, 1974).

However, for several reasons states were not seen by all as the appropriate
or the best governmental level for making education policy. In the late 1800s
states were viewed as corrupt and unrepresentative (Mitchell, 1981), hardly
the place for deciding matters so close to the family. Since the dollars for
education came from the local property tax, it was assumed — and tradition
made it so — that the control should be at the local level. New state constitutions and reforms improved state legislatures, but they did not take on the
challenge of education policy issues.

Early this century there were signs of control — or at least financial
subsidy — from other levels. Federal vocational education law and tighter
state control over rural consolidation around World War I were the first
indications that local schooling could not do the job alone. For example,
'progressive education' sponsors got new ideas about curriculum and teacher
training into practice through state law in the 1920s and 1930s. After World
War II federal dollars and federal agencies multiplied for many policy services.
The Cold War stimulated fear into a federal drive to improve the local
education system in the National Defense Education Act, especially in its

math and science programs. Other issues stimulated other governmental concerns, such as curriculum and desegregation (Ravitch, 1983). From just the impetus of desegregation through the Kennedy and Johnson years, social agencies like schools became the recipients and agents for the federal monies to make education equitable, productive, and efficient. Court decisions at state and federal levels solidified the equity demands (McCarthy and Deignan, 1982).

Reaction against some elements of such change naturally occurred. In the 1970s taxpayers revolted against the local property tax burden that paid the burgeoning costs of schooling and other social programs. As a result, states took on a larger share of these costs. For example, California's Proposition 13 in 1978 resulted in a transfer of the responsibility from the local to the state level for funding and initiative in education. In 1981 President Ronald Reagan began to undo the federal programs for education by trying to dissolve the US Department of Education and by giving 'block grants' and responsibility for education back to the states (Verstegen, 1988; Astuto and Clark, 1986).

In 1983, when the federal government was devolving its policy responsibilities to state, local, and charitable organizations, *A Nation at Risk* caused a furor that stimulated more state reforms. It obliged someone to do something about schools, but it left the decision-making to state policy actors. They would have to decide how to combine the federal legislative and judicial mandates with the state-specific concerns and how to energize the local districts to implement these mandates and concerns at the local level.

The Great Society influx of federal monies in the 1960s increased the power and expertise of state departments of education (Murphy, 1976), especially with Title VI, designed to strengthen state education agencies (SEAs). *A Nation at Risk* obliged states to pay attention to education, so many governors and legislators, who once had focused only on school finance (Campbell and Mazzoni, 1976), were mandating homework, specifying programs for training and certifying teachers, and generally getting their feet wet and their hands dirty in making education policy. The state courts also consistently reasserted their power over policy. For example, when state education funding failed to provide equity, the courts intervened. By the mid-1980s states were the prime source of education policy initiatives.

These fluctuations have affected educational professionals as well as the various policy actors. A recurrent question throughout history has been the governance role of the professionals. From the early building of the professional model of schools, professionals have vied for the right to decide how the education system should be managed (Cremin, 1961; Callahan, 1962). For a long time educational administrators successfully promulgated the myth that education and politics were separate and that the school system should be managed by neutral, but technically competent, administrators (Tyack, 1974). But critics have noted that the very structure of the school organization contains implicit political agendas (Popkewitz, 1987; Katz, 1971; Marshall, 1989); and teachers' political action committees have exercised increasing and explicit influence in state and national elections. So professional control has been a constant theme in US educational history.

Historically these contentions over who should govern schooling have affected education, with power shifting among educators, federal agencies, localities, and states. In the 1980s demands for action fell on the state policy actors and agencies. They had been strengthened by previous experience with federal programs, directed by Reagan's 'new federalism', and stimulated by the demand for reform in *A Nation at Risk*. All of these changes mean that there is a great need to understand the state policy system, for it is the arena with the greatest capacity and responsibility for reforming education.

However, scholars have been frustrated in trying to understand state education policy in any comprehensive fashion. Their methods, models, and theories have not adequately encompassed what William James called 'the buzzing, booming confusion of reality' of this field. Clearly there are many questions about the interrelationships among governmental structures, values, policy choices, and culture in the American states that affect what occurs in states' education policy-making. It is possible to encompass much of this diversity by use of a cultural paradigm that focuses centrally upon how cultural values enter into the structure of policy-making in states. We show how, as Garms, Guthrie, and Pierce (1978, p. 12) said, 'the outcomes of public policy can be predicted to some extent by careful examination of the cultural system in which they are made.'

A Cultural Paradigm for Understanding Policy Action

Thousands of *facts* about education policy exist: budget numbers, lists of organizations and coalitions, and charts depicting the states' progress in reforms. However, there is no usable, encompassing theory for explaining them. Long ago Easton set out the problem: 'in and of themselves facts do not enable us to explain or understand an event. Facts must be ordered in some way so that we can see their connection' (Easton, 1953, p. 4). What is needed is a theory that encompasses the facts so that we may explain, analyze, and predict the 'confusion of reality'. Theories about policy have emphasized structure, inputs, outputs, and roles. But in this book we shift our thinking toward a cultural paradigm, emphasizing the various ways values are manifested in the policy arena, seeking methods to understand the phenomena culturally. Like the cultural anthropologist, we seek to understand the 'cognitive organization of material phenomena' (Tyler, 1969, p. 3), to identify the phenomena that are significant in the culture, and to understand how participants organize these phenomena.

The lenses from a cultural paradigm focus on cultural views and meanings held by actors and ways these drive the policy system, both its processes and results. Culture refers to distinctive patterns of behavior, such as ways of eating, expressing affection, reacting to death, and so on. 'Culture is expressed by these patterns of behavior; the patterns reflect the codes or rules that guide how people behave — how they speak, make love, wage war, greet strangers . . . ' (Edgerton and Langness, 1974, p. 1).

To study culture, one must study systems of meaning, because 'systems of meaning constitute culture' (Spradley, 1979, p. 5). A cultural paradigm leads one to raise certain questions about meaning and behavior in patterns associated with policy-making:

1 What are the meanings associated with the formal offices, rules, and ritualized behaviors in policy-making?
2 What are the informal institutions, rules, and processes for gaining power and influence, namely, the right to decide which ideas, opinions, and values will guide behavior?
3 Is there an order to the policy activity that fits with the cognitive maps of policy-makers and is useful to the policy analyst tracking policy activity?
4 What are the sources of values? How do policy actors represent the values of their culture?
5 What is valued, that is, what preferences dominate behavior and activities, and how are preferences fashioned into real policy which will then authoritatively guide behaviors, attitudes, and actions toward these preferences?
6 How can we understand the meaning of the cultural forces that persist over time and the artifacts left behind from previous activity?

The paradigm has two central propositions: (a) culture shapes institutions and traditions, and (b) culture is reflected in written and unwritten codes of behavior. Therefore, institutions like governorships, executive agencies, political parties, or labor unions are the cultural stage set built by the prior and present understandings of culture held by policy actors.

On that stage set exists a subculture — that of the policy-makers, who are authorized and empowered to reflect societal goals when they make policy, but who are also constrained by the rules of their subculture. Within the subculture of the state capital, policy actors' behaviors are influenced by their socialization there. They develop shared understandings that are cognitive and affective screens that constrain their actions and refine their beliefs. This subculture teaches them, for example, that certain values are more important, that certain policy actors' power must not be directly challenged (as explained in chapter 2). In this subculture, power and influence are the coveted commodities so that policy-makers' interactions are guided by the drive for power. Those with the most power are those who are best able to have their values incorporated in policy. Also, as their ideas become state policy, they are the ones whose concerns and priorities will guide the actions of educators. Chapter 2 focuses on the first two questions raised by the cultural paradigm. It describes the power, influence structures, and rules that guide behavior in this state policy-making subculture.

The ongoing activity of the policy actors is to transform cultural values into policy — to allocate values. To track that transformation, one can identify the policies getting attention and the values that dominate the choices. The new statutes and budgets are the concrete outcomes of values transformed into policy. Chapters 3 and 4 demonstrate a taxonomy for organizing and tracking the cultural values in policy activity.

The purposes and activities of the political system cohere around the need to formulate and implement social policy. Easton (1953) provided the seminal notion of policy-making as the authoritative allocation of values and resources for a society. A policy 'consists of a web of decisions and actions that allocates values' (Easton, 1953, p. 130). The outcome of the activity and interaction in state capitals is public policy, found in codes, regulations, and monies to be distributed. A policy, then, is a set of values expressed in words, issued with authority, and reinforced with power (often money or penalties) in order to induce a shift toward these values.

In state capitals, when policies are formulated to change education systems, the values of *people* (elected or appointed to represent the values of particular groups) are transformed into a set of statements (policy) about the way things *must be done.* We can learn a great deal about a culture by understanding those values, by understanding the iterative process through which they are formed and reinforced, and by understanding the ways in which values are built into policy. However, these values and the processes are not neatly arranged and ordered for us to observe. A system is needed to make order and to track values, a system that is derived from real-world activity but is abstract enough to encompass all of the ways that values are transformed into policy. Chapters 3 and 4 present a theoretical taxonomy and demonstrate its efficacy for tracking the ways by which values are incorporated in education policy.

The religious, social, and ethnic values of those who populated a state have also evolved to contribute to the state's political culture. Chapter 5 demonstrates a method for using the lens of political culture to understand the meaning of persistent cultural forces. Finally, values are carried from the past in the accepted history, the traditions, rules, and structures of institutions (e.g., political parties, churches, schools, bureaucracies). These values affected those who wrote the state constitution and all the extant statutes, codes, and regulations. The education codes, those voluminous books that tell school boards and superintendents what they can and cannot do, reflect cultural agreements of the past that were arrived at through earlier policy-making. Chapter 6 will focus on this aspect of culture — the codes as ways of thinking about values. Chapter 6 demonstrates a method for tracking the cultural values in education codes.

The cultural paradigm's emphasis on patterns, values, and rules of behavior and on understanding the role of power and influence points to a view of policy-making as the way that cultural values are authorized and confirmed. As we apply the cultural questions to the activity, the institutions, and the artifacts of state policy systems, a model emerges. The model of the cultural paradigm, shown in figure 1.1, calls attention to the various sources and manifestations of values. This model suggests how culture remains stable even though it is continuously undergoing transformation. As new policy choices emerge (for reform, innovation, or restructuring), they become in time a part of the values background and historical context.

Figure 1.1   A Model of a Cultural Paradigm as a Way of Understanding the Public Policy System (derived from the study of state education policy-making)

Cultural Variables Affecting Policy	The Subculture of the State Capital	Policy: The Cultural Values Choices
Historical 'facts':	Policy-makers' shared understandings about:	Policy attention
Constitutions		Values priorities
Existing statutes and codes	1. what is desirable in their political culture	Policy choices
Political practices	2. policy alternatives available to them	New codes and regulations
Institutions	3. policy priorities (individual and generalized)	Budgets
Political culture	4. power and influence of different groups	
	5. assumptive worlds	
	6. values (individual and generalized)	

We are quite conscious about not only our paradigm but also its utilities. A paradigm influences the kinds of questions asked, the 'fit' of theory and evidence, and the relevance and validity of facts and methodologies. Our cultural paradigm guides us to ask questions about the meaning of institutions, rituals of behavior, and values. In chapter 7 we draw together major findings in the book to demonstrate the validity of their meanings that emerge in a structural anthropology. As cultures involve values, these must conflict due to differences in meanings, or polarities. The struggle over these polarities underlies any cultural explanation of American education policy.

The Persistent Questions about State Education Policy-making

Educators, citizens, politicians, and scholars persistently ask questions about the meaning of the activity in state education policy-making. The questions range from 'Who's in charge?' to 'How does what we're doing compare to other states?' to 'Can I expect to get anything good out of the policy activity?' This section discusses the persistent questions as a way of framing the political aspects of this activity which pervade a diverse system.

How Do History and Tradition Affect Policy-making?

In the American federal system each state has its own constitution and structures for administering public education, and the result is a diverse set of requirements for school services that are commonly offered in all states. For example, teachers and administrators certified in Alabama cannot automatically assume they can be teachers and administrators in California. Textbook agents travelling from state to state will encounter quite different laws, customs, finance systems, procedures, and beliefs about who should choose curriculum materials. California elects its chief state school officer (CSSO), but in most stages the CSSO is appointed by the governor or state board. West Virginia's legislature meets only sixty days per year, leaving most policy responsibility to the state board and department of education. Two persistent questions arise from such differences. Empirically, why do states develop different systems and policies? Normatively, is there a system that works best?

A beginning to answers lies in the fact that states have distinguishable political cultures, developed from the influence of their histories. They differ in their regional geography, migration patterns and resultant demography, and value orientations toward the role of government (Elazar, 1984). Chapter 5 shows that political culture in each state is a potent force shaping the institutions of government and bureaucracy, the meaning of politics, and the value of participation in government. Chapter 2 identifies systems of meaning that exist in the subculture that develops in each state capital. The 'best' system for each state seems to be the very one which evolved as it was shaped by its own culture; and the 'best' policies are those that fit its own value system and tradition. In short, a system and policies that do not serve the culture cannot, by definition, be 'best'.

How Do Policy Actors Gain Power?

The question of who has real power arises in all the states. Within the state, what is the power of the federal government? Of the judiciary? Who takes the initiative in, and so has the power to shape, education policy? Are they governors, state boards, interest group coalitions, or bureaucracies? How do competing agencies, officers, interest groups, and individuals gain power and influence to decide which values should prevail in policy?

Previous researchers have developed models for understanding facets of power in state education. Early on Iannaccone (1967) focused on interest groups' effects on the education policy system, theorizing that such groups evolve through stages that result in increasing coalescing in order to exercise power. Campbell and Mazzoni (1976) later examined the power sources and effectiveness of education policy actors in twelve states. Even later Rosenthal and Fuhrman (1981) used case studies of six states to provide rich descriptions of the interplay among policy actors. In these studies, who governs, that is, whose values are incorporated into policy, is contingent on the changing influence of government officials, interest groups and coalitions, and bureaucracies.

While the 'who governs' issue is influenced by outside pressures, like federal programs and national reports, it is the internal state policy culture that much more often determines this issue, as chapter 2 demonstrates. We will show that some commonalities exist among the states in the hierarchy of influence; the legislature as a whole and its education committees and staffs are everywhere in the highest rung. But each state has its individualized hierarchy. In one state the governor ranks highest; in another teachers' organizations; and in another the courts.

Chapter 2's report on influence rankings is our attempt to answer the question, 'who governs'. Power and influence ratings do fluctuate, but the chapter shows the importance of knowing the individual state's power structures as a way of understanding the subculture of state capitals. Those who live in these worlds know that they must live by unstated rules if they are to gain and maintain influence. Chapter 2 leads us to expand the question of 'who governs' by asking another pervasive query — by what rules do they govern?

What Are the Real Rules of Policy-making?

In senior high school most of us were treated to a course on civics, a unit on government. This invariably included a diagram on 'How a Bill Becomes a Law' and perhaps a local legislator as a guest speaker. People in the arena of politics learn that the real story is not told in these formal and public presentations. The complex and relatively closed culture of policy-making requires particular ways of operating. It is actually a subculture, entered by only a few policy actors who are socialized to the rules before entering it, all with the goal of gaining policy influence.

Role theory has guided one strand of analysis of such behavior in the legislative subculture. A quarter-century ago Wahlke, Buchanan and Ferguson (1962) identified the roles and 'rules of the game' that guide the interactions among state legislators, mapping networks and strategies through which policy action occurs. Others have followed that tradition in the Congress (Barber, 1965; Fenno, 1973; Smallwood, 1976), trying to understand how policy-makers learn to understand their own world. More recently Muir (1982) used the metaphor of schooling to understand how legislators get 'a first-rate political education' (p. 180) that disciplines them for public service through their participation in the state legislature. In doing so, he attacks Mayhew's (1974) assumption that congressional legislators are motivated most by the external forces concerning re-election.

In our research we asked insiders to describe how education policy is actually made. What emerged from their stories was a set of understandings drawn from their points of view about the interplay between the formal requirements and the informal understandings about how things are done within each capital subculture.

Special state conditions affect these understandings of policy-making regarding which state policy actors are socialized within that subculture.

This socialization constrains their proposals. For example, in Arizona policies involving minority issues must be dealt with indirectly. The melting pot approach will not work there. In Illinois Chicago's needs, in education or other state services, are a primary consideration shaping all policy. In Wisconsin a passion for quality and equity or for honesty and openness pervades all school policy formulations. Policy actors in these states can anticipate difficulty, perhaps even scorn and ridicule from their peers, if they propose policies that run counter to these understandings.

Chapter 2 delineates these 'assumptive worlds' — the understandings of the rules among those who participate in state education policy-making. This cultural approach also expands political socialization theory by demonstrating that, among policy élites, a particular set of rules must be learned in order to work in the culture of state education politics. We believe that these are new contributions to theory and methodology which use anthropological and linguistic analysis to discover these assumptive worlds of policy-makers.

Can Policy Activity Be Tracked?

The plethora of state school policies invites analytical schemes that permit categorization of reality in order to explain a policy issue. So a continuing question, applicable among all state policy systems, is whether school policy can be 'tracked' in some systematic fashion. For example, the study of education especially focusing on the state emerged as a field with Bailey, Frost, Marsh, and Wood (1962) exploring which state structures and conditions lead to more expenditures for education. There is a long scholarly tradition of tracking inputs and outputs, often with a normative bias toward finding ways to increase state school funding. This tradition has been greatly enhanced by the new methods for describing and measuring the expectations citizens have for their schools. This is most evident recently in the National Education Association's and the Council of Chief State School Officers' charts of inputs and, starting in 1984, the federal government's 'Wall Chart' of the inputs and outputs of each state's education system (Ginzburg, Noell, and Plisko, 1988).

This is a readily usable method of comparing education policy among states. Similarly one finds charts showing what each state is doing in a particular reform issue. This approach provides a simple answer to the problem of tracking and organizing state education policy action. But as H. L. Mencken once noted, 'For every complex question there's a simple answer, and it is wrong.' Charts and checklists do not capture the differences in goals, budgets, meanings, and contexts of each state's policies. How, for example, can one differentiate between 'school improvement programs' and 'effective schools projects'? After all, policy is embedded with much more meaning than its name can express. The state context involves such background variables as political culture, recent history, current fiscal status, and hierarchies of power and influence. All these will greatly affect the state and local meanings behind a policy. Checklists too often treat the policy-making process as a kind of black box in which inputs are mysteriously transformed into outputs. They tear the life out of the process, and they rely on official statistics which, even if they are compiled in a consistent manner within states from year to year (a doubtful assumption), will not be based on common between-state definitions. As Coombs points out, 'Each state has, to some extent, its own history and its own cultural coloring of the meanings which respondents attach to the concepts we are attempting to measure and the terms we use to elicit their response' (1980, p. 20).

Another difficulty in understanding occurs because policy issue areas have not been cleanly arrayed. How does one decide what is important? How do issues relate to each other? One can quickly list dozens of education policy issues of more or less importance: student testing, teacher salaries, growth, reorganization, bureaucratization, curricular revision, vocational education, religious conflict, racial and ethnic strife, competing urban, suburban, rural interests, international competition (e.g., Sputnik), tracking, bilingual education, unionization, decentralization, access and participation in school management, and so on. However, given scarce research and documentation resources by scholars and government, which ones warrant tracking? What are the relevant questions to ask?

Finally, simple enumeration of quantifiable inputs and outputs does not capture and organize the complex and value-laden dynamics of education policy. A large literature of case studies, sometimes comparative (Rosenthal and Fuhrman, 1981; Burlingame and Geske, 1979), clearly demonstrates that knowledge does not live by budget data alone. Because measures of budgets and state effort are not simple, one cannot make simple comparisons of them among states.

Thus we are left with a rarely treated question: What are sensible and useful ways to track and compare what states are doing in education? It is fairly easy to recognize across the states common themes and issues underlying many different policy actions. But it has proven far from easy to develop a classification scheme that meets the twin requirements of a taxonomy: *exhaustive* and *mutually exclusive* classification of all policy actions. Chapter 3 presents a taxonomy, demonstrating how it allows for the organization of policy choices and actions. This chapter also demonstrates the power of the taxonomy as a theoretical tool for conceptually organizing, comparing, and tracking policy direction. To know how policies are being shaped by various social forces they must be accurately classified. Similar and dissimilar types of action have to be identified before systematic regularities associated with each can be studied. Also, from a practical perspective, the dramatic outpouring of recent state policy initiatives is threatening and confusing to many educators (Mitchell, Wirt, and Marshall, 1986). It is equally confusing to many state policy-makers who, whether they wish to or not, must resolve numerous issues and decide what proposals to give the force of law and the power of public tax money. In the absence of a basic policy taxonomy, however, neither policy sponsors nor the school personnel toward whom they are directed can predict the effects of state actions.

One answer to these questions is the development and clarification of a theoretically consistent and operationally powerful taxonomy of *state policy mechanisms* (hereafter SPMs). Our book presents a taxonomy that serves this need for a tracking method. The taxonomy is the answer to several problems. First, it enables us to track policy action over the years and across the states by providing an outline of abstract and mutually exclusive categories of state policy action. Second, it is a step in the right direction for policy researchers who wish to be useful by bringing to bear a conceptual tool in policy analysis.

Which Values Predominate?

Politics can be seen as an arena for conflict over value allocations, so another pervasive question arises among the states over the nature of these values. Besides the desire for raw power, what basic values do people pursue when they vie for control of education policy-making?

Beyond the 'who governs' question is the analyst's question: 'toward what values?' Scholars who ask what happens to policy may employ organization theory, economic models, or neo-Marxist analysis, all designed to explain who gets what and how schools relate to societal power. While we drew insights from these scholars, the cultural paradigm has led to the focus on values. So we reframe the question and try to devise methods to identify and track persistent values and value shifts that are incorporated into policy.

The fundamental and sometimes competing values for education policy are Quality, Equity, Efficiency (Garms *et al.*, 1978), and Choice. Policy-makers constantly face dilemmas when they must choose among these values. Thus a vote for standardizing the curriculum materials may increase Efficiency and Quality, but the bilingual student's opportunity to *choose* and have equity of access to the curriculum is compromised. 'An intent to achieve equality frequently decreases school efficiency . . . racial integration usually entails added transportation costs' (Garms *et al.*, 1978, p. 27).

The larger culture of America shapes how educational resources are employed, what educational goals are pursued, and what politics of education in the American states is like (Wirt and Kirst, 1989). For example, most twentieth-century Americans take for granted that education is so valuable that one's children should have as much of it as private and public resources can afford. That value has underlain the 'free public schools' concept that has educated far more of our children, in absolute or proportional numbers, than in any other nation. For almost 150 years cultural agreements around this value have engaged family and government resources in ever-increasing amounts; school expenditures are the largest for any service in every one of the fifty states, far outranking welfare costs. This value has been so strong that it could survive a divisive split over a century ago between Protestants and Roman Catholics about schooling; the valuing of free public schools prevailed.

In spite of the overarching national cultural agreements, conflicts arise from subgroups, subcultures, and partisan interests with different values. Conflicts have occurred, for example, over the appropriate curriculum. Many states agree on the value of teaching American civics, but not on whether it is the student's duty to accept uncritically what government does or to question government's use of power (Litt, 1965; Morgan, 1977). Similarly the current conflict over teaching evolution versus creationism is rooted in value differences; and, of course, *states* have different cultural values. These fragmented value demands constantly confront policy-makers who must choose among the conflicting values of citizens with different needs, priorities, and backgrounds. Policy-makers' choices, more often than not, will both *reflect* as well as *shape* the values of the culture.

This larger picture of national and state cultures of values helps in a focus upon the search for particular values amid ongoing change in educational policy. In the pursuit of a few key values, most states have changed the overall direction of their education. Broadly put, *Efficiency* was the pre-eminent educational policy goal from the 1920s until the 1950s, the 'cult of efficiency' era (Callahan, 1962; Tyack, 1974); however, at the same time there was a search for *Quality* that underlay a child-centered, or 'progressive', curriculum (Ravitch, 1983). Even as Efficiency was reaching its apogee, the dedication to social *Equity* by some Americans was expanding the base of the school system by bringing mass education to the great majority of children. Equity emerged as the dominant issue with the *Brown v. Board of Education* decisions in the mid-1950s and remained the most important problem facing education through the 1970s.

In the wake of the Sputnik launching in 1957 the issue of *Quality* rose as a major concern of state policy-makers. During the 1960s and 1970s declining test scores, lack of positive findings from major evaluation studies, concern over declining productivity in American industry, and criticism of the skill of entering college freshman and army recruits all combined to raise, in the policy debate, new *Quality* terms like 'excellence,' 'achievement', and 'competency.' Throughout these decades, though, the value of *Choice* also persisted in the form of private school options; experiments with open transfer, alternative schools and vouchers; election of boards and superintendents; referenda on bonds and levies; and direct participation of citizens in school program planning and accountability schemes. Obviously there are some tensions among these four values, witnessed by policy actors battling over policies that encompass conflicting values.

The cultural paradigm directs our attention to the role of values in this policy conflict. These four values of Efficiency, Equity, Quality, and Choice will be defined fully in later chapters. Chapter 4 provides an analysis of the values of key education policy-makers in the 1980s. Chapter 5 demonstrates a method for measuring the cultural values of past education policy-making via content analysis of education codes and exploration of the way in which differing state political cultures produce different priorities among these four values. Chapters 4 and 5 demonstrate how these values are incorporated into policy preferences and actual policy choices of these policy-makers.

Is There a Workable Way of Understanding Policy-making?

In twenty years of studying politics of education, scholars still have not devised an approach that encompasses the reality of the world of education politics and that is experientially *useful*. Scholars have used decision-making, systems, social-psychological, and group theories to develop some coherent, albeit rough, pictures of education politics (Peterson, 1984).

How can policy research and analysis be used? The aim of much research on politics of education and policy analysis is to get a handle on the actual policy actions. But this purpose has not been achieved. Researchers do not understand enough about state education policy-making to survive in the policy subculture, even if they seek to enter it. Research is seldom used in the current spate of reform; indeed, as Boyd recently pointed out with alarm, the reforms run counter to what we *do* know about effective policy implementation (Boyd, 1987). So the question remains: how good are our ideas in the *real politique* of state policy-making? We need to find conceptual lenses that enable us to have credibility with policy-makers. We need to understand their world and to provide useful and relevant tools for analyzing it. This must be done within the canons of good scholarship.

This book develops abstract tools that are useful for policy analysis and for political analysis in tracing trends in policy action. The taxonomy *may* be useful when utilized in tracking and improving policy. We *need* it to compare policies among states in order to compare efforts, initiatives, trends, and so on. Chapter 7, placing this taxonomy in the context of theory and policy analysis, recommends its utility for tracking trends, organizing policy discussion, and building analysis and theory.

However, the taxonomy alone is a policy analysis tool and, as such, is limited to study of the policy world. It organizes phenomena by employing an overarching framework which generates the important questions about what goes into the process of making policy that leads to policy choices. But the taxonomy, while derived from the real world, does not capture the dynamic interactions and cognitive maps of policy élites. Cultural lenses add those dimensions. When one wishes to *act*, be heard, have influence, and work in policy environments, policy analysis tools are less relevant and cultural understandings are essential. Therefore, this book speaks directly out of the understandings of policy actors themselves as they understand the political culture, the power and influence systems, and the assumptive worlds within which they operate. The thinking within this cultural paradigm always brings us back to viewing the entire policy scene as the place where cultural values are made manifest in policy.

New understandings from the cultural paradigm. Reviewing and reflecting on the questions, the methodologies, and the findings in the book, chapter 7 presents and solves a puzzle. Reflecting on the array of conflicting forces that have been identified, described, measured, and tracked, chapter 7 asserts that we have discovered a fundamental truth about the American cultural structures. The cultural paradigm enables us to reframe the persistent questions about education politics; it directs us to certain concepts, guides our research methods, and, finally, provides us with the large overarching framework for making meaning of our findings. It directs us to see that the polarities and conflicts in our values are the locus of cultural meaning-making for Americans. We come to understand who we are; we construct our meanings and values through the conflictual interactions of politics. Finally, it shows how the cultural paradigm fits in the evolving theory and research on policy. It places the political, cultural, and assumptive worlds developments in a structural framework for understanding the politics of education. Chapter 7 makes the case that the cultural paradigm can encompass the insights of previous research, provide methods and frameworks for answering persistent questions, and permit us enough understanding to enter into and act upon the state policy environment.

Notes

1 The National Institute of Education funded our two-year research project, entitled 'Alternative State Policy Mechanisms for Pursuing Educational Quality, Equity, Efficiency and Choice Goals' (Mitchell, Wirt, and Marshall, 1986). The research design and instruments are included in the Appendix of this report and in our Appendices (Grant No. NIE-G-83-0138).
2 These policy actors included legislators, legislative aides, education journalists, education interest groups' representatives, governors' education advisors, chief state school officers and department of education staff.

Chapter 2

The Subculture of State Education Policy-makers

Watch the state superintendent of schools conferring with legislative staff. Follow the actions of the lobbyist for the state school boards association. Look to see whether the governor works closely with the teachers' associations. Who has power? Who governs? Who are the actors? What are the meanings of the rules and rituals? What is the purpose of their behavior? How would aspiring politicians fit in? The world of state education policy is populated with élites who were elected or appointed to maintain a certain cultural view — a preferred way of structuring schooling to achieve a preferred set of values. These élites understand the values of their culture and were elected or appointed to ensure that those values would be promoted. They enter the policy subculture with some understanding of the larger cultural context of their state's history, pressing needs, previous policies, and the particular constituency they represent. Each has been socialized, upon entering the state capital subculture, to fit within the particular understandings about power, roles, and rules of that subculture. This behavioral culture sets the broad framework in which pursuit of values in policy is carried out.

We began the exploration of state education policy culture by having these élites instruct us in their roles and rules of policy-maker behavior. Like previous observers, we saw much frenetic and intense activity, with value sets constantly in conflict. What we realized was that the purpose of this frenetic activity was to transform prevailing values into school policy always within a state capital subculture. The policy élites whose activities result in their amassing power are the ones whose values will become the policy for the state, structuring the way the schools will operate.

Identifying the Hierarchies of the Subcultures

Each policy actor enters the policy subculture with standing in an influence hierarchy, and each manipulates interactions in order to gain enough influence to be the group whose values dominate. Do policy élites recognize such a hierarchy, and how do these state hierarchies compare with each other? Answering these questions leads to more questions: how do policy actors gain and lose power; what is the game being played and what are the rules; and what do we know about policy-making as a result of examining this subculture?

Certain assumptions governed our exploration of the subculture of state capitals. We assumed that state constitutions and formal charts of power in policy-making do not portray the entire picture of influence. We also assumed tht state policy élites were well aware of the hierarchy in their own state. We generated a list of policy actors most likely to be involved in education policy-making based on previous research (Rosenthal and Fuhrman, 1981; Campbell and Mazzoni, 1976; Milstein and Jennings, 1973; Iannaccone, 1967; Wirt and Kirst, 1989; Mitchell, 1981). In interviews we asked them to identify others influential in education policy-making. This set of individuals constituted our 'state policy élite' — our key informants in each state. They informed us, first, about the hierarchy of policy influence (see Appendix E for this instrument).

The National Perspective on Power and Influence in States

Does agreement exist about a recognizable hierarchy? We found, when we aggregated the data on rankings from the six states, that respondents recognized clearly sharp differences in levels of power and influence. In fact, clusters of élites would be identified. Table 2.1 displays those data.

These were élite types with similar rankings of influence (their means had no significant difference). The members of each cluster have roughly comparable levels of influence in education policy development. Naming these clusters helps to display the meaning. For example, those élites who were always involved in education policy-making were named 'The Insiders'. Figure 2.1 demonstrates the centrality of certain groups to key education policy-making.

The Insiders

Individual states vary (sometimes markedly) but there was, nevertheless, a national picture of the rankings of power of certain élites.[1]

We labelled the most influential group in education policy-making as the Insiders. *Individual members of the legislature* have the highest ranking, on the average, across the six states; in Pennsylvania, West Virginia, Arizona, and Wisconsin they rank even higher than the legislature as a whole. This finding is consistent with a decades-old finding about the power of specialists in the legislatures. Specializing in a policy area, they guide the votes of other legislators, have the power to affect budget items, and spend their legislative careers in education committees (Wahlke, Eulau, Buchanan and Ferguson, 1962). For example, Pennsylvania policy élites identify the chairperson of the

Table 2.1   Ranking of Policy Influentials in Six States

Six-state Rank	Policy group	Group Mean★	Standard deviation	Cluster
1	Individual members of the legislature	5.85	0.98	Insiders
2	The state legislature as a whole	5.73	1.03	
3	Chief State School Officer	5.21	1.57	
4	Education interest groups combined	5.14	1.10	Near
5	Teacher organizations	5.10	1.54	Circle
6	Governor and executive staff	4.88	1.63	
7	Legislative staff	4.66	1.41	
8	State board of education★★	4.51	1.60	Far circle
9	School boards' associations	4.18	1.36	Sometime
10	Administrators' association	4.00	1.32	players
11	Courts	3.92	1.89	
12	Federal government	3.89	1.49	Often
13	Non-educator groups	3.87	1.31	forgotten
14	Lay groups	3.10	1.26	players
15	Education researcher organizations	2.66	1.48	
16	Referenda	2.13	1.64	
17	Producers of educational materials	2.11	1.20	

Notes: ★ Based on data collected from an instrument with a scale of 1–7, with seven being highest.
★★ Based on Arizona, California, Illinois, Pennsylvania and West Virginia. Wisconsin has no State Board of Education.

House Education Committee as the one who is knowledgeable, interested, expert, and powerful enough to make or break education policy, having chaired the committee for twenty years.

While most legislators devote only sporadic attention to education, the *legislature as a whole*, nevertheless, ranks just *below* individual members of the legislature in influence. That result confirms the legitimacy of elective bodies in policy-making which flows from our constitutional system. Figure 2.2 graphically shows the relative ranking of all groups and the Insiders tower over the other groups.

Figure 2.1   A Model of Power and Influence in Education Policy-making

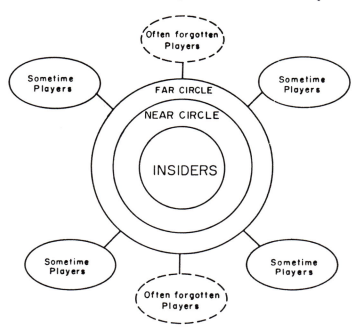

The Near Circle

Among policy actors, some make it a full-time occupation, the professionals. A group, including the *Chief State School Officer* (CSSO), the *State Department of Education (SDE), senior staff, the teachers' associations,* and '*all education interest groups combined*' have the next most influence. These actors, members of the Near Circle, are distinguished from other policy group professionals by their high influence.

The CSSO is third in influence across the six states, but there is a wide range of state rankings. In Wisconsin, with no State Board of Education (SBE), the CSSO has the highest ranking of all eighteen types of policy élites. In Pennsylvania, where the CSSO is viewed as the governor's education adviser, the CSSO ranks third, right after the governor.

It is important to remember that those who are in for the long term, such as the bureaucrats, may accrue long-term influence which is less obvious than that of legislators or governors who must show results and get attention to maintain their positions. The data show that the CSSO and SDE senior staff (the only policy group with full-time, legitimate, expert, and authoritative responsibility for managing state education policy-making) have lower power than legislators; however, that finding may be misleading.

The teachers' influence ranking is just below that of the CSSO and senior staff of the SDE. State affiliates of the American Federation of Teachers and the National Education Association are not always congruent on policy

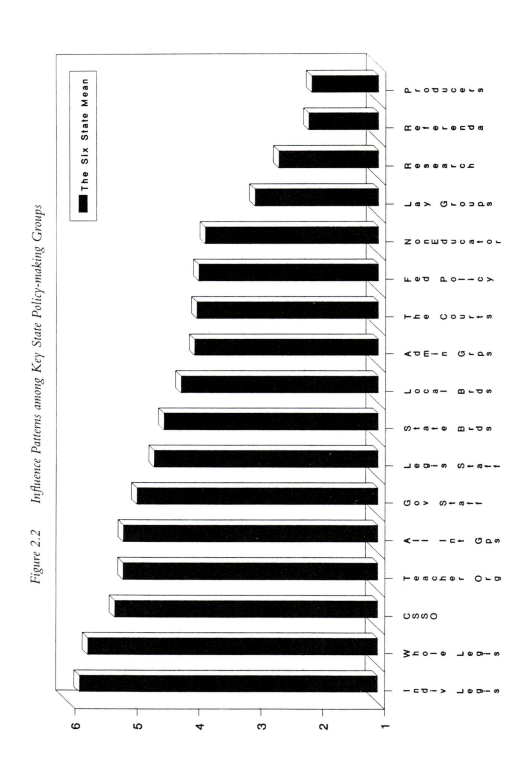

Figure 2.2   Influence Patterns among Key State Policy-making Groups

matters, but their political action committees, numerous lobbyists, and campaign funds allow them to wield high political influence.

A bit lower yet are the *governor and executive staff* whose involvement and influence were substantial enough to group them in the Near Circle. The findings confirm other studies of the governor and education. In the past governor and executive staff interest and expertise in education have been focused mainly on education finance (Campbell and Mazzoni, 1976). Constrained budgets, their rising political responsibility for education, and the pressure from interest groups have obligated all governors to pay attention to education issues in a reactive mode. Governors' proactive agenda-setting in education has become a phenomenon of the 1980s.

Finally, in the Near Circle are the *legislative staff*, just below governors but significantly higher than SBEs. Their influence increases because legislators and interest groups depend upon their expertise and information. In field work we often observed close relationships among these three.

Far Circle

The policy groups in the next set are influential but not crucial in policy-making, and so we termed them the Far Circle. The *state boards of education* have the lowest ranking of any *formal* state policy group. That status may arise because in our states (as in a majority) the governor appoints the SBE. Again there is some variation; the SBEs in Arizona and West Virginia have a rather high rank.

Sometime Players

At a level of influence significantly lower than the Far Circle lie the Sometime Players, the *state school boards' associations* and *administrators' associations*. These are policy actors and agencies that are formally involved but, by all accounts, are less influential in all six states.

Often Forgotten Players

The *courts, federal statutes*, and *non-education groups* earned the label of Often Forgotten Players by these rankings. Ranking of state and federal courts places them twelfth of the eighteen types. Court influence is construed by observers as immediate and direct, but not continuous, involvement. For example, Pennsylvanians frequently comment that the courts have been a major influence in the past but that they are no longer so powerful. Perhaps this influence is more pervasive than our data gathering instrument would tap. After all, policy-makers' choices, particularly in school finance policy, are made with clear knowledge of previous court decisions.

The influence of federal statutes is even less. From the perspectives of these key participants in policy-making, the *state* policy groups are in control and they like it that way. Non-educator interest groups such as business leaders and taxpayer groups are ranked fourteenth. Of the remaining types, *lay groups*, such as parent-teacher associations and advisory councils, are ranked fifteenth in the mean rankings in the states, while *educational researchers* are near the bottom ranking.

The lowest ranking is for *producers of education-related products* (such as textbook manufacturers and test producers). Some of our states avoid involvement in curriculum materials selection; but even in California, with a strong state policy for curriculum materials approval, producers still have the lowest ranking.

Surprises, Exploded Myths, and Intriguing Differences

There are surprises in these rankings. The myth of the power of producers of education materials is demolished — at least policy actors do not acknowledge it. Also policy actors in state capitals see federal mandates and court influence as waning in the 1980s; a similar study a decade earlier might well show greater influence. Further, policy actors see little or no influence from lay citizen groups or referenda. Also surprising — even in the era of school reform governors — governors rank *below* teacher organizations and barely above legislative staff. As for the SBE, no doubt it is an honor to be appointed, but it certainly does not signify high influence.

It is not surprising, though, that individual legislators — chairpersons mainly — dominate policy. They have higher power than the CSSO, SDE, and the SBE (actors officially assigned to education in their appointments). In democracies influence comes from being elected, and being appointed or having expertise even as a state school superintendent or a highly educated analyst of education policy cannot equal that power.

Relative Ranking of Policy Groups' Influence by State

The most intriguing finding is the wide range of rankings of each élite group in each of the six individual states. Table 2.2 displays these differences. These differences are seen when we look at each state's individual power and influence hierarchy.[2]

Why is the school boards' association ranked so low in West Virginia but high in Arizona? Why do the teachers' associations in Arizona and Pennsylvania have the lowest relative ranking in any of the state teachers' associations? Why do the CSSO/SBE policy groups rank higher in West Virginia than in any other state? Delving into these questions and puzzles, we learned a great deal about how formal power and structure are shaped differently by a history of political events and underlying cultural outlooks. The hierarchies of each state are displayed in Figures 2.3 to 2.8.

Table 2.2   Comparison of Individual States to the Six-State Rankings

Policy group	6-state rank**	AZ	WV	CA	WI	PA	IL
				States			
Individual members of legislature	1+	1	3+	2	4--	1	3
State legislature as whole	2+	2	5	1	6	4	2
CSSO	3	4	2++	7	1++	3	12--
Education interest groups combined	4	9	8	3+	5	6	4
Teacher organizations	5	12	6	4	2++	7	1++
Governor and executive staff	6	13--	9	6	3+	2++	5
Legislative staff	7	7	11	5+	9-	5++	6
State board of education	8	3++	4++	16	*	9	14--
Others	9	10	7	8	13	18	7
School boards' association	10	6	15--	11	7+	11	8
Administrators' association	11	15	12	9+	8	8+	13-
Courts	12	11	1++	10+	14	12	11
Federal policy mandates	13	8+	10++	13	11	10	9
Non-education groups	14	5++	13	12	10	13	10
Lay groups	15	14	16	15	12	14	15
Education researcher organizations	16	16	14	17	15	15	17
Referenda	17	18	18	14+	17	17	16
Production of educational materials	18	17+	17	18	16	16	18

Notes: * WI has no State Board of Education.
** ++ Ranked much higher than other states.
      + Ranked higher than other states.
      - Ranked lower than other states.
      – Ranked much lower than other states.

Some of the differences among states are statistically significant. West Virginia and Arizona rankings are particularly different from the mean of the total sample. One possible explanation (discussed in chapter 5) is that these states are examples of traditionalistic policy cultures emphasizing rule by élites in agrarian societies. We searched our case studies for further explanation of how culture shapes formal arrangements. We examined the policy-making dynamics among the key actors in each state. From that search we found that the history and the formal and informal political processes help explain the power and influence rankings. Descriptive data from two states — Arizona and California — serve to illustrate these dynamics.

Special Features in the Arizona Education Policy Context

Arizona's Insiders are legislators, the State Board, and the CSSO. Among even these a few players are most potent, often thought of in terms of their individual personalities, backgrounds, and specific interests. Our respondents provided us with a clearly differentiated set of rankings for the major actor groups as shown in Figure 2.3.

The legislature, especially its leading members, is the prime mover in

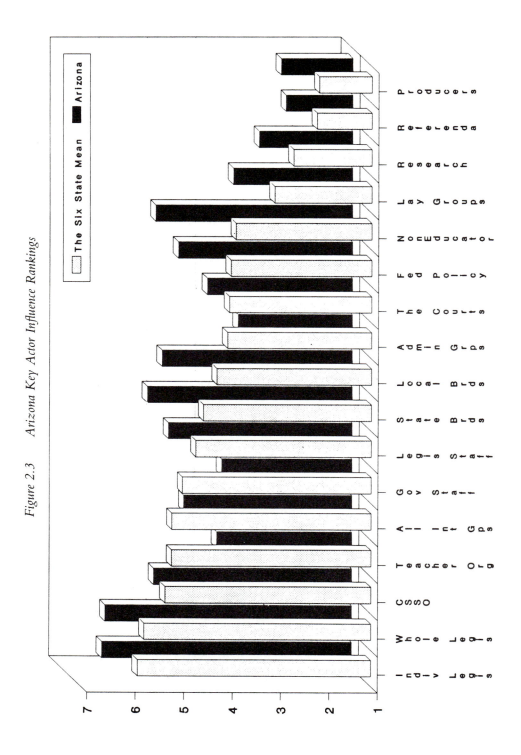

Figure 2.3   Arizona Key Actor Influence Rankings

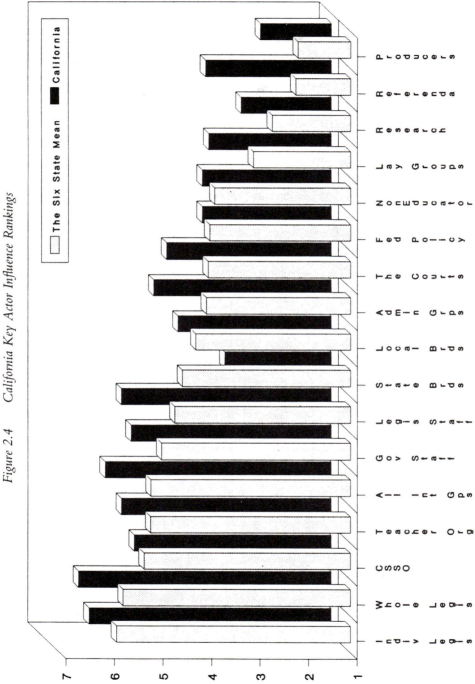

Figure 2.4   *California Key Actor Influence Rankings*

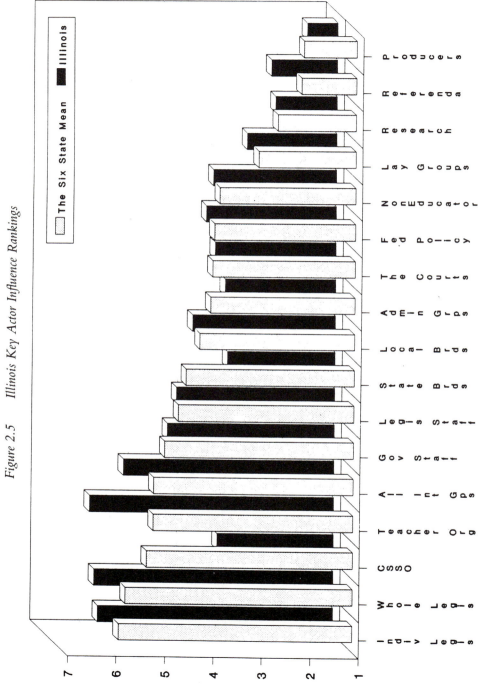

Figure 2.5   Illinois Key Actor Influence Rankings

Legend:
The Six State Mean
Illinois

Categories:
Indiv Legis, Whole Legis, CSSO, Teacher Org, All Int Grps, Gov Staff, Legis Staff, State Brd, Local Brds, Admin Grps, The Courts, Fed Policy, NonEducator, Lay Groups, Research, Referenda, Producers

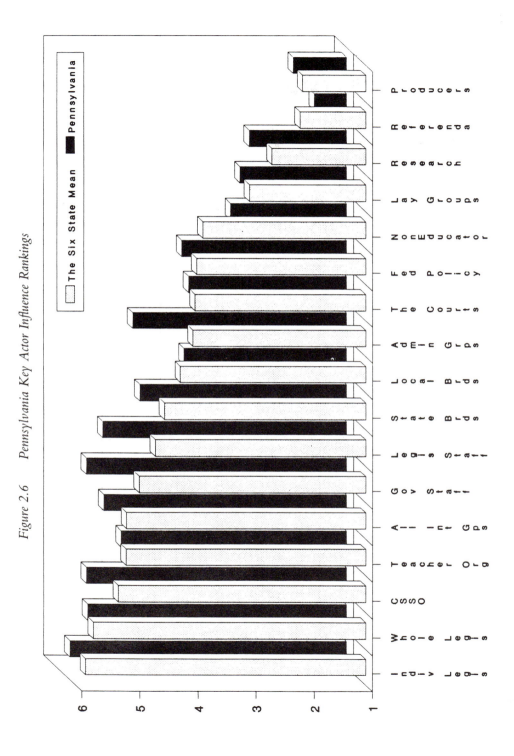

Figure 2.6   Pennsylvania Key Actor Influence Rankings

Figure 2.7   *West Virginia Key Actor Influence Rankings*

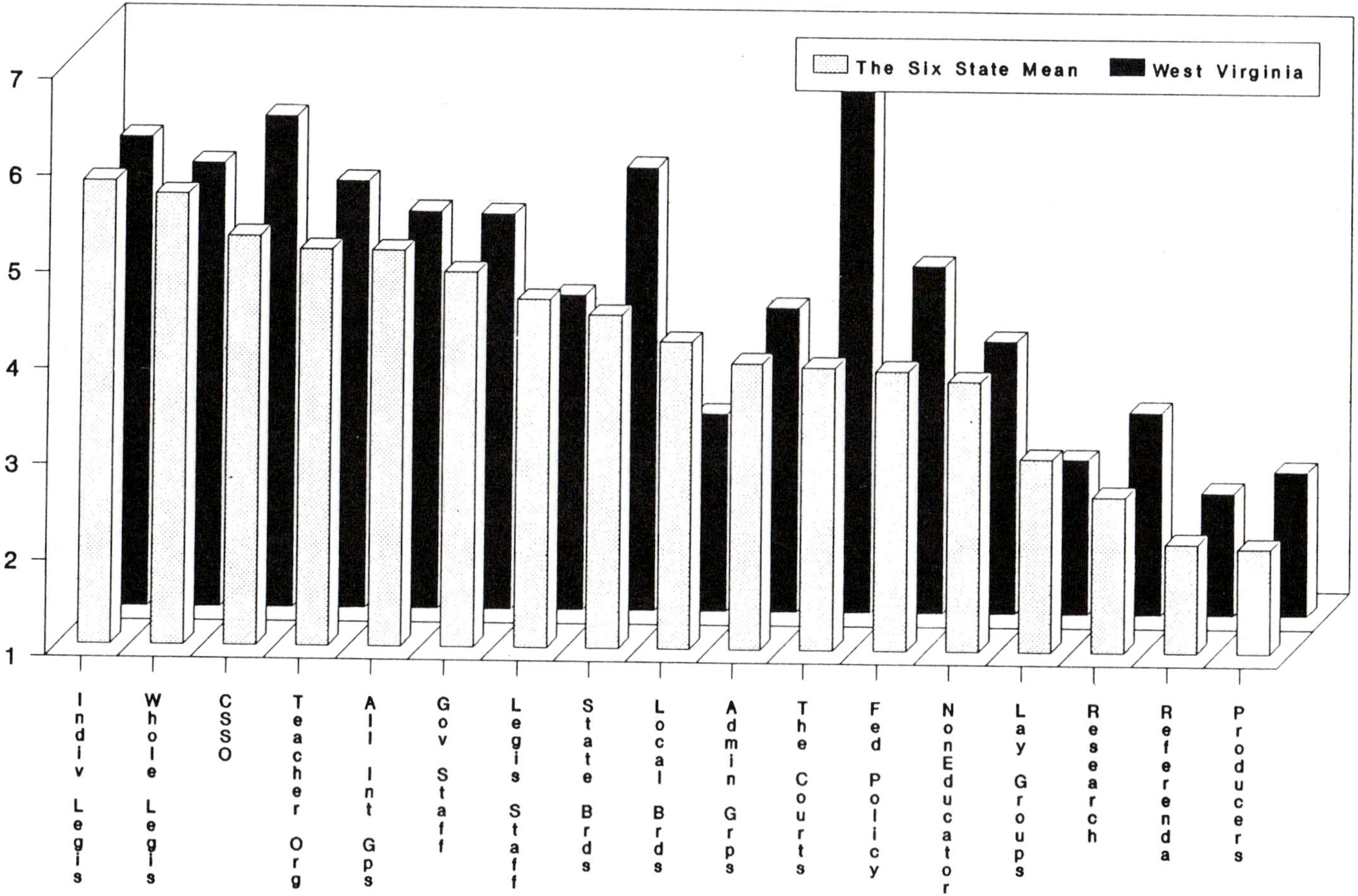

Legend:
- The Six State Mean
- West Virginia

Categories (bottom axis):
Indiv Legis, Whole Legis, CSSO, Teacher Org, All Int Gps, Gov Staff, Legis Staff, State Brds, Local Brds, Admin Grps, The Courts, Fed Policy, NonEducator, Lay Groups, Research, Referenda, Producers

Vertical axis: 1, 2, 3, 4, 5, 6, 7

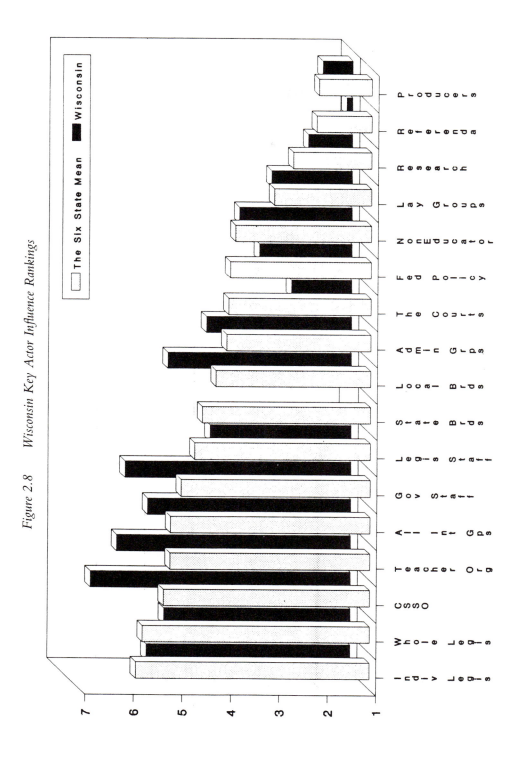

Figure 2.8   Wisconsin Key Actor Influence Rankings

education policy for the state. On a seven-point scale the legislative members' score is nearly a full point above the State Board of Education, which is ranked as the most influential non-legislative actor.

Arizonans give a significantly higher ranking to the State Board than the SBE ranking in other states. Its broad mandate from the legislature to develop programs and regulations has allowed it to pursue actively curriculum policy improvements and to adopt expansive school personnel policies such as its pilot program for extended supervision and assessment of teachers, its Centers for Excellence across the state for both pre-service and in-service training of teachers and administrators, and the Arizona Principals' Academy. The board has succeeded in bringing business and industrial interests into a coalition with key school administrators. Nearly identical in rank with the board is the vigorous and widely regarded Superintendent of Public Instruction.

Arizona's rankings differ from the other states in its ranking highly the non-educator interest groups (business leaders, taxpayer groups, etc.), because they were in the Near Circle. Our interviews identified the prestigious 'Phoenix 40' group business leaders, meeting monthly on an informal basis, and the technically competent, but less obviously powerful, Arizona Tax Payers' Association.

Among the state's education interest groups, the association of local school boards ranks higher than counterparts in other states. It possesses a well organized staff of professionals and a senior executive widely known as one who has paid close attention to state policy formation and implementation. Federal policy mandates have substantially stronger influence in state policy in Arizona than in other states. We relate this more to the general ideological conservatism of this state than to any specially strong federal intrusions into Arizona education. Also a very large part of Arizona's land area is in federal lands and Indian reservations with influence from the Bureau of Indian Affairs and federal impact aid (PL 81-874). Widely publicized problems have brought Arizona's financing for special education into line with the standards in the Education for All Handicapped Act (PL 94-142). No doubt, all of these factors heighten sensitivity to the impact of federal action on state policy.

Arizona respondents identify four groups as having less influence than do their counterparts in other states. We were not at all surprised to find teachers' organizations rank low. The Arizona Education Association is extraordinarily active in the state policy arena, but its efforts are generally unsuccessful. It uses a variety of tactics including direct lobbying, campaign contributions, highly publicized surveys of members and of the general public, and identification of key legislators and staffers to support or oppose. The organization has acquired a reputation for being tough and aggressive, but also for being 'politicized' and 'self-serving'. The latter elements in their reputation have seriously damaged their ability to influence policy. We suspect also that in traditionalistic culture teachers are viewed as being subservient to élites, so their 'uppitty' manner here touches a tender nerve of influence.

Why is the governor's influence less than elsewhere? Two factors contribute substantially to a reduction in this incumbent's (then George Babbitt) influence. First, he was seen as much more interested in non-education issues and so left little mark here. Second, he was a Democrat while the Republicans controlled both houses of the legislature; structurally, he could not do much to rate higher influence.

The general weakness of all education interest groups is quite evident. The school administrators' organization does not express the activist, reform orientation that we found in other states when we talked with teacher and school boards' association representatives.

Arizona policy-makers generally agree that education policy is directly related to the state's overall economic development process. Thus in Arizona policy is more a matter for political officials and community-based business and industry leaders than for professional educators. In short, here in a traditionalistic culture, élites are thought to have legitimate power to act — and they do.

Special Features in the Policy Context in California

In California there is a decided tendency for individual personalities to rise to prominence, overshadowing formal processes or identifiable political resources in the formation of education policy. As Figure 2.4 shows, the legislature is the prime mover in education policy matters, and major education programs are frequently known by the name of the legislator who introduced them — the Ryan Act for teacher certification, the Rodda Act for labor relations, the comprehensive Hughes-Hart Reform Act of 1983, etc. The legislature is surrounded by some of the most sophisticated, energetic, and well financed lobbyists to be found in any state.

The governor, George Deukmehian, was not noted for strong initiatives in any policy area. He did, however, have very substantial powers over the development of an executive budget and line item veto over legislative appropriations, and he gave good budgetary support of schools. The relationship between the governor and the legislature was especially complex during Deukmehian's term because of partisan struggles for the control of legislative houses.

The state superintendent, William Honig, whose ultimate influence was still being proven, was elected in a highly visible campaign emphasizing an accountability-focused 'basic education' approach to educational quality. This contrasted with the theme of innovation and equity that dominated the policies and rhetoric of Wilson Riles, his predecessor.

In California the tendency of all key policy groups to be strong and active led to policy proposals being more plentiful, heavily contested, and comprehensive than those in most other states. Only in this state do we find 500 to 700 bills on education policy topics being introduced in every legislative session. California's omnibus reform bills are typically longer and more complex than those in other states. At 290 pages, SB 813 (1983) clearly set the record for length in education policy legislation.

A close look at the mean influence ratings shown in Figure 2.4 for California suggests four special aspects of the policy influence system in this state. First, the State Board of Education drops to sixteenth rank in the California list. The board, appointed by the governor and forced to live with a popularly elected superintendent of public instruction, has little formal power. It is not as effective in the intensely political environment of this state as in others. Interview data suggest that Governor Deukmehian's predecessor, Jerry Brown, opened up the board to minority groups and women who brought less prestige and informal power to their positions.

The second point of interest in the California influence rankings is the fact that 'the state legislature as a whole' receives the top ranking, rather than the 'leading members of legislative committees'. This overall influence of the legislature taken as a whole is directly attributable to the recognition of California's strong legislative staff who are ranked fifth in California.

A third difference between California respondents and those in the other states is the strong showing of the education interest groups. In this state the school administrators and lay groups are given particularly strong ratings, raising the ranking of 'all education interest groups combined' to third place in the overall ranking. The strongest special interest groups in the state are the teacher organizations. They rank right behind the legislature and are viewed as more influential than all other groups, including the governor's office and the CSSO.

The courts and direct referenda are viewed as substantial sources of influence in this state. The courts' influence shows in the finance reform process (the *Serrano* case) and special education and labor relations policy decisions. The referendum process has been especially important in California, having produced a dramatic shift in funding from local property taxes to the state's general fund and initiated a state lottery expected to put significant new money into the schools.

Summary and Implications of Influence Rankings

It is important to focus on key findings in this six-state study. First, legislatures are the arenas where the education policy fight is carried out. The leaders lead the fights, and their staff carries much weight. Second, the strongest participants outside it are those most benefitting from its actions — all education pressure groups, especially teachers — and the single state-wide education administrator, the CSSO. Closely allied are the governors and their staff, because of their increasing concern about two matters: (1) state budgets have to be kept under control, and (2) education accounts for the single largest cost. Also governors are leading in educational innovation ideas during the 1980s. Thus the political authorities most responsible under the constitutions of the states are seen as the ones with most influence. All the others who have a continuing, or even occasional, interest in school policy usually cannot approach this degree of influence; they lack the legitimacy bestowed by the political system on the Insiders.

While the six-state sample provides a national perspective on influence, each state has its own hierarchy, shaped by history, current crises, recent power shifts, and pervasive informal rules for action. Although each shares much with the other states, each has its special context of influence where policy is made. No matter the variety of toppings, a pizza is a pizza.

It is clear that state policy élites recognize an influence hierarchy, that each state has its own hierarchy which varies from the total, and that the formal and informal policy histories help explain the differences. The differences suggest the presence of distinctive decisional systems shaped by each state's general political culture.

But we need to know more about these effects. Rosenthal (1981) notes that 'the legislative process cannot be considered in isolation from the prevailing ethos, the political ethics, and the capital community in which it operates' (p. 111). We wanted to know how the actors in each state gain (or lose) their power. We now turn to identifying the game being played and the rules of that game in the state capital's policy subculture. That analysis will demonstrate the cultural norms that shape education policy-makers' actions.

Assumptive Worlds of Education Policy-makers

In the influence hierarchies in each state capital just noted, distinctions are not static. Over particular policy issues and political events, policy actors have gained or lost influence. Some factors are constants, however. Actors' behaviors have been influenced by their own personal values and by their understanding of the policy subculture in which they operate. Values and subcultures interact. Through socialization, policy actors are taught roles and rules that will facilitate satisfaction of those values in the form of agreeable policy.

What are these rules and roles, and how can they be identified? How do they affect policy choices? We raised these questions in examining the political science concept of 'the rules of the game'. Our examination used methodology drawn from both political science and social anthropology. We also expanded upon Young's (1977) theory of assumptive worlds, that is, 'policy makers' subjective understandings of their environment' composed of 'the several intermingled elements of belief, perception, evaluation, and intention' that are 'responses to the reality' "out there"' (p. 3).

This analysis of assumptive worlds uses observational and interview data to obtain insiders' stories about how the powerful act, both in front of and behind the scenes. Such stories provide us with the understandings, values, and perceptions of what is possible and proper in policy-making. Choosing their own words, our policy élites offer open, extensive descriptions of subculture activity. The data set is replete with stories, values, assessments of personalities, groups, history, and common understandings. From these we can deduce a set of necessary questions with which all policy processes must deal.

Conceptualization of Assumptive Worlds

The focal question in this research became: What are the assumptive worlds and how do they affect the policy actors' educational policy-making in state capitals?

Political science traditions. Working in settings ranging from the Politburo to Parliament to the US Senate and using methods ranging from participant observation to survey, political scientists have identified the existence of expected patterns of behavior among policy-makers to which newcomers are socialized. The theoretical underpinnings for the research are several and complex: structural-functional analysis, role analysis, game or social choice theory, and organization theory. Case studies are the richest source of data. But Patterson (1968) critiques these approaches, saying 'so-called organizational theory has never informed legislative research very effectively . . . because it was conceived with the bureaucracy, or the firm, in mind' (p. 328).

Fenno (1978) also criticizes the bureaucratic framework of organization theory in previous research, saying that we must focus on the cognitive systems of policy actors: 'The key problem is perception' (p. xiii), that is, how policy actors see their actions and their consequences. Fenno utilized qualitative methodology to gain insiders' interpretations in the culture he was studying, using participant observation of relationships among members of the House of Representatives and their constituencies.

Lasswell, Lerner, and Rothwell (1952) report on 'social circulation' among political leaders in more theoretical terms. Matthews (1960) describes the folkways of the Senate, revealing such rules as reciprocity, apprentice behavior for freshmen senators, institutional patriotism, courtesy, and so on. He also analyzes how senators learn these rules, the functions of these folkways, and the motivations and outcomes when senators violate the folkways (for example, when senators lose effectiveness by 'going around the country demagoguing and calling their fellow senators names' (p. 99).)

To identify 'the crucial features which determine how well or poorly (legislative) functions are performed', Wahlke *et al.* (1962) interviewed legislators in four American states in order to 'inferentially construct portions of their cognitive and evaluative maps' (p. 31). They found forty-two rules of the game, such as exhibiting impersonality, respecting other members' legislative rights, and giving advance notice of a changed stand. Like those in Matthews' study, they described how some rules function to promote group cohesion and solidarity, to promote predictability of behavior within the system, and to expedite performance of legislative business. Sharkansky (1970) identifies policy 'routines'. More recently Hedlund (1985) reviews the research on organizational settings of legislatures — the environment within which the behavior occurs. He agrees with Carl Cheif (1977) that 'how things are done may well affect what is done . . . ' (p. 57).

Role theory guides another strand of analysis of role behavior. In addition to Wahlke, Eulau, Buchanan and Ferguson's (1962) identification of the roles and rules among state legislators, role theory has been used by others (Barber, 1965; Fenno, 1973; Smallwood, 1976) to understand how policy-makers themselves learn to understand their own world. For example, Muir (1982) uses the metaphor of schooling to understand how legislators get 'a first-rate political education' (p. 180) that disciplines them for public service through their participation in the legislature.

The political science traditions indicate that a focus on socialization to role orientations and rules of the policy-making game promises to get inside the thought processes and cognitive maps of policy actors in our states.

Social anthropology and sociolinguistics. We were also guided by political and social anthropological traditions 'to perceive regularities and similarities and differences in behavior, institutions and systems of behavior, and to develop therefrom correlations and principles of behavior' (Merritt, 1970, p. 200). In this tradition, policy-making can be viewed as a dramaturgy of ceremonial and ritual behavior that is regular behavior whose authority rests upon the authenticity with which it expresses key symbols and values. Thus Weatherford's (1981) *Tribes on the Hill* shows the need to understand the intricate cultural values and rules guiding behavior in the national capitol. Edelman's (1977) earlier work emphasizes the symbolism and dramaturgy in political settings which not only condition political acts, but also mold the very personalities of the actors.

While the social realities of state policy culture were the focus of this analysis, we used an analysis of language to discover unstated elements in the policy culture. We used an anthropological approach to identify these normative and cognitive bases for action as well as Glaser and Strauss' (1967) constant comparative method of analysis to reveal grounded theory (building upon and exploring beyond previous theory). In this way we saw policy-makers' talk, their choices of symbols and metaphors, and their choices of conflict-expanding or conflict-reducing strategies were also revealing their role orientations, group affiliations, and values. They also were displaying their understanding of how the policy process is affected by the control, authority, and reward systems in their policy environments. Edelman (1977) emphasizes that language is 'the key to the universe of the speaker and audience . . . It is all the more potent because it operates unconsciously for the most part, permeating perception, conceptions, and experiences' (p. 131).

Linguistic theory thus provided us insight into the world of action. Language can be a most powerful tool for embedding values and enforcing norms. Highly symbolic linguistic moves and face-to-face interaction are the ways reality and meaning are created in the policy subculture. The focus on words and language has great potential for understanding latent operational values in the cultures of policy-making. This method provides insights into actors' world views (perceptions), ways of feeling about that world (affect), and their way of wending through it in order to achieve their own ends (strategy). Power is enacted through language. Language shapes the meaning and interpretations attached to events and behaviors (Pfeffer, 1981a, 1981b). In the policy culure, where values and assumptions are necessarily being contested, language is also a tool for determining which group's definition of the emergent order prevails. Language also tells us how values are allocated in a system. Edelman (1977) alludes to such a process when he writes that with the naming and simultaneous classification of a problem 'we unconsciously establish the status and the roles of those involved with it, including their self-conceptions' (p. 29).

Linguistic theory assumes that every activity has built-in understandings about common goals and constraints. Even when in competition, policy actors exist, talk, are inspired to act, and constrain their actions and options according to unstated mutual, reciprocal understandings shared with consociates, those people who occupy the same social world (Schutz, 1958).

Language domain analysis is the most appropriate explicit methodology for discovering how people construct their world of experience from the way they talk about it (Donmoyer 1984a, 1984b). Ethnographic semantics enables us to examine thought as it is mirrored in language. Linguistic structures emerge which are keys to subjects' cognitive structures; this method is a way to 'discover a set of categories subjects themselves use to characterize signific-ant findings, as well as a means to explicate the specialized meanings partici-pants attributed to the terms they used' (Donmoyer, 1984b, pp. 25–6).

In particular, stories can reveal culture and values. As Burlingame (1983) says: 'Stories . . . tell us how power is distributed in our society. The story both creates and displays a universe of 'facts' and 'values.' We are able to ground our construction of life because the story tells us what 'is' and what 'ought' to be . . . ' (p. 2).

So we sought to uncover policy actors' assumptive worlds and to identify the categories of rules and the functions served by the rules. Our data enable us to reveal policy-makers' cognitive maps. Our data contain policy actors' stories collected in a relaxed, non-directed questioning format. The analysis explicitly focuses on policy actors' words — their modes of expression, of obfuscation, and of bias. In short, our approach was to use their utterances as a key to understanding their assumptive worlds. This provides insights into the way that their values are introduced, translated, interpreted, and mobilized within a policy system.

We operated under two assumptions about policy actors: (1) that they have to attune to the rules of their culture if they are to be successful, and (2) that they seek to gain power and influence in order to assure that their values become part of policy. Their stories reveal within each state a language and common understandings about what does and does not work in their subcul-ture. Tapping into the policy actors' words and stories, then, our analysis pursues four tasks:

1   examination of how the dominant story emerges within the assumptive worlds of policy actors;
2   discovery of how policy-makers come to agreement on their collective stories as they work toward agreement on policy;
3   identification of the functions of assumptive worlds; and
4   development of a grounded theory of policy culture based upon comparative analysis of six state policy cultures.

Our analysis reveals definite rules for the exercise of influence. These rules serve to establish and control definitions of rights and responsibilities among policy groups. The stories of policy-making illuminate how specific activities allow policy groups to gain (or lose) power. Stories also reveal shared, state-specific understandings about the cultural constraints on policy behavior and choice. These findings constitute the assumptions about operating within the policy world of education. We found that in these distinctive assumptive worlds of the states the actors share a common language about the processes, constraints, and rituals that have to be observed during policy-making. Analysis of this language shows how the assumptive worlds interact with particular policy initiatives and consequently function in the policy culture.

The Findings on Assumptive Worlds

Our analysis was generated from an intensive look at two states' data and then testing the analysis through comparison with the other six. West Virginia and Pennsylvania data provide answers to two questions: (1) What are domains of a policy-maker's assumptive world and (2) What are the functions and consequences of assumptive worlds in education policy formation?

Four domains have been identified inferentially:

1   Who has the right and responsibility to initiate policy?
2   What policy ideas are deemed unacceptable?
3   What policy mobilizing activities are deemed appropriate?
4   What are the special conditions of each state?

These domains are action guides in the policy subculture. Policy actors, to function successfully, must continuously consider them, for they generate operational principles, shared understandings about how to act and think. These domains and their operational principles are described below, with examples showing how they guide action in policy cultures. Interviews revealed the operational principles and the domains were developed as conceptual categories in building grounded theory.[3]

Domain 1: Who Has the Right and Responsibility to Initiate

In any political system there are understandings about who or what agency has authority to use the power of government. So one of the domains of policy-makers' assumptive worlds must specify who is *obliged* and who has the *right* to initiate action on policy issues. These are prescriptions for action relevant for particular policy-makers. This general domain yields a set of operational principles for education policy, which we illustrate from Pennsylvania and West Virginia.

The prescription for the CSSO role. Policy actors live within prescriptions of power and responsibility, and the most visible pinnacle administrative position in the state — the CSSO — certainly knows what can and cannot be done. For example, the Pennsylvania policy culture visibly constrained its CSSO (then Robert Wilburn), but certain role behavior on his part could overcome the constraints. As a former chief budget advisor to the governor, Wilburn had worked closely with key legislators. When the governor publicly took the initiative to set a major policy agenda for education, Wilburn sought legislative approval for it. Respected, he was viewed as having the full confidence of the governor and the ability to work with key legislators. As a result policy agenda was approved. He was viewed as 'right and proper', the sort of CSSO who could 'butt heads' over the budget at 4.00 a.m. inner-office meetings, and who understood that that was the way the 'game' should be played.

The importance of this pattern of expectations for Pennsylvania policy actors is reinforced by stories of an 'errant' CSSO who had aggressively urged new directions in education philosophy and initiated mandated reforms at the district level without adequately consulting the legislature. Instead he used educational experts and research to plan his reform. His recommendations were viewed by legislators as manipulative and out of line. In short, he was *violating* the pattern of expectations. Several legislators' words demonstrate their view that 'Bob Scanlon wasn't wanted any longer because he tried to be too activist, to do too much' (PA, 3, 11).[4] One legislator recalled this conflict by saying, 'We'd have to remind him: 'Mr Scanlon, there's a legislature!' (PA, 1, 10).[5]

In short, the CSSO's role must be carried out, not simply within the constraints of a formal constitution or law, but within the expectations of legislators who are quite willing to undermine one who takes initiative 'improperly'.

Prescription for the SDE role. Limits on agency action are fully understood in any policy culture. In education one operational principle is that SDE staff are not expected to initiate policy, to lobby directly for proposals, or to try to manipulate other policy groups. Rather they are expected only to provide service and information to interest groups, legislators, and other policy actors who *do* initiate and lobby.

For example, the SDE in Pennsylvania lost stature when its staff violated this principle. In the past legislative staff, lobbyists, and SDE staff had always met together to plan strategy. But once legislative staffers suspected that the SDE was providing false and inadequate information and statistics, sanctions were applied. Legislators and staffers refused to use SDE information. They denied it any access to policy formulation, and the SDE could no longer use the tactic of framing the issues by providing the information. Legislators actually found a clandestine way to obtain SDE data, and the legislative staff developed their own information-gathering expertise independent of the SDE.[6]

On the other hand, the SDE in West Virginia successfully maintained an image of working within the rules. As a result, it could function as a quite subtle lobbyist. In some cases it coordinated pressure groups, as one staff person explained, 'We developed pre-school and handicapped programs with the support of lobby groups. We developed a lobby for it. I should say *the people* developed a lobby' (WVA, 1, 1). A West Virginia SDE staffer described the elaborate process by which a policy thrust, over a three-year period, evolved from being just an idea to an SDE proposal to an SBE priority and, finally, to a Board regulation or legislative action. He spoke of building 'packages', and of 'feeling out the internal processes and prioritizing in relationship to what you can get.' He recalled:

> I put the Principal's Academy on my list two years ago. It came at about a ten in the SBE's priority list. People saw it and talked about it. The next year, before the budget process came in, we called in all associations and laid out what we were going to do, told them what would be on our list, and if they wanted to support it we'd appreciate it. We also involved key members of the legislature in that discussion . . . We had internal and external people and had them put it into their legislative programs. Eventually it came out high on the SBE's list. [He concluded] We [SDE] don't officially lobby (WVA, 1, 1).

This is a conscious, patient sort of control, a slow building up by the SDE staff in order to turn initiatives into policy. Those who are in for the long term — the bureaucrats — exercise a long-term power and influence as long as they work within the assumptive worlds understandings.

Boundary disputes. When multiple jurisdictions of authority exist, there always arises a boundary problem. Who may act vis-à-vis another? An operational principle develops in this conflict within the authority domain. Where authority is disputed, much of the policy activity will be a struggle for authority, not for educational reform. One example is the boundary problem between the legislature and school board. They are often the two agencies vested in a state constitution, hence they possess formally independent authority. But if the board is vested only in legislation, the legislature is the final authority.

For example, in Pennsylvania the SBE was created through legislative act. The boundaries among areas of responsibility, credit, and control of education have been contentious among the House Education Committees, the Senate Education Committees, and the State Board. James Gallagher,

House Education Committee Chair, said in early 1984, 'I tell the State Board "We created you and we could dissolve you."' Subsequently, new legislation expanded the state board to include as members the legislators who headed the education committees, including our respondent Gallagher. Through this maneuvre, legislators both took more control over the board and also headed off the competition between board and legislature. In another Pennsylvania example, legislators' suspicion that SDE regulations were remaking policy intent led to establishment of the Regulatory Review Board. This board's task was to ensure that neither executive agency nor bureaucracy could take away legislators' authority.

Always, then, some principle about control — a pecking hierarchy — is established when authority conflicts.

Variations in initiative within the legislature. The role of legislatures in policy initiatives is problematic, in contrast to the certainty of their constitutional role. That is, in the matter of initiatives, what the legislature *may* do is not always what it *will* do, because other agencies may take on this task. In this authority domain, state expectations may vary so that no operational principle is fixed.

There has been a shift emerging in the assumptive world in Pennsylvania, with the legislature increasingly taking initiatives which were once the SBE's prerogative. The struggle for new definition of school program is an example. Senators thought that the State Board should make such policy, one saying: 'I can't see the legislature standing up and deciding how much time you spend on each course, what courses to teach; I'm not sure that's our function' (PA, 1, 8). Or, as one of the Senate Education Committee Chairs said, 'I have a tendency to wait until the wrath of battle passes and then make my decision based upon the result . . . ' (PA, 1, 11).

Senators thought the SBE should take initiative. *House* Committees, by comparison, were far more activist, initiating reform while the SBE still debated. On the other hand, in West Virginia there was a common agreement that legislators should *not* get involved in curriculum or program definition. Their assumptions dictated that the state board and the SDE should have the right to initiate in these domains. A legislator explained, 'The Department of Education makes the program definition and curriculum decisions . . . I think we only *react* as a legislature' (WVA, 1, 18).

Thus there are state-specific definitions of operational principles that bind the behavior of policy actors within each state's assumptive world.

Domain 2: What Policy Ideas Are Deemed Unacceptable?

Assumptive worlds include a common understanding of another domain, what policy proposals are unacceptable in that policy culture. Many understandings are unstated, but implicit in their reported perceptions. For example, in Pennsylvania policy actors assert that they never had a court case attacking inequity in school finance because every year their state-aid formula-weightings strove to promote equity. Pennsylvania's assumptive world accepted and acted on the understanding that school finance equalization must be assured. However, in West Virginia this assumption about what was acceptable was *not* part of their policy world, which is why it required a state supreme court decision to put it on the policy agenda. While what is unacceptable may vary among states, there is an understanding of what the unacceptable is in every state. Some behavioral principles follow from it.

Policies that trample on powerful interests. This principle arises when recognizably powerful interests are directly threatened. For example, in Pennsylvania some policy actors were upset about unanticipated consequences of legislation that provided transportation of students to non-public schools. To the chagrin of those who supported the legislation in order to support Catholic schools, wealthy parents had used this transportation to send their children to exclusive private schools, some of which were located in Delaware and New Jersey. Legislators on key committees had constituents benefitting from that policy. At a strategy session, when the possibility of changing this was discussed, a legislative staffer said: 'As long as we've got those legislators from those districts there, no [reform] proposal will see the light of day' (PA, 3, 11). Given the political reality that legislators must protect the interests of their constituents, to propose such a policy would be regarded as non-rational.

Other examples arise regularly with policy proposals which hurt a state's big city, as we had in all our six states. For example, in Pennsylvania it is said, 'No matter what it is, if it's not going to help Philadelphia, then it won't fly.' In short, there is an historical acceptance of Philadelphia's special needs, backed by the fact that the Philadelphia delegation consists of thirty-six members out of 253. The same attitude, backed by equivalent power, affects Chicago in Illinois and Los Angeles in California.

Policies that lead to open defiance. Some policies that are formally already in place are deemed unacceptable because actors will not implement them for various reasons. For example, the Pennsylvania and Illinois policies that mandated state support of 50 per cent of local education costs have never been achieved. There are arguments in both places about whether the state was paying only 39 per cent or 42 per cent, but all agreed that they were not close to the required 50 per cent. Despite the common knowledge that the law is traditionally violated (in a cloud of contrary argument by violators), there have been ritual debates over it. Legislators or lobbyists supporting the 50 per cent mandate will regularly provide figures showing the state falling far below that figure; then the governor's representatives or opposed legislators will give quite different figures, but little happens to improve the figure. All this has become an operational principle that there will be a continuing discrepancy.

Policies that defy dominant traditions. Traditions vary greatly about how the state should or should not use its vested authority. In education particularly there is great difference in state control of education (Wirt, 1980). As a result, these traditions define what groups' policy interests are dominant. In West Virginia, for example, school finance equalization illustrates this assumptive world principle. Until State Supreme Court Judge Arthur Recht's finance equity decision, the state spending large amounts of money and seeking equity of access to educational services had been unthinkable. In the years before that case a few legislators had tried to work toward equalizing educational facilities and programs by altering the school-aid formula. But the court's solution—a massive reform of the tax system, re-evaluation of the property holdings in all counties (particularly those with large corporate mining holdings), and use of state power to collect and distribute monies to aid less property rich districts — was seen as outrageous. When state supreme court created such an outrageous policy, reactions were extreme. One policy actor explained, 'Recht excited anger because it required okay counties to pay for non-okay counties' (W Va, 3, 3). A senator recalled:

All the politicians screamed all of this will cost millions of dollars and we just can't afford it and it's a terrible thing that the judge could be so impractical. It's not common sense as to what can be done in education. He's coming up with all these hyper ideas for bilingual studies and paying teachers all the same! (WVA, 1, 18).

In West Virginia these policy thrusts were against the logic of the state's assumptive worlds; that such policy thrusts were commonplace in other states was irrelevant. Change required a policy actor who defied the assumptive worlds — a state supreme court judge — backed by the testimony of experts and the precedent of other states to issue such a policy. Not surprisingly the reaction of policy actors in West Virginia to the Recht decision has been slow compliance, on the one hand, and articulation of an anti-outsider sentiment, on the other hand. In his 1984 State of the State address, the governor asserted that West Virginians can make policy for schools without the intrusion of outsiders. That statement drew the loudest applause of the evening. Recht violated the West Virginia assumptive world.

Policy debates that diverge from the prevailing dominant values. A parallel operational principle exists to affect actors who challenge dominant values. Policy actors who attempt policy debate on goals that are out of fashion risk appearing ridiculous. As a result, policy debates will normally center on acceptable policy mechanisms and goals, a process that helps focus any policy discussion.

For example, the current fashionable goal in Pennsylvania during the 1980s was quality. 'The present push to raise the standards, with the state board and the legislators all trying to get their stamp on new regulations, is kind of a rush to toughness — they all want to be perceived as standing for higher quality' (PA, 1, 18). This statement acknowledges the ritual of competition for dominance in articulating the prevailing values. This competition is competition for the obvious, for no one would strive for the mediocre. This statement, though, demonstrates that the assumptive world included an agreement among dominant actors that the fundamental goal was *Quality*. Key policy actors could focus their attention on the same goal, identifying where the current game would be played, and other values would be tossed aside. Others could not successfully offer policy proposals based on competing goals that would alter this assumptive world. Those who articulated policies promoting different values sounded irrelevant, were thus unheard, and were even likely to lose power by this effort.

Domain 3: What Uses of Power in Policy-making Activities Are Appropriate?

Policy groups employ power guided by understood operational principles in the state policy culture. In general some uses of power will enhance one's influence in making policy but others will not. Successful policy actors are guided by operational principles, thus demonstrating the domain of power in action.

Know your place and cooperate with those in power. Authority systems consist of roles, each interacting with others, but often distinguished in terms of deference that combine to form patterns. Failure to observe deference patterns will block effective use of power, but working with the deference pattern will enhance effectiveness. For example, in Pennsylvania's state policy culture, the school boards association's inappropriate policy mobilizing methods are evidence of their inability to work within the assumptive worlds. As a result they have low influence. Respondents noted:

> Their lobbyist will go to our meetings, and they'll start espousing positions and issues *against* everything that we do. They were always against recodification. They always would fight us tooth and nail . . . They would try to say that it cost too much money, we're mandating too many things. They'd just like to wipe out the whole code and just do it themselves, just at the local level (PA, 1, 13).

The school boards' associations in both Pennsylvania and West Virginia were not seen as cooperative members of education interest group coalitions; consequently they had low power. The West Virginia association brought in out-of-state consultants (an affront to state experts linked to policy-makers).

On the other hand, the School Service Personnel Association exercised power in West Virginia by observing deference patterns. Walking through the capitol with the director of this 11,337-member organization, one could observe legislators' respect for him in greetings. More important, though, was the director's alliance with the coalition of all other education interest groups except the Teachers' Associations and the School Boards' Association. This association claimed that it obtained 'the best fringe benefit package in the country' (WVA, 2) through negotiating directly with the legislature. The office of the association organized by the director combined the homey presence of an office cat with the clout of full-time lawyers fighting for members' rights in court. His behavior fitted elements of this traditionalistic culture. For example, he carried his Bible and quoted pertinent passages when speaking to his members about their agendas. This group had the power to put into the state-wide school calendar a week's vacation during fall hunting season.

The success of influential interest groups exists in part because they mirror a predominant values system but also adopt perferred styles of interaction. Knowing one's place and working cooperatively combine into an operational principle that enhances groups' policy interests.

Observe all proprieties and boundaries. Knowing one's place implies knowing the boundaries of protocol or areas of responsibility. Also it means knowing that, when these are violated, there must be restitution. If one group gets out of line, the others will punish and restore the boundaries. Policy élite carry maps in their heads of the geography of influence and responsibility, and they have a vested interest in maintaining those boundaries. For example, the chair of an education committee recalled, 'The Governor called a press conference when I was in New Orleans . . . to annouce his major initiative for education. He should have known better than to do that when I was out of town' (PA, 1, 8). The chairman made it clear that legislative action would not proceed as long as such violations continued.

One implication of this operational principle is that policy actors can rarely make major innovations because these innovations, by definition, might threaten the domain of some partner in policy-making. This situation is produced by separation of power constitutions that fragment policy leadership. The deeper implication of innovations means that aware actors are constrained in their power to mobilize policy by the propriety that all relevant actors must be involved. Policy actors who behave otherwise are upsetting the rules, and they will be sanctioned.

Something for everyone. Mobilization of policy is hampered when policy actors' needs are not met or when proposals would harm their constituents or members. For proposals to advance, therefore, policy actors must be convinced that they will benefit. The consequent operational principle in the use of power involves distribution of benefits and losses among actors. A Pennslyvania CSSO explained the necessary strategy for building consensus, given the competition among education interest groups during formulation of new curriculum regulations.

> The process was interesting because no one got everything he wanted, but they [all group representatives] were able to see that no one else got everything they wanted either . . . I think some of the groups care as much about what other people are getting as what they themselves want . . . Consequently, there was very little resistance to its passage (PA, 1, 18).

Bet on the winner. In a democracy elections are the prime source for legitimately obtaining power to exercise constitutional authority. One must always support the winner of elections, chancy though the results may be. A major implication is that culture makes policy-making most successful when it is distributive. That occurs when nobody gets everything, nobody gets nothing, and everybody gets something. Unfortunately not all needed policy is distributive, for equity needs call for special resources, or redistribution, that violate this operative principle. Hence it is sometimes difficult to implement redistributive policy at all levels of government — unless an outside authority compels it (thus the Recht decision in West Virginia).

It follows that deciding who winners of legitimating elections will be — and supporting them — is an operational principle to enhance policy-making effectiveness. Campaigning for the candidate who loses is a sure way to reduce opportunities to have one's values and needs incorporated in policy. For example, the Pennsylvania teachers' association had enjoyed easy access to Governor Richard Thornburg's office in his first term, but that disappeared when it supported his challenger in the next election. When Thornburg won, the association lost the power to present its positions to the man who was becoming the most influential education policy actor in that state. Also the chairs of two West Virginia committees not only lost their chair position, they also lost staff, office, and even membership on their committee when they supported the losing candidate for governor. Their successors were relative newcomers to education issues; one said that he took the chair because nobody else wanted it among those who had campaigned for the winners. In these cases the principle of betting on the winner outweighed any logic regarding the authority of expertise.

Limit social relationships. A policy actor's formal role is overlain with his or her qualities as a human being who must necessarily engage in social relationship with other actors. The role and the social relationship can complement one another, of course, but an operational principle arises when they conflict. Wahlke *et al.*'s (1962) analysis of legislators' bonds of friendship noted that 'the political roles of a legislator, as a member of a party, an officer of the chamber, or chairman of a committee, are more compelling than his social role as a friend, a good fellow, and a dinner companion' (p. 235).

With their frequent sharing of policy campaigns, information, and work space, policy actors inevitably develop friendships. However, when policy or career interests demand abrogating these relationships, it is done with impunity and clear conscience. For example, several Pennsylvania policy actors shared ownership in a racehorse and enjoyed the camaraderie that accompanies this sport. This lent the public appearance that they were sharing information and working together in policies. However, one was surprised when his friend withheld information and took an opposing position on a policy matter. He learned that policy actors' guiding principles will usually put maintenance of a political career above maintenance of friendship. This principle follows from how political systems select their leaders. Loyalty to king overrode bonds of friendship in earlier systems, and democracy's claims are just as demanding on its elected leaders.

Staffers' constraints. The last two decades have seen the rise of staff in all legislatures and a growth in their influence, as noted earlier in this chapter. But while legislative staff are close to true power, they must work within historically set operational principles. They also have the task of ensuring that their bosses do not violate these norms and that their information and assistance are keyed into the framework of the dominant values.

For example, several key Pennsylvania legislators, even those who were education specialists, reported that their staff were the ones who really knew education policy but that they must work with legislators in gauging the perspectives of colleagues and in tracing the movement in consensus formation. Staffers cannot offer ideas and analyses that veer from that consensus. One West Virginia staffer's analysis of effective schools research was important as it tied into key legislators' consensus with SDE and SBE proposals on principals' academies. But no matter how expert, the legislative staff must carefully assess the drift of opinion as consensus forms around policy alternatives and then limit their analyses to this framework.

Work with tricks and constraints. In maneuvering to build coalitions within any political system, some ways of doing so are acceptable ('tricks'), while others are not. So one operational principle consists of a schedule of do's and don'ts appropriate to build evaluations. The schedule varies across states because different cultures define what is 'right', but some items are more similar than others. For example, West Virginia and Pennsylvania policy actors 'close their eyes' to their departments of education when they overestimate the cost of bus transportation in their budget so that the SDE can 'enjoy that flexibility' (WVA, 3, 15). Underlying this understanding among the departments' key lobbyists and legislative staff is the realization that this trick is functional in allowing the departments needed slack in dealing with the uncertainties of energy costs for transportation. Further West Virginia's budgeting processes could be upset by massive mine workers' strikes, so policy actors there have built into their budget the expectation that there will be a coal miners' strike every four years, which always reduces state revenue. Historical practices, coal miners' solidarity, and the constitutional mandate to balance the budget combine to require this familiar trick in the budgeting process. Everyone knows and accepts such stratagems in these state's policy culture.

Policy issue network sponsorship. Because no state 'is an island, alone unto itself', the presence of other states has led to intergovernmental connections which may be used in policy-making. These connections do not determine what policies result, but they are a proper use of power within the states under some conditions.

Kirst (1981) has identified the existence of policy issue networks for education whose value assumptions, ways of framing policy issues, research reports, and issue consultants have spread ideas for policy innovation among the states. A few policy actors do participate in such networks, particularly through their contacts with research institutions, universities, Education Commission of the States, National Conference of State Legislators, and the like. Policy actors use these contacts to get information on new ideas and on their state's standing on different educational measures and initiatives. Legislators' participation in Education Commission of the States and, for

West Virginia, in the Southern Regional Education Conference, has enhanced the spread of policy ideas in education by all accounts.

Policy issue networks exist for national education interest groups, but they also exist within regions. Thus a Pennsylvania teachers' association lobbyist gleans information about salary and pension policies, as well as ways of conceptualizing issues, from counterparts in other states at their regional meetings. Sharkansky (1970) identified a policy 'routine' which he labelled 'regional consolidation: copy your neighbor', but this is a very little studied aspect of the regionalization of policy ideas in state government. We suggest several elements operate on this diffusion of innovation. First, key policy actors' sponsorship is essential before outside information will be used. Such sponsorship requires perception of the importance of research and of seeking it through interstate communication. Moreover, one's position may be more important than the expertise used. This was shown in West Virginia, whose principals' academy policy was offered based on research, however, the coalition of dominant actors promoting the policy was more effective in policy mobilization than was this research. Another limit on outside information exists. Outside expertise that could challenge the power base of dominant actors is not welcome and can easily be discounted as irrelevant. In short, knowledge is often used like a hired gun, to defend dominant groups and their policy values. But the spread of certain ideas about conditions in education and about remedies for them — the nationalization of information — can in time affect those most resistant to remedy.

Limit experimentation. States are sometimes pressed to experiment with new policy ventures. While some state policy cultures are open to experimenting, others are not. What makes a difference may be the availability of resources. The operative principle is not to experiment unless it is affordable. For example, part of the assumptive worlds in West Virginia is the understanding that, with its characteristic low resources, there will be no outright experimentation in education policy. While discussing innovative ideas for policy, one legislative staffer said:

> Such things won't happen real fast because if you propose it, the first thing they'll have to know is what other states are doing it and how did it work and how much did it cost and what are the results. They won't consider it without that kind of information (WVA, 2, 21).

This comment was buttressed by an SDE senior staffer's description of the laborious process of pulling principals' academy policy through a maze of resistance from conception to implementation. In contrast, California, with its greater resources, takes great pride in being innovative and experimental.

This principle is rooted in a state's expectations of the possible and the desirable, and both stem from cultural learning about such problematic matters. State culture thus resists or encourages experimentation in recent reform initiatives (Kirst, 1981). Some reforms, though, can engulf all states, as followed *A Nation at Risk* report. But usually the bias against experimentation is another operational principle that militates against major innovating in state educators' policy systems.

Therefore, within the domain of uses of power in policy-making, certain operational principles guide policy action. Those actors who do not work within these guides are unlikely to achieve the power to have their values incorporated in policy. While there is variation in the exact form each principle takes among the states, the principles always appear in the policy culture.

Domain 4: What Special State Conditions Affect Policy-making

State policy actors often assume there are unique features of their states that shape their policy-making, and these emerge from their own accounts or stories. This belief in each state's uniqueness is a systemic quality of all states, and generates another set of operational principles.

State resources drive policy. One principle is awareness that available resources will always drive policy. More resources mean more policy options which are feasible, and less mean less. For example, West Virginia's policy actors were constantly aware that they ranked near the bottom of all states on teacher salary, dropouts, and so on. Consequently many of their policy options were offered with the justifications of reference to those state comparisons. This principle was illustrated on the walls of the House Education Committee meeting room where a huge chart, with West Virginia highlighted, showed US Department of Education statistics on inputs and outputs in the education systems of all the states. Many West Virginia policy actors cited these statistics as they explained education policy issues. In California, on the other hand, awareness of large resources meant their policy-makers could point out that they had the funds to drive many program options.

Attitude toward education. Another operational principle in the domain of special conditions is that each state has a fundamental (but often differing) belief about the importance of education. This judgment is so broadly shared within a state that it may be termed a cultural expectation. Perhaps the most intriguing data on how cultural expectations and socio-economic realities affect policy-making came in West Virginia. A legislative staffer told a widely expressed joke about West Virginia's attitude toward improvement through education. 'There's an old saying about the West Virginian who said, "I went to first grade, then I went to second grade, and by golly, by then I decided that going on to higher education was not for me!"' (WVA, 3). Many West Virginians have mixed emotions about the value of higher education since it usually results in upward mobility out of their state.

On the other hand, Wisconsin policy-makers would not understand this outlook. For them, more education, including the higher kind, is expected of citizens and expected to be funded by the state. In their moralistic culture education is the key road to self-enhancement. California also shares the expectation that more is better in education.

These implicit understandings of the limits and opportunities in state policy cultures reflect both tradition and societal realities and also provide insight into the process of value-translation. The sense of the unique features of states is part of the web of cultural meanings that shape perceptions about the possible and so modify educational policy choices that translate the possible into the actual.

The Effects of Assumptive Worlds in the Policy Cultures

We have specified the nature and consequences of four domains of action, guides to policy-making, and their attendant operational principles that constitute the assumptive worlds. Policy élites understand these principles and act in accordance. Now it is important to discuss their effects on policy-making. We believe that there are two general effects: maintaining predictability and building coalitions. Table 2.3 sets these out. The operational rules reviewed to this point will facilitate one or the other general effect.

Table 2.3   Functions of the Operational Principles of Assumptive Worlds

Action guide domains and operational principles	Maintain power and predictability	Promote cohesion
Who has the right and responsibility to initiate?		
The prescription for the CSSO role	X	
The prescription for the SDE role	X	
Legislative—SBE boundaries	X	
What policy ideas are deemed unacceptable?		
Policies that trample on powerful interests		X
Policies that lead to open defiance		X
Policies that defy tradition and dominant interests		X
Policy debates that diverge from the prevailing value		X
Untested 'unworkable' policy		X
What uses of power in policy-making activities are appropriate?		
Know your place and cooperate with the powerful	X	
Something for everyone	X	
Observe proprieties and boundaries	X	
Bet on the winner	X	
Limit social relationships	X	
Staffers' constraints	X	
Work with constraints and tricks		X
Policy issue network sponsorship		X
Limit experimentation		X
What special state conditions affect policy-making?		
Cultural characteristics		X
Geographical demographic characteristics		X

The Effect of Maintaining a Predictable Environment

'Cultures (shared values justifying social relationships) post lookouts and give warnings just as assuredly as armies post pickets' (Wildavsky, 1987b, p. 8). Cultures are durable and stable. They change slowly, and the changes seldom require veering away from a culturally stable and approved set of values and behaviors.

Order in society and predictability in human life are basic goals of all political systems in all times. Even in state policy cultures where there is an abundance of active, seething values conflicts, order and predictability are maintained by the operational rules located in two of our four domains: the right and responsibility to initiate and the using of power to achieve policy consensus. These parts of the assumptive worlds are understood and acted on by insiders in the policy arena. In an environment where the competition for control is the main game, a system must exist which defines renegade behavior. The interviews are replete with statements about what is 'proper' behavior and even more with stories about remembered violations. Policy actors' stories about their own acculturation in the policy arena are full of examples of learning from their own *faux pas*. They are upset when others violate the rules, overstep the boundaries, or fail to observe the rituals.

As a result, in the policy world there is a predictability of behavior generated by the assumptive world. Stability and satisfactory control of the policy environment occur when all involved understand what sorts of people will be allowed to share in agenda-building. There is security in knowing that the rituals of touching all bases, becoming involved, and sharing information will be observed by all effective players. Behavior that would be distressful in another setting (e.g., undermining a friend's position) is not only acceptable, but necessary, in this setting. Policy actors who do not observe such principles threaten the stability of all and risk losing their own power in the informal structure of the policy culture. Consequently maintaining predictability enhances existing power. Rules, roles, proper behavior, and boundaries are important for power maintenance. While some groups and individuals can gain power if they challenge the rules and change the culture (e.g., the courts in West Virginia), part of their new ability to maintain power is their observance of the new rules. Both the maintainers and the challengers, those enhancing and threatening predictability, seek the same goal: to have their values embodied in policy in a predictable policy culture.

The Effect of Building Cohesion

The policy culture is made up of individuals with different personal values and biographies *and* of groups with different positions, demands, and competing values. Despite such difference, policy actors do come to agreement from time to time, even if only temporarily, on a policy choice. The range of options for policy-making is theoretically infinite, but state policy actors' choices fit within a much more limited range. The assumptive world is one of the factors that limit the range of options and so focus debate within certain understood parameters. In effect, common understandings constrain policy choices to the common biases about what threatens and what enhances dominant values in a particular system.

This cohesion-building function allows a shorthand of communication among policy insiders. Dissonant ideas are not articulated, and policies that promote unfashionable values are not formulated. Cohesion-building also functions to exlude those who know only the surface language, without the deeper meaning and symbolic import. That result further facilitates policy-making by excluding people and ideas that do not fit within the values reflected in local language and stories.

Implications of Assumptive Worlds

Assumptive Worlds as Value-translators

The values and preferences that policy actors represent must be translated so that they will be recognized, included, and responded to in the policy culture. Policies must be recreated to fit within the assumptive worlds.

For example, the Pennsylvania teachers' association's preference for a state-wide minimum salary could not pass. It was not translated to fit into an assumptive world where they had lost power by betting on a loser, and in Pennsylvania a predictable brake on policy was the demand that the state pay for every cost of a state mandate to the locals. In addition, the proposal was not part of the governor's initiative at a time when he, the CSSO, and the key legislators were coalescing around quality as the understood goal, with personnel policy (not finance policy) as the appropriate approach to that goal.

On the other hand, the West Virginia School Service Personnel Association's policy positions, mobilizing, and coalitional behaviors apparently fit within the understandings of language, rules, and values in that state's policy culture. Although it was a labor association, it affiliated with key education lobbies, took an anti-collective bargaining position, and succeeded in maintaining the power to meet members' needs. This association thus translated its goals to fit successfully within assumptive worlds in West Virginia.

In such ways, then, policy actors rephrase and recreate the image and symbols — and change the content and goals — of policy preferences in order to maintain power and have their needs met. Symbols — and their language — shape perceptions of the feasible, independent of any objective criteria of need. Rather the needs to be met (short of outsiders' intrusions) are defined by what the policy culture teaches as the possible. Underlying these assumptive worlds in action are basic agreements on the nature of society of human beings. It is the difference among states about these underlying agreements that stimulates other differences which result in policy differences.

Assumptive Worlds as Barometers of Change

The action guides of assumptive worlds come to policy actors through social-ization. However, when there is a shift in the policy culture, their assumptive worlds are jarred and even upset. Such upset is revealed in stories of 'outrage-ous' behavior, 'wild' proposals, and policies that shake tradition. For example, when Pennsylvania's Governor Thornburg announced in 1983 a comprehen-sive agenda for education, he upset the hierarchy and boundaries of power and responsibility in that policy culture. Similarly the West Virginia Supreme Court decree that the legislature must equalize its children's access to quality education signalled the intrusion of new values. In these cases state policy actors had defied the assumptive worlds, and they did so with enough force and power to change the assumptive worlds. Thornburg's action signalled a new alignment which legislators, the CSSO, and other policy actors had to consider in all future policy mobilization. The court's decision forced the West Virginia policy culture to alter its values and reshape its ideas of the feasible to include equity goals tied to the state tax system. In these examples powerful actors, applying the force of formal authority, were able to upset the stable hierarchy and alter the values in the policy culture. However, less powerful actors attempting to defy the assumptive worlds would risk sanctions — loss of power and exclusion from policy deliberations.

The *Nation at Risk* report illustrates another and major outside influence that upset assumptive worlds in most states. Such national attention on the quality of education obligated formal policy actors to respond. In states where only CSSOs and legislators had formulated education policy agendas that were not challenged, governors like Thornburg had to respond. The *Risk* report contains policy proposals for controlling implementation of quality improvements (e.g., required homework, competency exams). Those pro-posals obligated policy actors in the states to demonstrate an assertive, con-trolled program of school improvement, or else, in effect, admit to constitu-ents that there was no leadership seeking excellence in education. Not for the fist time, then, national action within the federal system pushed state élites to act or lose political standing locally — particularly when the broader public desired change.

Upsets in the assumptive worlds — boundary crossing, defiance of norms, policy proposals that veer away from tradition — are indicators of significant shifts in values, power alignments, and understandings about what is possible and preferable. Assumptive worlds' changes are barometers that predict change in state policy. Policy changes arise not from objective criteria of need but from changes in assumptive worlds.

Contribution to a Cultural Theory

Predominant values and policy choices are filtered through the assumptive worlds of a state. Policy-makers make different choices of policy mechanisms

Figure 2.9   Assumptive Worlds' Fit with Other Approaches to Understanding Policy-making

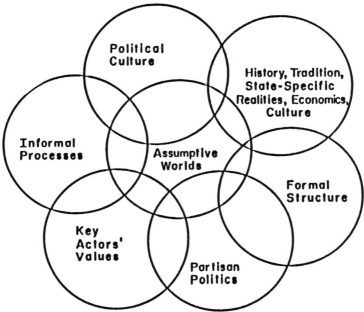

and approaches to education reform because they are working in different assumptive worlds. Having been socialized to their particular subculture, they know how to act to maintain their good standing. To maintain their power position policy actors reword, translate, and alter their positions; they modify their behaviors and constrain their preferences to work within the assumptive worlds.

Any model or theory of education policy-making must incorporate the assumptive world concept. Indeed, this concept touches and coheres the other elements of the policy-making world, as Figure 2.9 suggests.

This concept derives from and binds together the history, values and role obligations of key actors, political culture, formal structure, partisan politics, and informal processes of the policy world. The assumptive worlds are revealed by policy-makers' words and stories about policy-making, and by key actors' endorsement of these enduring cultural factors. Their socialization into the subculture of their capitals teaches them what values, behaviors, and choices are possible.

Wirt and Kirst (1989), reflecting on the varied separate research traditions for studying policy-making, said, 'As a consequence of these different approaches, what is known is much like the four blind persons who describe an elephant in terms of the particular parts touched' (p. 216). The assumptive world model provides connective tissue that pulls together various models of policy-making. A state subculture's assumptive worlds are to shape and transform values to fit with certain constants.

The focus in this chapter on the subcultures — their hierarchies and the assumptive worlds — is useful for understanding the hidden meanings behind the frenetic activity and words in state capitals. However, it leaves us with the need to find ways to track the effects of culture on specific policy choices. The next chapter tackles that problem, presenting a taxonomy of policy alternatives and enabling us to identify trends in policy priorities.

Notes

1 In all but one case mean scores for all members of each of the six cluster groups differed significantly from all members of the other five clusters (i.e., yield paired t-test probability values less than .01). Thus in each case the most influential member of the lower cluster has significantly *less* influence than the least influential member of the cluster above it. The one exception to this general rule is the separation between the three groups in the cluster we call the Near Circle (the CSSOs, teacher organizations, and the coalition of all education interest groups combined) and those in the Far Circle cluster (the governors and their executive advisors, legislative staffers, and the state boards of education). The lower two groups in the Far Circle (legislative staff and state boards of education) are ranked significantly lower than all members of the Near Circle, but the mean score for the governor and his advisors is only significantly lower than that for the CSSOs. Hence it is appropriate to think of the governor and executive staff as a transitional group, closer to the Near Circle than the legislative staff and state board, but still not among the most influential participants.

2 Detailed display of statistical data can be seen in Marshall, Mitchell, and Wirt, (1986) or Mitchell, Wirt and Marshall, (1986).

3 Ironically, the richest data were from stories of mistakes, violations of the rules, and failures to act and think within the assumed parameters in a particular policy culture.

4 To protect anonymity, subjects are given labels; first their state is identified, then the type of data collection, then the number assigned to that particular informant. Thus PA, 1, 11 means this Pennsylvania quote is from round 1 of data collection, code number is 11. W VA, 2, 22 is a West Virginia quote from round 2 of data collection, and her code number is 22. Data collected from participant observation were designated as round 3. Thus W VA, 3, 14 is West Virginia data collected during informal participant observation 3 and the person providing the datum was code number 14.

5 This CSSO initiated change using his own personal sense of what were legitimate sources of ideas rather that the assumptive world's sense of the legitimate sources of ideas.

6 By trying to manipulate other groups and 'manage' information, this SDE

staff lost power. Their violation excluded them from the coalition that had shared information and strategy with them.

Chapter 3

State Policy Mechanisms as Cultural Products

Try to compare Pennsylvania's School Improvement Program with California's. Try to identify all the states with principals' academies. A thoughtful person will realize that policies may have the same name, even focus on the same element, but still be very different. After all each came from a different culture. How can state policies be tracked, organized, and compared? This chapter answers that question.

The social relationships among state élites involved in the formation of education policy for the nation's schools were the subject of the last chapter. Attention was focused on the cultural assumptions these leaders used to orient themselves to decision-making processes and power relationships found in the statehouses of the American states. The subculture in state capitols provides action guides. But methods for organizing the products of the activities — the policy decision — are still needed. This chapter and the next examine the decisions which result from the interactions in state capitols. This chapter focuses on the immediate content of the policy deliberations undertaken by the leaders described in chapter 2. The analysis identifies and classifies common elements in school policy debates and develops a taxonomy of basic policy actions. Once the taxonomic structure of state policies has been delineated, the taxonomy is used to identify the prevailing policy choices and the values embedded in these choices. Elements of a national culture affecting policy priorities are identified, and the analysis shows how state cultural values create distinct state priorities. In chapter 4, the taxonomy is used to track the influence of individuals' values on policy choices. In chapter 5 the taxonomy helps in analyzing the relationship between political culture and policy choices. Finally, the taxonomy is used in chapter 6 to trace cultural artifacts — the codes that embody the values that dominated in earlier policy-making. Thus the taxonomy demonstrates its power as a theoretical tool for analyzing the transformation of cultural values into policy.

The cultural paradigm led us to view the activities of those in the state capital as rituals that follow certain rules and that have the purpose of creating policy. To understand this purposeful behavior we sought to develop a taxonomic framework for classifying and comparing state mechanisms supporting and controlling public education. This mirrors the efforts of anthropologists who have developed taxonomic systems to help them organize the myriad activities, norms, hierarchies, and objects in cultures.[1] A taxonomy to organize the activity state education policy cultures will assist in organizing — to know what fits where and what it means. With a taxonomy we can know what to focus on and how to track changes and differences. Policies are products of state policy culture activity. That is, they are the manufactured results of purposeful human activity — implements or instruments used by political leaders to structure and control the physical and social environment of the schools.

Viewing policies as cultural artifacts (or products) provides a framework for defining policy. This framework contrasts sharply with research work approaching the study of school policy from traditional political or economic interest theories. Political and economic interest theories fail to specify what counts as policy. As Mitchell (1985) notes, definitions of policy vary widely. In most studies the term is used without explicit definition, with the result that education policy research generally fails to produce cumulative insights or explicit tests of overall theory. Divergent cultures define policies differently and look at different facets of human behavior whenever they try to document the link between policy and action. Absence of a consistent policy definition has resulted in a failure to generate a key element in any science — a systematic taxonomy of the objects of study.

Of course, knowing that a taxonomy is important does not guarantee that one will be developed. Policy definitions are grounded in the overall analytic framework or paradigm one uses to account for human activity (Mitchell, 1985). These paradigms are, in turn, linked to underlying sets of cultural norms and presuppositions. These presuppositions reflect, as the theologian Paul Tillich (1952) reminds us, competing conceptions of the eternal human search for the Good, the True, and the Beautiful.

But the problem should not be hopelessly complex. The tradition in anthropology of identifying common elements among cultures assumes that there are discernable and limited categories for analyzing patterns of behavior across cultures. An orderly taxonomy of education policy options is possible if, as Wildavsky (1987c, p. 6) asserts, 'there are only a limited number of cultures that between them categorize most human relations.' If the variety of cultural beliefs and norms is limited, policy actors' concepts of control will be similarly limited. They will recognize only a limited number of instruments for shaping school performance. In policy actors' cognitive processes, in their policy preferences, and in their actual policy choices, the array of mechanisms and approaches to education policy should be evident. Just as anthropologists seek to identify the domains of human behavior and accompanying cognitive systems (e.g., childrearing practices or beliefs about afterlife), we should be able to identify the array of alternatives and overarching domains of education policy-making. Policy taxonomies, like the assumptive worlds used to guide decision-making activities, exist in the minds of the key actors within each state's policy-making community. In other words they are structures of thought rather than objective physical phenomena. Hence the development of a classification scheme depends on understanding how state policy-makers think about the relationship between state action and school performance.

A Taxonomy of State Control Mechanisms

In the last few years policy-makers in a number of states have undertaken what they describe as 'comprehensive' school improvement programs. These comprehensive policy initiatives are aimed at integrating into a unified strategy various combinations of fiscal, organizational, staff development, curriculum, and student assessment elements (among the most active are California, Colorado, Connecticut, Delaware, Florida, Kentucky, Maryland, Missouri, and Pennsylvania — see Odden and Dougherty, 1982; McLaughlin, 1981).

In most states recent policy initiatives have been conceived more narrowly. Reforms have been less vigorous and more focused on a narrow range of issues and activities. Student and/or teacher testing and assessment programs are the most frequent targets of these narrower program initiatives. Assessment and testing have been especially prominent in recent policy debates in Arizona, Nebraska, New Mexico, South Carolina, and Wisconsin.

Once the states with so-called 'comprehensive programs' and those following a 'testing strategy' have been identified, it is difficult to discern systematic distinctions among the myriad of other policies adopted in the name of school improvement. Even the easily recognized distinction between comprehensive school improvement programs and narrower testing and assessment policies is not very helpful if we are trying to understand why states adopt particular policies or predict whether adopted policies will be effectively implemented. 'Comprehensive programs' and 'student assessment policies' are not mutually exclusive categories: every comprehensive program has to deal with testing issues in some way, and every testing policy is part of some form of overall policy framework, even if it has been adopted piecemeal over a period of years. Moreover, the content of various comprehensive reform programs differs so much from one state to the next that it is hard to justify treating them as comparable policy mechanisms in any sense other than that they represent a bundle of policies all adopted at about the same time.

Problems in classifying states' policy action spring largely from the lack of a classification scheme — a mapping system separating different types of policy and providing a basis for comparing them. We concluded, therefore, that development of a formal taxonomy, one that would systematically classify all major policies and appropriately distinguish among them would be an invaluable contribution to the ongoing study of state policy systems. The needed taxonomy, we reasoned, might be constructed through interpretation of empirical data or by direct theoretical analysis of policy alternatives. If empirical, the taxonomy would be constructed by closely examining the similarities and differences in the way policy-makers describe existing policies and clustering them into meaningful groups based on these empirically observed characteristics. A theoretical taxonomy would be constructed by identifying a set of analytical concepts capable of describing and accounting for the ways decision-makers think about possible education policy variations. Some examples of empirical taxonomic frameworks can be found in the literature, but they tend to be neither consistently developed nor comprehensively applied (see, for example, Odden and Dougherty, 1982; McLaughlin, 1981; Berman, 1981; Mitchell, 1981; Kirst, 1981). The problem with empirically constructed taxonomies is that typically they have only instrumental value to the researchers who develop them — used as a handy means of summarizing data but not intended to meet the basic criteria of a sound taxonomic structure.

To be of lasting value a taxonomy must use classification categories that are simultaneously exhaustive (covering all elements) and mutually exclusive (allowing particular policies to be classified as belonging to one and only one category). The theoretical approach to taxonomy construction begins with this principle of exhaustive, mutually exclusive classification categories and searches for an underlying characteristic, common to all policy elements, that can serve as the basis for developing those categories.

We found three different approaches to identifying theoretical classification schemes in the literature on public policy. The first approach, illustrated in Garms, Guthrie, and Pierce (1978), distinguished taxonomic categories on the basis of the fundamental social values which they embody. These authors asserted that school finance policies can be distinguished on the basis of whether they contribute to the 'equality', 'efficiency,' or 'liberty' values that underlie all policy decisions. Herbert Kaufman (1956) originated this approach to a social value-based taxonomy of public policies. He argued that the three values of 'democratic legitimacy', 'organizational efficiency', and 'neutral technical competence' are held in constant tension in American politics — and that particular policy choices must at least implicitly embrace one of these values at the expense of the others.

Lowi's (1964) provocative work presents a second theoretical approach to taxonomy development. He emphasized the importance of looking to the economic consequences of various policy choices in order to classify them. He originated the distinction among 'distributive', 'redistributive', and 'regulatory' policies, later adding a fourth policy category, 'constituency', to this list. This taxonomic structure classifies policy actions according to their impact on the distribution of costs and benefits resulting from their enactment. Lowi's categorical scheme has been widely used. It has been especially well applied by Paul Peterson and several of his students (see, for example, Rabe and Peterson, 1982).

The third theoretical principle of classification found in the literature — and the one which we found most appropriate for this study — focuses on the basic control mechanisms available to state-level policy-makers. Mitchell and Iannaccone (1980) used this principle of classification in looking at the impact of legislative policy on school operations. They distinguished only three basic mechanisms: 'resource allocation', 'rule making', and 'ideological belief articulation'. A few years later Mitchell and Encarnation (1984) argued that the control mechanism principle could be used to distinguish among seven different state policy mechanisms. Their work became the starting point for the taxonomic structure developed in this research.

The Seven Basic Policy Mechanisms

As we set about the task of identifying the mechanism we began with the intent to identify the basic control mechanisms. We started with the Mitchell and Encarnation (1984) framework and made modifications based on our early field work.[2]

Preliminary field interviews revealed that the Mitchell and Encarnation framework was flawed in two important respects. First, one important policy domain, identified during interviews in California and West Virginia — the construction of school buildings and facilities — was missing from the original list. Follow-up interviews showed that decisions in this area were seen as important in the overall repertoire of state-level decisions by a small, but significant, group of respondents in all of our sample states. It was probably missed earlier because building and facilities decisions generally have a very low political profile and tend to change rather slowly. The second change was required when early field interviews documented the extent to which generation of education revenues is entangled with the generation of overall revenue for the states' general funds. A clear description of how this mechanism operates would require a comprehensive analysis of all state finance policies, carrying us far beyond the education arena under study. We reluctantly decided, therefore, to limit our analysis of school finance policies to those that deal with resource allocation, leaving revenue generation for later study.

Operational definitions for the identified policy variables required distinguishing between two levels or types of education policy. On a macroscale seven alternative *state policy mechanisms* or domains comprehensively differentiate among the basic themes or arenas for action. Individual policymakers tend to specialize in one or more of these domains. Moreover, decisions in one domain tend to be made with little concern for those involving the other mechanisms. The following operational definitions serve to distinguish among these seven basic state policy mechanisms in education:

1 *School finance*: controlling how education funds are distributed and how human and fiscal resources are allocated to the schools;
2 *School personnel training and certification*: controlling the conditions for getting or keeping various jobs in the school system;
3 *Student testing and assessment*: fixing the timing and consequences of testing, including subjects covered and the distribution of test data;
4 *School program definition*: controlling program planning and

accreditation or otherwise specifying what schools must teach and how long they must teach it;

5 *School organization and governance*: the assignment of authority and responsibility to various groups and individuals;

6 *Curriculum materials*: controlling the development and/or selection of textbooks and other instructional materials;

7 *School buildings and facilities*: determination of architecture, placement, and maintenance for buildings and other school facilities.

Within each of these seven domains we found that policy debates and decisions tend to focus on a relatively small number of competing *approaches* to the formulation of specific policies or programs. Each approach provides a unique mix of public resources, social values, and assignments of governing authority for dealing with problems. Across the seven mechanisms, thirty-three specific approaches were identified. In some areas alternatives were few in number and easy to identify; in others larger numbers of less well defined alternatives were found.

Thus a taxonomy for conceptually organizing and tracking policy action was developed, building on previous theory and altering it to encompass the observations and actions reported in the data. The taxonomy comfortably fitted policy actors' descriptions of their state policy system. The following sections describe the verification procedures used to test the resulting taxonomy of state policy mechanisms and alternative approaches.

Verifying the Taxonomy

Data collected during preliminary field interviews with key actors in six sample states produced clear definitions for the seven basic state policy mechanisms described above. The important question, however, was whether these categories actually applied to the cognitive processes used by policy-makers in their contemplation of optional mechanisms that might be used to shape school performance. To test the ability of the seven domains to capture the thinking of policy actors, we used the domains as the framework for a second round of interviews, this time asking four broad questions:

Question 1: How much attention is being given to each policy mechanism in your state? To assist them in answering this question, respondents were given a list of the seven policy mechanisms (see Appendix D), each accompanied by examples of several policy actions that fit the definition. They were asked to review the list carefully and then rank order the mechanisms from 1 to 7 on the basis of the relative amount of attention that was being given to each within their own state's overall school policy-making system.

Question 2: Are the various policy mechanisms being given too much, too little, or about the right amount of attention by policy-makers in this state? In responding to this question, respondents were asked to review the list and indicate which policy mechanisms, if any, were in need of more (or less) attention. They were encouraged to offer their own personal judgment, rather than adopting the state policy system reporting stance requested when responding to the first question.

Question 3: Which policy mechanisms do you feel most knowledgeable about? This question was posed as a way of preparing for more detailed discussion of the alternative approaches to policy-making within each core area, covered in the fourth question.

Question 4: How would you rank the amount of attention given to the listed alternative approaches? Finally, respondents were asked to review alternative policy approaches in the domains with which they were most familiar. Specific policy approaches used by state decision-makers to formulate state actions in each of the seven basic taxonomic categories were identified through analysis of preliminary field interviews, the content of state statutes, newspaper accounts of policy debates, and the general tenor of state policy activity throughout the nation. Using these alternative approaches to stimulate discussion, policy-makers were asked to provide a conceptual interpretation of recent policy activity in their home state, and to rank order the alternative policy approaches.

Interpreting Policy-maker Views

The data gathered in response to these four questions were analyzed in three steps. First, a determination was made of the extent to which respondents from all of the sample states hold similar views regarding the nature and level of state policy activity in each of the seven core policy domains. By looking at commonalities across all six states, we were able to gain a national perspective — to discover the extent to which policy-makers in all states confront similar education problems and develop similar responses. Second, with this national view in mind, we disaggregated the data into state subgroups and examined the extent to which views in one state differ from those in others. Using a simple analysis of variance (ANOVA) technique, we examined the extent to which policy-makers report systematic differences among states in: (1) the amount of attention given to each policy mechanism; (2) the belief that some mechanisms are getting more or less attention than needed; and (3) the degree to which they feel knowledgeable about each of the policy domains. Third, since interstate differences were very large, we applied multiple discriminant analysis to the data; this permitted a more precise description of the unique character of each state.

What the Taxonomy Reveals

National Agreement on Priorities

There was substantial agreement among policy-makers in all six sample states regarding the amounts of attention being given to each of the policy domains.

The mean scores for each policy domain for all 140 policy-makers interviewed are shown in table 3.1.

Table 3.1   Average Priority Ranking Given to Each of the Seven State Policy Mechanisms

Policy mechanism	Mean rank, current level of state-wide attention	Percentage reporting adequate knowledge	Net percentage urging greater attention
Top priority			
Finance	1.56 *****	79	28
High priority			
Personnel	3.34 **********	55	36
Student testing	3.37 *********	49	04
Program definition	3.53 **********	46	13
Low priority			
Organization goveranance	5.11 ***************	40	26
Curriculum materials	5.04 ***************	17	20
Lowest priority			
Building facilities	5.89 ******************	19	26

Several important conclusions can be drawn from the data in this table. The first and most obvious is that school finance receives much more attention than issues related to school building and plant and facilities. Indeed, the overall mean scores shown in the first column of the table reveal a remarkably high level of agreement among all respondents regarding the distribution of state-level attention to various mechanisms for influencing school performance. The mean rank of 1.56 for school finance indicates an overwhelming agreement that this is the most frequently used mechanism for influencing school performance. Had respondents randomly ranked each of the seven policy mechanisms, all would have produced the same mean scores of about 4.0 — half-way between 1 and 7.

The average rank assigned to each of the seven basic policy mechanisms indicates that there are four distinct *clusters* of policy mechanisms within the minds of state decision-makers. *School finance* stands alone as the highest priority domain. Well below the finance ranking three broad policy mechanisms — *personnel training and certification, student testing and assessment, and school program definition* — are given similar scores. The mean rankings of these policy mechanisms (3.34, 3.37, and 3.53 respectively) do not differ from each other, but all three are significantly above the 5.11 mean rank for school organization and governance policies. The third cluster of mechanisms includes *school organization and governance* issues and those related to *curriculum materials* selection and development. Attention given to these two mechanisms is about equal, but differs significantly from all others. At the bottom of the list the 140 respondents agreed that states pay least attention to school *building and facilities* policies. The mean of 5.89 for this mechanism reflects a very strong agreement that it is rarely accorded a prominent place in state decision-making (the average rank is only a little more than one point above the 7.00 last place given by individual respondents).[3] On average each respondent agreed 46 per cent of the time with the ranking given by all other respondents — a remarkable degree of agreement when we consider that these respondents represent six different states with large expenditure histories and diverse decision-making traditions.

To what extent did policy élites want greater attention for each policy domain? The second column in table 3.1 reports on the extent to which policy élites in all sample states believe greater attention should be given to each of the various domains. The scores in this column report the *net percentage* of respondents urging greater attention to each of the seven policy domains (i.e., the number urging more attention minus the number urging less). All of these net percentage scores are positive, indicating that most state policy-makers believe *all* seven policy mechanisms are in need of greater attention.

To what extent did policy élites feel knowledgeable about the policy domains? At least 35 per cent of all respondents believe that personnel training and certification policies need greater attention. More than 25 per cent feel that finance, governance, and school building policies should be pursued more energetically, and over 20 per cent feel that curriculum materials should receive more state-level action. Only the student testing and assessment policy domain appears to be getting about as much attention as the respondents in this study felt is appropriate. With two exceptions this pattern is found in each of the six states under study. Arizona leaders were unique in believing that on balance student testing is getting too much attention, and Californians tend to believe that finance policies receive a bit more attention than is appropriate.

The extent to which policy élites feel knowledgeable about each policy domain is indicated in the third column of table 3.1. The mean scores in this column show that policy-makers tend to feel most knowledgeable about the same policy domains they see as most frequently addressed by the policy system. Nearly 80 per cent of all respondents feel that they understand school finance issues. By contrast, less than 20 per cent feel comfortable discussing either school building or curriculum materials policies. Statistically the knowledgeability mean scores reveal the existence of three distinct levels of familiarity with the seven policy domains. Finance issues are clearly in a class by themselves; a large majority of élites claim knowledge of this domain. Behind finance, roughly half the respondents are comfortable discussing *personnel training and certification*, *student assessment program definition*, and *school governance*. Substantially fewer respondents indicated they are familiar with either *school building* and facilities or *curriculum materials* policies.

Today's policy actors firmly believe that they can alter school performance most effectively through close attention to finance and personnel reform. That was not always the case, however. For most of the 1950s and 1960s school governance was the hot topic, with a broad range of policy actors pressing their authority in that policy domain. We suspect governance would have been a more familiar topic among policy-makers if our study had been conducted thirty years ago. Cultural rather than intellectual or political variables appear to account for the pattern of decision-makers' familiarity with the seven policy domains. It is certainly no easier to understand school finance than building policies, and the professionally arcane issues of student testing seem to be just as broadly understood as the more obviously political questions of school governance. The culture of state capitals in the 1980s has focused the attention of key members of each state's policy élites on matters of finance, personnel, student testing, and program definition.

Interstate Contrasts

Since policy-makers from all six sample states indicated substantial agreement regarding: (1) the level of attention being given to each of the policy mechanisms, (2) the need for more attention to some issues, and (3) overall knowledge about policy domains, we undertook to examine whether their survey responses indicated significant interstate differences as well. Multiple discriminant analysis was applied to the views expressed by the 140 respondents in order to provide an overall summary of interstate differences.

Though interpretation is complicated, multiple discriminant analysis provides the most powerful tool available for summarizing major differences among élite groups representing the six states in our sample. Table 3.2 illustrates the power of this technique. It shows highly significant differences among the six states' policy-maker groups regarding the amount of attention being given to each of the policy domains.[4]

In particular the discriminant function coefficients and the state policy group centroid of the first discriminant function in table 3.2 show that:

1 West Virginia policy-makers differ markedly from others in that they are especially concerned about school building and facilities policies but relatively unconcerned about student testing issues;
2 Pennsylvania and Wisconsin policy-makers reverse these priorities, giving selectively more attention to student assessment while neglecting facilities issues.

These findings are fully confirmed by field interviews. A recent West Virginia court case held that inequality of educational opportunity is directly tied to inequities in access to adequate school facilities. Consequently the court mandated significant new school facilities development. This court decision was repeatedly identified as the most important recent school policy event in the state (*Pauley v. Bailey* 324 S.E. 2d 128, 1984). The Pennsylvania and Wisconsin cases are less dramatic, but interviews in both of these states confirm the emphasis on student assessment as a major reform and important strategy.

Table 3.2   Multiple Discriminant Analysis of State Policy Priorities (groups defined by state)

	Standardized canonical discriminant function coefficients		
	Func #1	Func #2	Func #3
	R=.75, p=.00	R=.54, p=.00	R=.39, p=.00
Policy mechanism	X=188.6, df=35	X=79.6, df=24	X=34.3, df=15
Student testing	.79	.10	-.18
Buildings facilities	-.69	-.18	-.28
Curriculum materials	.11	-.69	-.27
Organization governance	-.24	.61	-.02
Program definition	.29	-.20	.01
School finance	-.12	.15	-.04
Personnel	.16	-.06	.94

| | Canonical discriminant functions evaluated at group centroids | | |
State	Func #1	Func #2	Func #3
Arizona	-.54	.37	-.61
California	.42	.59	-.13
Illinois	.75	-1.32	-.23
Pennsylvania	-.94	.15	.30
West Virginia	2.35	.51	.34
Wisconsin	-1.05	-.23	.50

| | | | | Group means | | | |
State	Fin.	Pers.	Tstng	Prgm	Gov	Curr.	Bldg
AZ	1.917	2.383	3.083	3.817	5.417	4.850	6.533
CA	1.000	3.324	3.912	3.971	5.706	4.647	5.441
IL	1.182	3.318	3.909	3.045	3.773	6.545	5.591
PA	1.704	3.426	2.259	3.593	5.537	5.019	6.352
WV	1.556	4.222	5.172	3.639	4.556	4.833	3.722
WI	1.674	3.848	2.500	3.130	5.087	4.717	6.848
Total	1.555	3.343	3.372	3.529	5.044	4.106	5.894

The second multiple discriminant function shown in table 3.2 identifies another set of statistically significant differences among the states.[5] It supports the conclusion that:

Illinois respondents have the strongest views regarding curriculum and governance mechanisms — they are most concerned with governance questions and least concerned with curriculum materials issues.

This focus on governance issues in Illinois was vividly manifested in a recent controversy over reorganization of the office of the state superintendent of public instruction. The office was shifted from an elected to an appointed post. Governance controversy also surfaced during deliberations on a hard fought collective bargaining statute for teachers. Governance issues have had a long history of importance in Illinois, with traditional tensions between the city of Chicago and 'downstate' interests creating a labyrinthine dual governance system for most public services in the state.

The third discriminant function shown in table 3.2 is also highly significant and accounts for about 15 per cent of the remaining respondent variance. A single policy mechanism — school personnel training and certification — provides most of the explanatory power for this function. As seen in the centroid scores:

Arizona policy-makers gave the highest ranking to personnel policies.

They gave a mean score of 2.38 to personnel training and certification policy issues — more than a full rank higher than any other state. West Virginia and Wisconsin occupy the other extreme, giving personnel questions a relatively low ranking. Arizona's interest in personnel matters is clearly documented in the field interviews. This state recently adopted merit pay, career ladders, teacher evaluation, and staff development reforms — all accompanied by highly visible public debate over how best to improve teacher and administrative training and performance.

Summarizing the National Policy Culture

As the foregoing analysis reveals, there is a powerful national consensus on the meaning and relative importance of each policy mechanism. This broad consensus is accompanied by equally powerful and unique state profiles of reliance on these basic mechanisms for supporting and controlling school performance. It is safe to conclude, therefore, that a national policy culture exists, and that state subcultures exert equally powerful influence over the policy-making process, giving each state a specific profile of responses to core elements in the national taxonomy of policy control mechanisms.

Differences among the six sample states are summarized in figure 3.1. This figure is a three-dimensional plot of the state centroids shown on table 3.2. West Virginia and Illinois are visibly the 'outliers' on this graph. West Virginians, with their traditional reluctance to provide substantial funding or state-level direction to education, have been dramatically affected by the *Pauley v. Bailey* decision. They have responded to this court mandate by giving unusually intense attention to building facilities and curriculum materials policy issues, while giving commensurately less attention to student testing and governance matters. Illinois, less concerned about these issues, gives more attention than any other state to problems of governance. California shares with West Virginia a higher than average interest in curriculum and building issues. California policy-makers reported the highest level of attention to curriculum matters (though still ranking this domain fifth, with a modest mean of 4.647), and the lowest interest in governance (ranked last in this state). Wisconsin and Pennsylvania are close together in their views, and farthest from the West Virginia and Illinois group centroids. These states share intense concern with student testing policies and a relatively low level of interest in personnel matters. Arizona respondents reported that an unusually high level of attention is given to the personnel issue. The prominence

Figure 3.1   State Policy Mechanisms: Attention Level in Each State

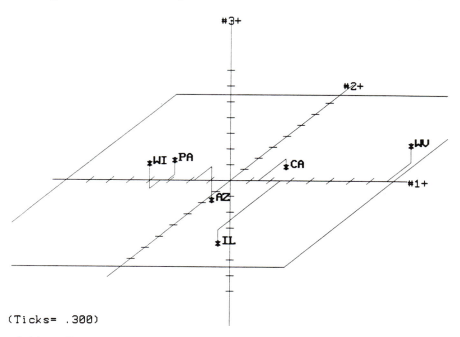

(Ticks= .300)

of this policy activity in Arizona is largely responsible for the explanatory power of the third discriminant function.

Competing Approaches within Policy Domains

Behind the broad picture of control over education framed by the taxonomy described above lie substantive policy debates regarding how best to utilize each of the seven core mechanisms to support and direct public school programs and services. The next step in our analysis was to look at competing approaches to control found within each of the seven domains.

As indicated above, each policy-maker in the study was asked to review the small group of frequently debated approaches to education policy in the policy domains with which they were most familiar. The respondents were asked to rank order the alternative approaches to three or more of the seven basic policy mechanisms. The approach identified as getting the most attention was given a score of 1.0, with successively larger scores going to approaches getting less attention during the last two to three years.[6]

Half of the policy-makers surveyed discussed alternative approaches in the areas of finance, personnel, student testing, and school program definition. The data on alternative approaches to these policy domains are examined below.

As with responses to the taxonomy of policy mechanisms, data analysis for the competing approaches was undertaken in two stages. First, the nature and extent of overall agreement among all respondents reporting on the same policy mechanism were explored. These agreements provided a relatively detailed account of the 'national perspective' affecting the way state decision-makers handle specific school policy questions.[7] Second, following the analysis of agreement among respondents, differences among respondents were examined in detail to reveal how states differ in their approach to each policy arena.

A cautionary note is in order before beginning this analysis. The data under review describe views held by the most active and informed members of each state's policy-making élite *at the time of our study*. Current actors in these or other states may hold rather different views. While this limitation is both real and important, our primary interest lies not in predicting how any particular state can or will act today. Reading newspapers, journals, and policy documents within each state, and conducting open ended interviews with today's key actors is the best way to go about that task. Our interest is more basic: we are seeking to show the cultural basis and taxonomic structure of education policy alternatives and to show how these alternatives are incorporated into specific policy decisions.[8]

School Finance Policy Approaches

Data covering the competing approaches to school finance provide clear evidence that there is a common, national perspective on how best to deal with this complex issue. The data also describe important subcultural differences among the states as each comes to grips with specific aspects of school funding policy.

Five competing finance policy approaches were identified. The first is the universal problem of fixing the total amount of money to be allocated to schooling. State policy-makers are endlessly challenged to fund schools 'adequately' while simultaneously 'cutting the fat' out of 'bloated' state budgets. A second issue driving school finance debates is the equalization of support for all children. Equalization has been a celebrated issue closely identified with court decisions like *Serrano* (California), *Cahill* (New Jersey), and *Rodriguez* (Texas). The third finance approach emphasizes targeting school funds on particular student populations. Categorical budget allocations and entitlement funding levels are often debated in an effort to use school finance policy to restructure educational opportunities for disadvantaged children. The fourth finance approach is a favorite among school districts facing high costs arising from special circumstances. Rural districts seek funds for transportation or to support very small schools. Urban districts seek higher cost of living allowances. Similarly those with rapidly declining or increasing enrollments seek special relief. These special pleadings are summarized in our data as a matter of 'offsetting specially burdensome costs' for various types of districts. Finally, the fifth approach to school finance policy covered in the data involves targeting funds on specific school functions. Textbook purchases, building funds, child nutrition, or library funds fall into this category. Each of these five finance approaches must compete with the others for scarce tax dollars and political support.

Overall Agreement on Finance Policy Approach

Across the six states under study *equalizing* the amount of money supporting each child in the schools was identified as the dominant approach to school finance. Attention to equalization questions is followed closely by concern with *fixing the total amount of money* spent on education in the state. As indicated in table 3.3, the third approach — *targeting* funds on population with special needs — receives significantly less attention than the first two approaches.[9] The two finance approaches ranked last — *offsetting burdensome costs* to school districts with special financial hardships and *financing special school functions*, such as transportation, textbook acquisition, or building programs — were significantly different from the higher ranked targeting approach.

Table 3.3   Average Priority Ranking Given to Alternative Approaches to Finance Policy

Finance policy approach	Mean rank given by policy-makers in all states
High priority	
Equalizing amount per child	2.191 ================
Fixing total amount spent	2.322 ================
Moderate priority	
Targeting on special groups	2.945 =========================
Low priority	
Offsetting burdensome costs	3.699 =============================
Financing particular functions	3.873 ===============================

The extent of agreement among respondents regarding the relative importance of the five competing approaches to school finance described in table 3.3 is less dramatic than that expressed when they ranked the seven core policy mechanisms (see table 3.1). Nevertheless, it is fair to conclude that a national culture supports a common perception that the dominant school finance problem facing public education continues to be guaranteeing equal support for all children.

Interstate Differences in Policy Approaches

Strong subcultures exist in each state strong enough to control thinking about the best approach for finance policy. The multiple discriminant analysis presented in table 3.4 highlights interstate differences in approach to school finance policy formation. The three discriminant functions in this table account for 47 per cent in the total variance among the states, indicating the presence of very strong subcultures in each state, capable of controlling overall finance policy orientation.

Table 3.4   Multiple Discriminant Analysis of Finance Policy Alternatives (groups defined by state)

	Standardized canonical discriminant function coefficients		
Finance Approach	Func #1 R=.53, p=.00 X=72.9,df=25	Func #2 R=.41, p=.00 X=36.5,df=16	Func #3 R=.33, p=.07 X=15.6,df=9
Equalizing amount/child	−.79	.24	−.16
Fixing total funding	.62	.17	−.08
Financing special functions	−.09	−.87	−.05
Targeting special groups	−.05	.14	.79
Offsetting high costs	.25	.37	−.56

	Canonical discriminant functions evaluated at group centroids		
State	Func #1	Func #2	Func #3
Arizona	−.16	−.50	.48
California	−1.08	.73	−.05
Illinois	−.17	.10	−.31
Pennsylvania	−.25	−.23	−.20
West Virginia	1.04	.68	.37
Wisconsin	.64	−.20	−.40

		Group means			
State	Equal	Fixing Amt	Target	Finance	Offset
AZ	2.077	2.058	3.308	4.288	3.192
CA	3.464	1.571	3.143	3.179	3.643
IL	2.300	2.000	2.825	3.775	4.050
PA	2.500	2.261	2.630	4.000	3.500
WV	1.333	3.467	3.267	3.333	4.000
WI	1.625	2.725	2.575	4.175	4.050
Total	2.191	2.322	2.945	3.873	3.699

Two sharp differences were revealed in the six states' finance policy approaches: (1) the amount of attention given to equalizing the amount of money spent on each child in the state; and (2) the extent of concern with fixing the overall level of funding for education within the state.

West Virginia, recently placed under court order to equalize educational opportunities across the state, reported that equalization is the number one finance policy priority. California, by contrast, was recently found to have adequately complied with the terms of the *Serrano* decision on equalization and reports that raising the overall level of funding is the primary thrust of recent finance policy decisions in that state. The other four states range between the extremes found in West Virginia and California. Wisconsin joins West Virginia in ranking equalization ahead of the problem of setting an overall funding level. The other three states join California respondents in reversing this order. We had expected Arizona policy-makers to report somewhat greater concern with funding level issues. Both constitutional and statutory limits on educational expenditures were passed in that state.

Disagreement exists among the states over how much attention is being given to the fiscal policy approach we have called 'financing special functions'. While no state views this approach as a high priority concern, there are substantial differences in states' willingness to earmark school funds for particular types of services or functions. State subcultures shape the thinking and the priority setting differently. California gives this approach third place among the five alternative approaches, while Arizona, Wisconsin, and Pennsylvania put it last. The relatively high California ranking is closely linked to policy events in that state; the 1983 omnibus education bill (SB 813) provided money for a broad array of specific district budget items ranging from textbooks to teacher salaries.

West Virginia joins California in placing the financing approach third. In the West Virginia case this concern is closely associated with an overall equity focus. With top priority being given to fiscal equalization and to targeting funds on specific student groups, West Virginia's interest in the development of financial resources for specific school functions becomes part of an equal opportunity policy debate of the sort that dominated decision-making in the larger industrial states (e.g., California, Florida, New Jersey, and Texas) during the 1970s.

Where equity issues are less prominent, states tend to differ over whether the funds should be targeted on the special needs of particular student populations or used to offset the burdensome costs associated with various school problems.[10] Generally state policy-makers give greater priority to targeting funds on special student needs. Arizona is an exception, however. Arizona policy-makers report giving greater attention to offsetting the extra costs associated with such problems as rural transportation and declining enrollments. This reported emphasis may be thought to clash with the fact that Arizona has recently adopted a fairly strong bilingual education program mandate, and incorporated extra funds for special education students into their school finance formula. The bilingual mandate is not tied directly to categorical funding, however, and the special education funding is built into the general finance formula in such a way that it may not be widely recognized as a technique for targeting funds on this special population. Wisconsin and Illinois are at the other end of the policy spectrum. They each give targeting a relatively prominent place in school finance; Wisconsin policy-makers ranked this approach second, just behind equalizing.

These findings are graphically displayed in figure 3.2. Note that only West Virginia and Wisconsin are to the right of center on the axis representing

Figure 3.2   Alternative Finance Policy Approaches: Attention Level in Each State

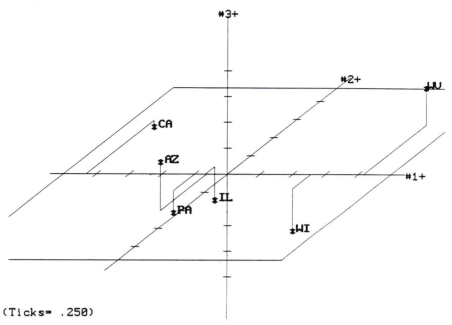

(Ticks= .250)

discriminant function #1, indicating that they alone have positive centroid scores for this function contrasting equalization with fixing total school funding levels.

California policy-makers have been so deeply involved in the fallout from the infamous Proposition 13 property tax relief referendum in 1978 that they have been largely indifferent to the ranking of all finance policy alternatives save the one concerned with fixing the overall level of school funding. They place this approach more than 1.5 ranks above all other alternatives.[11]

Personnel Policy Approaches

Four competing approaches to the formation of personnel policies were presented to state decision-makers willing to discuss this policy mechanism. In our research attention was limited to those policies aimed at shaping teacher quality and job performance. There are, of course, numerous state policies aimed at influencing the work of administrators and classified employees, but for the purposes of this study, we focused on teachers and their work roles.

The most obvious approach is state control over *pre-service training and certification*. Every state has a substantial body of law detailing pre-service credential requirements. All require specific courses; some specify mental and/or physical examinations. In recent years many states have adopted laws and regulations aimed at holding experienced teachers accountable for high quality job performance. These *accountability* policies include a variety of continuing education and examination requirements, evaluation and supervision mechanisms, and merit or bonus pay systems. A third approach to the development of teacher personnel systems goes under the general rubric of *professional development*. This includes support for in-service training, encouragement of advanced degree work, and enhancement of collegial working relationships. The fourth approach presented to policy-makers for discussion — *control over teacher job definitions* — is relatively recent in origin. Several states have developed career ladders, mentor teacher, or job enlargement programs aimed at expanding and enriching the scope of teacher work responsibilities. This policy approach appears to be motivated by a rather widespread belief that teachers are suffering alienation and 'burnout' in jobs that have become too narrow in scope and bureaucratic in form.

Overall Agreement on Alternative Personnel Policy Approaches

A national policy culture generates broad agreement among the states regarding the relative importance of the four different approaches to personnel policy formation. Eighty-two respondents ranked alternative approaches to school personnel policy. To a substantial degree they agreed that the four identified alternatives are rank ordered as shown in table 3.5. Pre-service certification and training issues were ranked as most important, professional development and accountability system development were ranked about equally, and issues related to changing teacher job definitions were clearly seen as the least frequent expression of this policy mechanism. Policy élites agreed with one another about 22 per cent of the time across all states as they described the relative amount of attention being given to these four alternative approaches to personnel training and certification. In statistical terms this level of agreement is a highly reliable indication of a national culture supporting a common view of how best to approach this important educational policy domain.

Table 3.5 Average Priority Ranking Given to Alternative Approaches to Personnel Policy

Personnel policy approach	Mean rank given by policy-makers in all states
High priority	
Pre-service certification/training	1.787 =============
Moderate priority	
Professional development	2.305 ===============
Accountability systems	2.683 ===============
Low priority	
Changing teacher job definitions	3.238 =======================

Interstate Differences in Personnel Policy Orientation

In spite of the sense of national agreement, a few significant state subculture differences emerged in personnel policy approaches. As indicated in Table 3.6, the strong differences emerged around the importance of using the approach of teacher job definition policies (e.g., career ladders, differentiated staffing, mentor teachers). Interest in teacher job definition policies varies substantially from state to state.

Table 3.6   Multiple Discriminant Analysis of Personnel Training and Certification Policy Alternatives (groups defined by state)

Standardized canonical discriminant function coefficients		
	Func #1	Func #2
	R=.59, p=.00	R=.39,p=.14
Personnel policy approach	X=49.8,df=20	X=13.3,df=12
Change Teacher Job Definitions	.94	-.33
Professional Development	-.44	-.36
Training & Certification	-.24	.67
Accountability	-.01	-.04

Canonical discriminant functions evaluated at group centroids		
	Func #1	Func #2
State		
Arizona	-.60	.23
California	-1.06	-.19
Illinois	.43	-.38
Pennsylvania	.79	-.41
West Virginia	1.13	1.04
Wisconsin	-.04	-.01

State	Certify	Group means Develop	Account	Job def.
AZ	2.200	2.440	2.600	2.760
CA	1.600	3.000	2.850	2.550
IL	1.429	2.357	2.571	3.643
PA	1.357	2.071	2.679	3.893
WV	2.000	1.571	2.786	3.786
WI	1.875	2.083	2.792	3.250
Total	1.787	2.305	2.683	3.238

While the entire group of respondents ranking alternative personnel policy approaches ranked the job definition approach well below the other three approaches, California respondents did not follow this general tendency. Californians reported that job definition policies were second in importance, exceeded only by issues of training and certification. Arizona respondents

Figure 3.3   Alternative Approaches to Personnel Policy: Attention Level in Each State

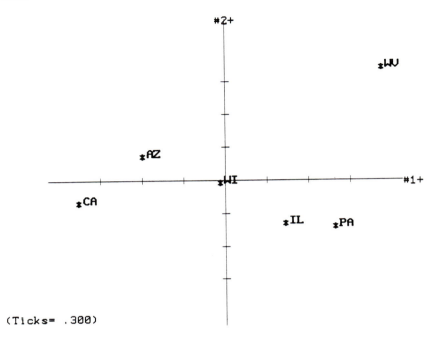

(Ticks= .300)

were also inclined to view job definition policies as relatively important. Arizonans were unique, however, in their tendency to view all of the teacher policy approaches as about equally important, with the first place mean of 2.20 for pre-service training and certification only .56 ranks above their last place 2.76 for the job definition policy approach. By contrast, Pennsylvanians showed the strongnet rank order preferences. In that state the policy élite ranked pre-service certification policies a full 2.5 ranks above job definition approaches.

As suggested by the second discriminant function shown in table 3.6, there is a decided tendency for states to see teacher improvement as a matter of *choosing* between reforming pre-service certification and training and an emphasis on professional development and job redefinition approaches. While job definition dominates the first personnel discriminant function, relative attention to the training and certification approach dominates the second order discrimination among the states.[12]

West Virginia policy-makers exhibited a distinctive state subculture pattern. This state reported a strong emphasis on professional development (more than half a rank higher than any other state). Pennsylvania, Illinois, and California contrast most sharply with the West Virginia view, reporting high interest in pre-service training and certification.[13] The relationships among the states are graphically depicted in figure 3.3.

Student Testing Policy Approaches

As with finance and personnel policies, the data reveal a national cultural agreement on the best way to approach student testing policy. Individual state subcultures deviate from the national pattern, each embracing a particular pattern of student testing policy approaches.

Overall Agreement on Student Testing Policy Approaches

Five alternative approaches to student testing and assessment policy were identified through analysis of preliminary interviews and documents. Seventy respondents told us about the relative amount of attention given to each of these five testing policy options in their respective states. As shown in table 3.7, a full 40 per cent of the average individual variance is shared by the seventy respondents reporting. Such strong agreement leaves little doubt regarding the existence of a national consensus on the relative importance of the various approaches to this key policy domain.

Respondents generally agree that *specifying the form or content of test instruments* is the most frequently used approach. They also agree that *measuring non-academic outcomes* of student learning activities is the least frequently used approach. The use of testing programs to *evaluate teachers or school programs* was ranked next to last by most respondents, but interview notes suggest that this approach was on the upswing at the time of our study.

Table 3.7   Average Priority Ranking Given to Alternative Approaches to Student Testing Policy

Student testing policy approach	Mean rank given by policy-makers in all states
Top priority	
Specifying test format or content	1.464 ================
Moderate priority	
Using tests for student placement	2.736 =========================
Mandating local test development	3.050 ==========================
Low priority	
Using tests to evaluate teachers/programs	3.586 ============================
Lowest priority	
Measuring non–academic outcomes	4.121 ==============================

Interstate Differences in Testing Policy Orientation

As in the other policy domains, multiple discriminant analysis reveals very sharp differences among the individual states in their approach to student testing policy. In combination the three discriminant functions shown in the top portion of table 3.8 account for nearly 63 per cent of the variation among the six states. Interpreting the three multiple discriminant functions shown in this table is complicated, however, because variations in state handling of the most prominent approach to testing policy — specification of the format or content of state-wide testing programs — play a substantial role in all three of the functions.[14] Careful scrutiny of the function coefficients, state centroids, and mean ranking scores for the five different approaches to testing policy is well worth the effort, however.

Table 3.8   Multiple Discriminant Analysis of Student Testing and Assessment Policy Alternatives (groups defined by state)

	Standardized canonical discriminant function coefficients		
	Func #1 $R=.59, p=.00$	Func #2 $R=.55, p=.00$	Func #3 $R=.45, p=.07$
Testing approach	$X=69.2, df=25$	$X=41.9, df=16$	$X=19.0, df=9$
Mandating local tests	-.75	-.19	-.05
Measuring non-academics	.74	-.57	-.19
Use tests for placement	-.14	.39	.27
Evaluating teachers/programs	.20	.18	.64
Specify format or content	.49	.48	-.51

	Canonical discriminant functions evaluated at group centroids		
State	Func #1	Func #2	Func #3
Arizona	-.08	-.78	-.28
California	-.90	1.02	-.84
Illinois	1.04	.78	-.52
Pennsylvania	-.78	-.17	.19
West Virginia	-.86	.98	.91
Wisconsin	.72	.13	.50

			Group means		
State	Format	Placement	Evaluating	Non-academic	Mandate
AZ	1.325	2.475	3.150	4.600	3.150
CA	1.667	3.250	3.000	3.250	3.333
IL	2.375	2.500	3.625	4.438	2.063
PA	1.125	2.594	3.656	3.656	3.969
WV	1.250	3.625	3.875	3.125	6.875
WI	1.500	2.906	4.188	4.406	2.188
Total	1.464	2.736	3.586	4.121	3.050

The sharpest differences in state testing policies are related to the three approaches dealing with specification of test content: mandating tests for local use, measuring non-academic achievements, and directly specifying test format or content. Statistically speaking, some states are significantly more likely to rely on local district content decisions than are others. By the same token some states are more likely directly to specify test content, while others are more interested in measuring non-academic outcomes.

The first discriminant function reported in table 3.8 traces these differences. The two approaches dealing with direct specification of test content (e.g., direct specification of the format or content of the tests, and concern with the measurement of non-academic achievements) have large positive coefficients on this function, while the use of state authority to require local districts to develop their own tests has a large negative coefficient.

Illinois and Wisconsin rely most heavily on mandatory local test development as indicated by their positive centroid scores. California, Pennsylvania, and West Virginia, by contrast, give relatively high priority to measuring non-academic subjects and specifying test format and content. Arizona policy-makers are relatively neutral on these approaches. Despite a strong tradition of local autonomy, however, this state was in the midst of selecting a new state-wide test at the time of our study. This accounts for the high ranking of the format and content specification approach in this state.

The second multiple discriminant function shown in table 3.8 is almost as powerful as the first (the multiple correlation coefficient drops from .59 to .55). The large coefficients in this second function are for: (1) non-academic assessment; (2) the use of tests to control student promotion or placement; and (3) state-level specification of state format and content. It is appropriate to conclude that states differ significantly in their inclination to use state-defined academic achievement tests to assess student educational progress. As indicated by the positive and negative signs attached to these large coefficients, states differ significantly in the way they use their authority to define test purposes. Some states give greater emphasis to assessing non-academic outcomes, others to specifying test content for use in student placement.

California, West Virginia, Illinois, and to some extent even Wisconsin policy-makers view state testing programs as less useful for monitoring academic progress than those in Arizona and Pennsylvania, as indicated by their centroid scores. Illinois respondents reported a higher than average ranking to the use of tests to control student placement and promotion, but they also were the only group to report that local test development takes precedence over state-wide testing programs.

The third multiple discriminant function shown in Table 3.8 is also highly significant (p = .03) and quite powerful.[15] The two largest coefficients in this function are those for: (1) using test scores to evaluate school programs or teachers, and once again (2) using state authority to define test format and content. While all states reported giving substantially greater attention to specifying the content or format of testing programs than to their use in evaluating school performance, the large coefficients indicate the presence of significant differences among the states in their inclination to mandate the use of test results.

Figure 3.4   Alternative Approaches to Student Testing: Attention Level in Each State

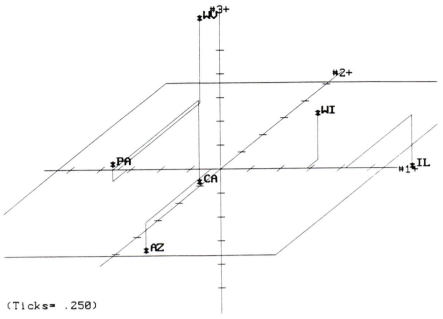

(Ticks= .250)

California tends to give the most emphasis to test utilization for personnel and program evaluation as indicated by the state centroid scores for this third function. West Virginia and Wisconsin give the least amount of attention to this policy approach.

A three-dimensional plot of the six state centroid scores is presented in figure 3.4. This figure assists in conceptualizing the combined effects of all three significant discriminant functions. Taken together, the three testing policy discriminant functions vividly describe the basic options available to all states.

As indicated in the figure, Californians (lower, left, rear) uniquely endorse for *broadening test content* to include non-academic assessments and show stronger than average interest in *using tests to evaluate school and teacher performance* rather than to control student placement. Only Californians reported the school/teacher evaluation approach to testing to be more prominent than the student assignment one.

West Virginia policy actors (upper, left, rear) were the only ones to show *no interest in using tests for either student placement or school program evaluation.* Only West Virginia respondents ranked non-academic assessment policies as more important than both placement and evaluation usage. Illinois policy actors were singularly *committed to local control over test content.* Only this state ranked mandates for local test development ahead of establishing state control over the format or content of tests. Wisconsin policy actors generally shared the Illinois view, but they reported that the balance of attention is shifted somewhat toward state-level test specification.

Arizona (lower, left, front) was unique in its emphasis on using *tests for evaluation of student progress combined with a rejection of non-academic assessments.* This state expressed the view that schools are intended to produce academic achievement and, therefore, testing that achievement should be a prominent state policy concern. Moreover, Arizonans believe test results should control both student progress and school evaluation more strongly than policy-makers in other states. Pennsylvania (upper, left, front) largely shared the Arizona pattern but gave greater emphasis to state-level test content specification and commensurately less attention to local test development.

Program Definition Approaches

School program definition is the fourth area where more than half of the policy élite in our study evaluated alternative policy approaches. As shown in table 3.9, four competing approaches to program definition were identified in early field interviews: (1) setting higher program standards; (2) mandating the teaching of particular courses or subjects; (3) developing programs for special groups of students; and (4) changing program time requirements (e.g., fixing the length of the school day, the school year, or specifying the number of minutes to be devoted to particular subjects. The policy-makers surveyed agreed overwhelmingly that setting higher program standards is the number one approach in this policy domain. The other three approaches (mandating particular subjects, developing programs for special groups of students, and changing time requirements) were ranked well below the 1.41 mean rank given to the standard setting approach.

Table 3.9   Average Priority Ranking Given to Alternative Approaches to Program Definition Policy

Program definition approach	Mean rank given by policy-makers in all states
High priority	
Setting higher standards	1.409 ================
Moderate priority	
Mandating particular subjects	2.675 ====================
Developing programs for special groups	2.916 =======================
Changing time requirements (day/year)	3.078 =======================

The mean scores for the four alternative approaches to program definition contain about 34 per cent as much variance as an average respondent. Statistically this level of agreement on the ranking of alternative approaches is highly significant. Once again the evidence is consistent with the existence of an effective national culture capable of strongly influencing policy options in all states. The thinking and priority setting of policy élites across the states have been shaped by a common culture and set of understandings.

Highest priority was reportedly given to using state authority to *set higher program standards* for local districts. This priority is manifested in specifying accreditation procedures, defining promotion and graduation requirements, or otherwise holding districts responsible for implementing particular program elements. The other three identified approaches were reported to be given roughly equal levels of state attention, more than a full rank below that assigned to the standards-setting approach.

Interstate Differences in Program Definition Orientation

While national agreement is strong, table 3.10 documents the existence of significant differences among state subcultures. The data in this table reveal that policy-makers differ most strongly in their assessments of the extent to which regulating the time requirements for school programs is an important approach to school program definition. As indicated in the table, a single significant discriminant function resulted when alternative program definition approaches were submitted to multiple discriminant analysis. This highly reliable function accounts for about 30 per cent of the respondent variance. The function coefficients shown in the top section of the table indicate strong interstate disagreement over: (1) approaching program definition through time and standard setting, versus (2) specifying particular subjects or targeting programs on special student groups. The coefficient for the time control approach to school programs is the largest (+0.82) and contrasts most sharply with the -0.56 coefficient for mandating particular school subjects. Though smaller in magnitude, the coefficient for the policy approach involving development of programs for special student groups is also negative. The coefficient for setting program performance standards is the smallest of the group, but has a positive sign like the time requirement approach.

Policy élites in Illinois, and to a lesser extent in Arizona, relied on the subject mandating and special program development approaches (as shown in the state centroids in the middle portion of the table). Californians were pre-eminently concerned with time requirement specification. In fact, California was the only state to rank time requirement changes second, ahead of subject specification and special group program development. Thus, while setting higher program standards is universally reported to be the most important approach to program definition, the data indicate the existence of substantial variations across the states in how that policy approach is combined with time or content specification. Once again state cultures have exerted a powerful influence on perceptions of the most important approaches to program definition policy formation.

Table 3.10   Multiple Discriminant Analysis of School Program Definition Policy Alternatives (groups defined by state)

Standardized canonical discriminant function coefficients	
Program definition approach	Func #1 R=.55,p=.01 X=37.5,df=20
Change time requirement	.80
Specify subjects	-.56
Programs for special groups	-.40
Set program standards	.36

Canonical discriminant functions evaluated at group centroids	
State	Func #1
Arizona	-.14
California	-1.28
Illinois	1.15
Pennsylvania	-.94
West Virginia	2.35
Wisconsin	-.22

	Group means			
State	Time	Subjects	Set Standards	Special
AZ	3.024	3.000	1.310	2.667
CA	1.938	3.313	1.375	3.375
IL	3.727	2.091	1.909	2.545
PA	3.385	2.269	1.423	2.923
WV	3.091	2.409	1.318	3.182
WI	3.000	2.885	1.231	3.115
Total	3.078	2.675	1.409	2.916

The Contribution to a Cultural Theory of School Policy Structure

In this chapter policy decisions are treated as cultural artifacts, the products of values preferences. A taxonomy of basic educational policy mechanisms was developed from interview data and confirmed through quantitative survey responses from 140 key policy actors in six states. The taxonomy was developed by asking these policy-makers to respond to broad questions about the attention given to each of seven basic policy mechanisms, their assessment of whether policy-makers should be giving more (or less) attention to each policy domain, and how they would rank the amount of attention given to various approaches within the seven basic policy domains. These questions elicited data confirming the role played by both national and state culture systems on policy choices. The method of study — using a taxonomy to organize thinking about policy preferences — also enabled us effectively to describe the unique character of each state's cultural pattern.

A strong national culture creates broad consensus about the relative importance of various policy mechanisms, while strong state-level subcultures create sharp differences regarding the amount of attention actually focused on specific policy domains. Moreover, policy-makers have systematically divergent views about how much attention the state *should* give to each policy mechanism. Differences in the degree to which individual policy-makers feel knowledgeable about various policy mechanisms are closely associated with their perception that the policy has been receiving significant attention within their own state policy system.

After reviewing policy-maker commonalities and differences regarding the degree of reliance on variance approaches to each of the seven basic state policy mechanisms, we concluded that the national culture shapes overall state orientations toward critical approaches within each policy domain. In the area of school finance national attention has been focused on equalization of expenditures, and the establishment of overall funding levels for the schools. In the personnel arena pre-service training and certification issues have been most important. Decisions in the arena of student testing policy have been dominated by concerns related to specifying the format or content of required tests. Setting higher standards for school performance dominated policy-making in the school program definition policy arena.

In sum, we found education policies to be products of both state and national cultures. These products have a taxonomic structure. While much more work remains to be done on the details of the taxonomy, it is clear that the taxonomy consists of two nested layers. The basic layer is a set of seven broad policy domains identifying the control mechanisms available to state policy leaders seeking to support or influence school performance. Policy élites agree that these seven domains describe their ways of thinking about how to alter or control school performance. A second layer of taxonomic categories distinguishes among alternative or competing approaches to policy formation within each of the seven basic domains. In responding to our questions policy élites revealed strong agreement regarding the policy approaches being utilized within their own states. Thus this chapter contributes answers to two persistent questions raised in chapter 1. It reveals important evidence of the influences of both national and state cultures, and it provides a grounded theoretical taxonomy for analyzing and tracking the products of the policy culture.[16] The taxonomy can be used to organize and track the trends. The taxonomy will be useful for organizing crosscultural (cross-state) comparison.

Notes

1 They developed the Human Relations Area Files to help organize the patterned activities that are the elements of a culture. They note, for example, that activities are always: (1) associated with particular *subjects* (e.g., priests, policy-makers); (2) directed toward specific *objectives* (e.g., food preparation, child care, school reform); (3) accomplished by use of an identifiable *means* (e.g., weapons, mutual aid and treaties, policy mechanisms); (4) aimed at general *purposes* or goals (e.g., socialization, bewitching, equalizing); and (5) producing concrete *results* (e.g., making ships, giving children equal access to schools).

2 Mitchell and Encarnation's (1984) tentative list of basic state policy domains guided our initial data collection in the field. Their list included:
 1 school organization and governance,
 2 personnel training and certification,
 3 school program definition,
 4 curriculum materials development and selection,
 5 student testing and assessment,
  and two finance policy domains:
 6 revenue generation, and
 7 resource allocation.

3 One way of assessing overall agreement among the respondents is to compare the variance of the mean scores for the total group with the variance in the typical 1 through 7 ranking given by individual respondents. The ranks 1 through 7 have an overall variance of 4.00. The group means shown in table 3.1 range from 1.56 to 5.89 and have a total variance of 1.86 — 46 per cent as large as the individual variance.

4 The first step in interpreting a multiple discriminant analysis is to look at the canonical correlation (R) for each of the reported discriminant functions and the associated probability (p-value) indicating whether the canonical correlations are significant. The square of each canonical correlation is an estimate of the variance in the data set that contributes to successful discrimination among respondents from each of the several states. For example, in table 3.2 the first discriminant function has a canonical R of .75 with a highly significant p-value (virtually zero). This means that this function accounts for approximately 56 per cent of the variations in group membership of the respondents (an extraordinarily high level of explained variance when using only seven predictor variables on a sample of 140 respondents).

 Once it is determined that a discriminant function is successful in significantly separating groups of respondents, it becomes appropriate to begin interpreting its substantive meaning. This is done by using both the standardized discriminant function coefficients (shown in the top portion of the table) and the group centroids (shown in the middle portion of the table). The large coefficients in the first function found in table 3.2 are those associated with student testing (0.79) and building and facilities (-0.69) policies. The fact that the coefficients have opposite signs indicates that the greatest differences among the states separate those who view one of these mechanisms as receiving less attention within their state while the other is receiving more. The group centroids (in the middle portion of the table) show which state was most likely to be represented in these competing views. Respondents from West Virginia with a centroid of 2.35 held the most dramatic position on this discriminant function. They gave small scores (i.e., tended to rank as quite prominent) to the building and facilities policy domain, while giving relatively large scores (indicating a lower rank) to student testing policy. This can be easily confirmed by looking at the mean scores for each state's respondents shown at the bottom of table 3.2. West Virginia gave the building and facilities policy arena an average rank of 5.47 (more than two ranks below the 3.7 average rank for all respondents). Looking back at the group centroids in the middle of the table, we see that West Virginia respondents contrasted in their views most sharply with those in Wisconsin and Pennsylvania who had group centroids of -1.05 and -0.94 respectively.

5 With a canonical correlation of .54, this function accounts for 29 per cent of the remaining response variance. The pattern of coefficients in the top portion of the table indicates that two different policy mechanisms account for most of the explanatory power of this function: curriculum materials (with a coefficient of -.69) and school organization/governance (with a coefficient of +.61).

6 Where respondents were unable or unwilling to give alternative approaches different ranks, each was given the average score for the ranks covered. Typically respondents did not rank the alternative approaches to all seven mechanisms. Rather each informant was first asked to report on the three about which he/she felt most knowledgeable. If interview time permitted, respondents were then asked to rank the approaches with which they were less familiar. The number of respondents evaluating each policy mechanism ranged from a low of thirty-eight who evaluated school building policies to a high of 118 who were prepared to rank alternative approaches to school finance. The average respondent provided data on about 3.5 domains — an average of about sixty-eight respondents per policy area.

7 We should note that sample sizes are relatively small in each policy domain. Moreover, the samples were selected to be representative of the most active and informed members of each state's decision-making élite. There are, no doubt, important sampling biases in this procedure. As a result, our findings should not be construed to reflect the views of a state or even of the average policy-maker within each state.

8 A paired t-test shows the difference between the 'targeting' mean and the 'fixing total amount' mean to be statistically significant.

9 This can be seen in the group centroid scores for the first multiple discriminant function in table 3.4, and confirmed in the group mean scores at the bottom of the table.

10 The third discriminant function shown in table 3.4 is weaker in

explanatory power and less statistically reliable than either of the other two (p-value of .07 falls just short of the traditional .05 used for assessing statistical significance). It provides some potentially important insights into finance policy debates, however, so we cautiously interpret it here.

11 The California centroid in figure 3.2 demonstrates that the state has a special, distinctive way of viewing finance.

12 This multiple discriminant function is shown in the second column of table 3.6. While assisting in our interpretation of the data, it is not a particularly reliable indicator — the p-value is only .14.

13 As indicated in figure 3.3, and confirmed in the mean scores shown at the bottom of table 3.6.

14 That is, this policy approach has a relatively large coefficient in each discriminant function (.49 in Function #1, .48 in Function #2, and -.51 in Function #3).

15 The third function has a multiple correlation coefficient (multiple R) of 0.45, meaning that about 20 per cent of the remaining variance in responses is explained by it.

16 Though it is impossible to be sure that all of the core policy control mechanisms are included in our list, we are confident that the vast bulk of state policy can be divided into seven domains: finance, personnel, student testing, school program definition, school governance and organization, curriculum materials specification, and school building and facilities. We are less confident that we have found all of the alternative approaches to state action used within these seven core domains. Further research is needed to discover whether the taxonomy of competing approaches and mutual exclusivity required of a reliable taxonomy. The needed research should be designed to refine the cultural theory developed here. More crosscultural analysis among state policy systems is needed to clarify and refine the taxonomic categories described in this chapter.

Chapter 4

Public Values in the Policy Culture[1]

Suppose you are a legislator who thinks schools should be managed more efficiently, or a teacher union lobbyist who thinks that schools (and teachers) should not be getting less money just because they are located in a poor district. What kind of policy would you push for: higher standards for school buildings, special training for superintendents, higher state definitions of minimums for school curriculum programs? How do policy actors choose a policy mechanism? Is there a defined pattern? Do policy actors use certain mechanisms for certain goals? This chapter identifies such patterns by examining policy-makers' values.

The most important distinguishing feature of any culture is its system of values. While cultural systems also provide their 'natives' with common ways of perceiving the everyday objects, persons, and events, these common perceptions of concrete events and observable phenomena can be communicated across cultural boundaries. Basic values are not so easily communicated. Aliens seeking to enter a foreign culture must devote considerable time and energy to discovering and understanding the nuances of ordinary activities before they can grasp the value system and gain access to the culture's underlying structure and meaning. The gap between universal experiences of concrete events and divergent ways of interpreting and evaluating those events is the most common source of cultural conflict.

This chapter inquires into the core values of state policy actors. Like ordinary citizens, public policy-makers rely on the core values of their culture in forming overall judgments about various proposed courses of action. Cultural norms tell them whether the anticipated activities are morally good or bad, socially important or trivial, politically purposeful or meaningless, personally fulfilling or aimless. This chapter shows policy preferences are shaped by the cultural values embraced by individual policy actors. Moreover, since cultures vary from state to state we should find systematic variations in the values embodied by key state actors; and these value variations should account for differences in policy orientation.

Policy analysts typically assume that public values are based on economic rationality, political interest, or both. As Wildavsky (1987a) notes, however, cultural influences on policy are powerful and operate in ways that contrast sharply with rational political or economic value systems. Drawing on Mary Douglas' provocative work, he asserts that there are four core cultural types: fatalism, collectivism, individualism, and egalitarianism. He traces some of the policy and public value implications of these four cultural types, and argues that cultural variation can explain policy actions that cannot be seen as either economically or politically rational.

Our own investigation shares Wildavsky's emphasis on culture but follows a somewhat different path to the identification of core values. The factors identified by Wildavsky as the sources of key cultural alternatives — élite power and degree of regulatory prescription — vary from state to state, but other aspects of the political culture in most American states also show great variation and can effectively explain important subcultural differences. There is, for example, a critical tension in all state policy systems among three social values described by Kaufman (1956) as: 'neutral technical competence', 'democratic legitimacy', and 'organizational efficiency'. As described below, these values are widely recognized in American political *Culture* by the more succinct names: *Quality, Equity,* and *Efficiency.* A fourth basic value — freedom of *Choice* or liberty — is described in some detail by Garms, Guthrie, and Pierce (1978).

This chapter takes on the difficult problem of trying to define and measure these four basic values as they operate in education policy systems. First, we provide philosophical definitions; then we develop a measurement procedure that allows us to identify patterns of values affecting policy action in the state. The taxonomy, described in chapter 3, serves as a tool for organizing our analysis of values. In chapter 6 we will see how the four core values are differently embodied in the education statutes adopted by each of the American states.

Political and Philosophical Bases of American Values

To understand how the four core social values shape policy maker behavior, we need to describe how each has its roots in a unique political ideology or philosophy.

1 Choice (or Liberty). This is arguably the most basic of all American public values. It was the passionate belief of the American Federalists that good government is defined by its ability to preserve freedom of choice for its citizens. This was the bedrock of classical liberalism as formulated by John Locke and John Stuart Mill. It was summed up succinctly by Thomas Jefferson in his declaration, 'That government governs best which governs least.'

Choice is a difficult value to pursue through governmental action; it seems generally to be supported more by inaction than by positive policy formation. A number of critical choice issues can be identified in current education policy debates, however. Probably the most prominent among them are vouchers and other strategies to allow families to choose among schools for their children. But many strategies for increasing choice are less dramatic and less controversial. Recent choice embracing strategies include alternative school program development, flexibility in local school planning, and greater decentralization of budget and management decisions.

2 Quality. Given the primary role played by choice or liberty in the American political system, positive public policy actions must be justified in terms of their ability to enhance the quality of life for citizens. Indeed, governmental action to provide direct services is defensible only if the quality of the services provided is on the whole at least as good as could be reasonably expected to arise through private action.

The argument that government is intrinsically superior to private action in some areas of service has a long and convincing history. In the modern period Rousseau's social contract theory best captured this argument. His theory is based on the proposition that citizens join together in collective action to achieve goals they would be incapable of reaching through private actions and thus enter into a contractual relationship with the State — securing improved life opportunities in exchange for reduced personal liberties.

As a practical matter, Americans have believed for about a century that the overall quality of life in this country is substantially increased through a system of free, compulsory mass education. For some the quality improvement is economic, measured by the greater productivity of well educated workers. For others the compelling rationale for public education is civic — schools provide an introduction to American culture and prepare responsible citizens. Still others see the benefits of public education in private terms — increased personal capacities and expanded sensitivity to culture, language, literature, and the arts.

However the goals of public education are defined, quality is destroyed if schools do not have the resources, the technical capacity, or the will to deliver services effectively. Hence, despite the variety of its ultimate ends, there is broad agreement that quality is an instrumental and immediate public value, one with which to judge school performance and formulate policies aimed at shaping their performance. This instrumental meaning of quality provides the positive basis for policy evaluation and informs strategic thinking about how to improve schools. Strategies for improving quality include increasing money and resources, increasing minimum requirements for teachers' and administrators' certification, and increasing the number of required courses in the school curricula.

3 Efficiency. Americans have had an intense love-hate relationship with efficiency as a public policy value since the founding of the Republic. The cruel efficiencies of totalitarian governments are recognized and feared. But the productive efficiency of American business and industry are just as frequently held out as the model after which to design public service agencies. Moreover, Americans feel a need for an orderly, predictable, and controlled system to contain private and interest group conflicts threatening the social order. Social unrest and the threat of anarchy fade when government provides for the orderly and efficient delivery of public services.

It was Thomas Hobbes who used the problem of efficiency and order as the cornerstone of modern political theory. Without government to create efficient order, Hobbes argued, life quickly becomes 'brutish, short and ugly'. For Hobbes the arbitrariness of efficient governmental authority is a small price to pay for the resulting security and order which make civilized life possible. In the American experience the efficiency of scientific management (Taylor, 1911) is more often presented as the legitimating reason for expansive governmental authority. But recent conservative political ideologues offer a straightforward embrace of Hobbesian argument in their call for 'law and order' in daily life.

As indicated in chapter 1, the embrace of efficiency in education was given a tremendous boost by scientific management theorists during the first three decades of this century (see Callahan, 1962). Regulating school operations in ways intended to keep costs down and order up has been a major concern of policy-makers in most states and localities. The strong presumption that expansive and generally centralized governmental authority is the proper means for achieving efficient control has recently come under attack but it remains a core value in most education programs.

4 Equity. Though the very first 'self-evident' truth set forth in the Declaration of Independence is that 'all men are created equal', Americans have had considerable difficulty embodying this core value in public policies. Nevertheless, equity is a core public value and one which can be powerfully invoked as a basis for creating or changing policy decisions.

Karl Marx framed the problem of equity for modern political theory. He argued that inequities in society are a governmental responsibility because private social relationships inevitably exacerbate the problem. In private society, Marx argued, there is a steady accumulation of wealth and privilege in the hands of one social class at the expense of others. Revolutionary warfare is, he asserted, the inevitable consequence of this instability in private social relationships. Hence the government must perform the most important function of interceding in this drift toward private domination by taking action to restore equality of opportunity to all citizens — giving everyone a chance to benefit from economic productivity and to share in the privileges of full citizenship.

The Marxist vision of inevitable revolution by disenfranchised groups against the privileged classes has not come to fruition in the United States. Political leaders, perhaps actively understanding Marx's argument, have acted to keep the process from following the natural tendency toward cumulative inequality. Without accepting Marxist theory, policy-makers in this country have recognized the importance of preventing alienation and abuse by political élites.

As a policy matter, equity is complicated. It is a matter of *redress* rather than one of *address*. That is, policy-makers cannot decree social equity, they can only create laws and social programs that relieve the effects of inequity *after* it has been identified. The need for governmental action cannot be recognized until some identifiable inequity has been shown to be serious and in need of remedy. Then action is only justified to the extent necessary to eliminate the identified inequity. In the schools educators have been asked to treat equity problems on two levels: (1) elimination of inequality of educational opportunity within and across all school programs; and (2) the provision of special educational resources to disadvantaged and handicapped children to enable them to achieve greater equity in society after they leave the school. These two equity problems do not always lend themselves to compatible policy solutions, but both are pressed as the basis for action.

Measuring Policy Actors' Values

Historically the goals of the American education system have been altered in response to shifts in values (see chapter 1). Which values prevail? To determine whether competition among the public values of choice, quality, efficiency, and equity is responsible for shaping state education policies, we must first find a way to measure the extent to which state policy-makers adhere to one or another of them. To assess policy-maker value preferences, we developed an eighteen-item survey instrument. The instrument was designed to allow respondents to provide a comparative assessment of the importance of a dozen educational problems. Each problem was phrased in such a way as to reflect the application of one of the core values to a particular school program or policy issue. Each item in the survey instrument consisted of two of these educational policy problems separated by a line divided into six segments, thus:

INCREASING   MAKING PROGRAMS
PROGRAM   —:   —:   —::   —:   —:   — MORE COST-EFFICIENT[2]
FLEXIBILITY

The 140 policymakers surveyed were asked to report their personal views regarding the relative importance of each policy problem within their home states by placing an 'x' on the line closest to the more important member of each pair. Decision-makers committed to the value of choice would be expected to endorse the item 'increasing program flexibility', while policy-makes preferring efficiency would mark closer to the item 'making programs more cost-efficient'.[3]

A summary of policy-maker response to the value preference survey is presented in figure 4.1. As indicated by the placement of the problem phrases in the columns of the figure, each phrase was designed to assess respondent value preference in one of three educational policy domains: program definition, finance, and school organization and governance. As the row labels indicate, one item in each policy domain was worded to express each of the four fundamental public values: Choice, Quality, Efficiency, and Equity. The instrument provides three separate measures of each policy-maker's relative value preference: once for educational program definition, once for finance, and one for school organization and governance. (Items were paired *within*, but not across, the three policy domains.)

Figure 4.1   Public Values Instrument Items

Value	Policy Domain		
	Program	Finance	Organization and Governance
Efficiency	Making programs more cost-effective [-2.01]	Improving the use of education tax dollars [0.82]	More efficient school management [0.91]
Equity	Giving more attention to children with special needs [0.36]	Greater equalization of resources [0.08]	Broader participation in decision-making [-1.12]
Quality	Setting higher academic standards [2.71]	Increasing the level of funding for schools [2.63]	Developing quality-conscious leadership [3.51]
Choice	Increasing program flexibility [-1.07]	Reducing restrictions on local expenditures [-3.53]	Providing more choices for families and children [-3.29]

Scores were assigned to each phrase in the instrument on the basis of the 'x' marks placed on the comparison lines. For each bipolar pair a positive score was assigned to the item closest to respondent's 'x' and an identical negative score for the other item. Responses were scored +1 when the 'x' was close to the center of the line, +2 when the 'x' was on the middle segment, and +3 when the 'x' was in the space closest to the end of the line. Thus the more powerful the preference of one item over the other, the larger the score difference between the items. Mean scores for all 140 policy-makers in the sample are shown in brackets under each phrase in figure 4.1.

Common Cultural Values

Several important observations about the cultural value system common to all states in our sample can be made on the basis of these item mean scores. Note, for example, that educational *quality items were ranked first in all three domains*, indicating that this value was widely held and was generally recognized as a critical concern in current educational policy debates.

Note also that the mean scores for *all items in the policy domains of finance and the organization/governance had the same rank order* — Quality was given top priority, followed by Efficiency and Equity, with Choice ranked a distant last. By contrast, in dealing with school program domain policy-makers ranked Efficiency (represented by the phrase 'Making programs more cost-effective') last, well behind both Equity and Choice values. Interview data suggest that this is not a measurement problem. The policy-makers simply did not view improved program efficiency as an important mechanism for raising overall school performance. They did believe, however, that more efficient management and financing are directly related to quality improvement. They saw removing regulations and increasing school program flexibility as less threatening to overall performance than increased emphasis on a cost-benefit approach to program development.

It was surprising to find so little priority given to approaches that would enhance the choice value. We found *consistently negative scores for all three choice items*. While the survey instrument forced respondents to rank order value preferences, interview data did not suggest that state policy-makers actually oppose expanding educational choice. When forced to choose, however, respondents give clear priority to quality, efficiency, and equity values. The high priority given to improving school quality found in the survey data was also a dominant theme in most policy-makers' remarks. Data from the instrument indicate that this emphasis on Quality leads most policy-makers to be willing to sacrifice Choice (especially in the fiscal and organization/governance domains). This is especially true when expanded choice is seen as competing with such direct approaches to quality improvement as setting higher academic standards, increasing school funding, and developing quality-conscious leadership. Thus at least in this sample policy-makers would sacrifice Choice before giving up any of the other values.

Receding support for educational equity is clearly evident in the data. The instrument offered policy-makers a chance to endorse three Equity oriented problem statements. The equity problems related to finance equalization and expanded participation in decision-making were ranked well behind Quality and Efficiency considerations. In the program domain, equity concerns associated with the development of programs for children with special needs ranked second, well behind the quality oriented problem of setting higher academic standards.

Additional insights into the national policy culture arise when we remember that scores on the education policy values instrument are ipsative; that is, positive scores on any one item are matched by negative scores on another, resulting in a grand mean of zero for each individual (and for the entire sample). This enables us to estimate the extent of overall agreement among policy-makers regarding the appropriate rank ordering of the four cultural values under study.[4] On the average nearly half the variance in each individual's ranking of the organization and governance policy values is shared by all policy-makers in the sample. This is a remarkable degree of consistency — clear evidence of a national consensus on the precedence of Quality over the other cultural values.

Agreement among respondents was less strong when they considered school finance policy, and value consensus was weakest of all in the program domain.[5] While consensus in these two domains is statistically very reliable, respondents agreed on the rank ordering of values only about 20 to 30 per cent of the time in these domains. That is, state policy-makers are much stronger in their agreement about the rank ordering of values in the organization/governance arena. Decentralization supporters should note that the item 'Reducing restrictions on local expenditures' received the lowest overall mean (-3.53) among all items in the questionnaire, indicating strong agreement that this was not currently a pressing problem with high priority for state policy-makers.

Policy-maker Value Preferences

We wondered whether there was a consensus on values cutting across all policy domains. We generated an overall preference score for each of the four competing cultural values by summing across the program, finance, and organization/governance domains. Distribution statistics for these four value preferences for the 140 policy-makers are shown in table 4.1. When all items are taken together, the data indicate that the cultural bias toward Quality dominates all of the alternatives by a wide margin. There is a clear cultural norm influencing the policy-makers in the six diverse states, a norm identifying quality as the dominant value perspective. Quality and Choice items are most antithetical. Policy-makers regularly picked the quality oriented problem statements over the choice items. Efficiency and Equity values are close to each other and not significantly different from the grand mean of zero. That is, while individual respondents were able clearly to distinguish equity and efficiency values, the total group displayed no consistent preference.

Table 4.1   Value Preference Statistics for All Policy-makers

Variable	Mean	Standard Deviation	Minimum	Maximum
Quality	8.85	8.01	– 9.0	27.0
Efficiency	-0.28	9.00	-19.0	20.0
Equity	-0.68	7.42	-21.0	22.0
Choice	-7.89	7.08	-23.0	15.0

By giving negative mean scores to all but the quality value option, respondents confirm the obvious fact that educational Quality is the dominant concern of state policy leaders in the 1980s. The quality value preference now holds the place reserved for Efficiency considerations in the 1920s and 1930s and has replaced the Equity thrust of the 1960s and 1970s.

Taken as a whole, the policy-makers in this study illuminate the national political culture. Despite variations from one domain to another, the values of Quality, Efficiency, Equity, and Choice are broadly shared, and a clear order of preference can be discerned.[6]

Comparisons among States

While the findings describe a robust national culture, indicating broad agreement on how the four core public values should be used to assess school problems, we wondered about the substantial disagreements among the policy-makers in our sample. The standard deviations, and especially the range data presented in table 4.1, document the extent of this disagreement. With possible minimum and maximum scores ranging from -27 to +27, we can see that individual policy-makers have taken nearly all possible value positions.

This evidence of policy-maker disagreement over values raises the question of whether subcultural norms in each state create distinctive state-level value patterns. Differences in state by state mean scores are reported in table 4.2 and displayed graphically in figure 4.2. As the graph indicates, all six states share the view that quality is the most pressing policy problem, and that choice is most easily sacrificed to get it.

Table 4.2   State by State Mean Value Preference Scores

Value	AZ	CA	IL	PA	WV	WI
Quality	6.53	10.35	10.56	8.78	8.53	9.38
Efficiency	2.33	-3.35	0.35	0.18	-2.00	-1.13
Equity	-2.93	-1.12	-1.30	-0.07	3.21	-0.71
Choice	-5.93	-5.88	-9.61	-8.89	-9.74	-7.54

Though the value of Quality was ranked first in every state, it was significantly above the national average in Illinois and California, and definitely less dominant in Arizona. The largest interstate differences are seen in the level of commitment to equity oriented policy approaches. Scores on the equity oriented policy approaches ranged from a high score of +3.21 in West Virginia (a state under court order to do something about equality of educational opportunity at the time of our study) to a low of -2.93 in Arizona.

Reasonably strong interstate variations were also found in Efficiency and Choice policy value preferences. Efficiency was most strongly embraced by Arizona policy-makers, while it was most frequently rejected by California respondents. Choice as a public value was rejected in all states, but the rejection in Arizona and California was much less pronounced than that in Illinois and West Virginia. Differences among individual policy-makers are apparently to be explained by the existence of consistent subcultural value preferences within each state.

Contrasting State Views of Public Values

Having discovered that states differ systematically, we wondered where the differences appeared — in which policy domains and in which values? Multiple

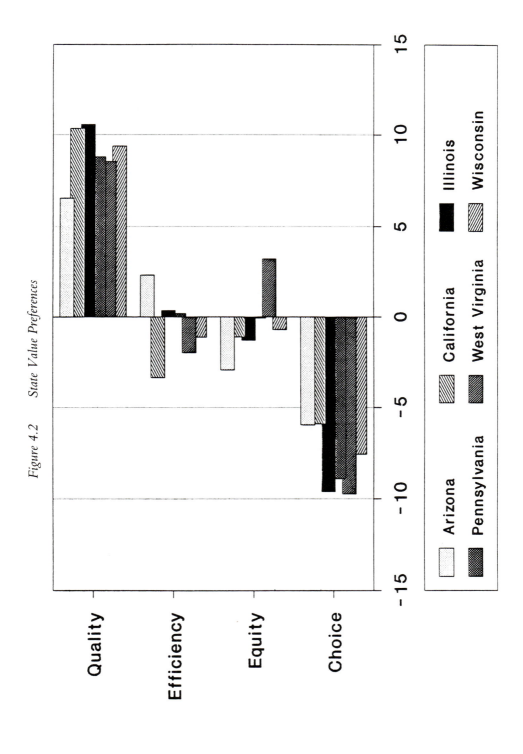

Figure 4.2   State Value Preferences

discriminant analysis is the most effective statistical tool for summarizing the interstate differences in policy value preference. Analysis of scores on the twelve survey items, with policy-makers grouped by their state of residence, is reported in table 4.3.[7] The most powerful finding supported by the data in this table is that state subcultures play a major role in determining how individuals will evaluate school finance policy problems.

Table 4.3   *Multiple Discriminant Analysis of Policy Problem Perceptions (Groups Defined by State)*

Problem		Standardized canonical discriminant function coefficients	
		Func #1 R=.50,p=.00 X2=79.5,df=45	Func #2 R=.43,p=.11 X2=42.1,df=32
Reducing restrictions	(FinChoice)	-0.773**	0.080
Greater equalization	(FinEquity)	0.474*	0.211
Increasing funding	(FinQuality)	0.383*	-0.370
Improving tax use	(FinEffency)	-0.230	0.114
Broader participation	(OrgEquity)	0.211	0.031
Cost-effective programs	(PgmEffency)	-0.088	0.068
Providing more choice	(OrgChoice)	0.000	-0.578**
Attend to special needs	(PgmEquity)	-0.047	-0.484*
Increase flexibility	(PgmChoice)	0.070	0.361*
More efficient management	(OrgEffency)	-0.118	0.257
Quality leadership	(OrgQuality)	-0.083	0.196
Higher academic standards	(PgmQuality)	0.070	0.098

State	Canonical Discriminant Functions Evaluated at Group Centroids	
	Func #1	Func #2
Arizona	-0.836	0.380
California	-0.210	-0.090
Illinois	0.594	0.619
Pennsylvania	-0.108	-0.221
West Virginia	0.853	0.091
Wisconsin	0.069	-0.828

	Group means											
	Program				Finance				Organization/Governance			
State	EFF	EQU	QUA	CHO	EFF	EQU	QUA	CHO	EFF	EQU	QUA	CHO
AZ	-1.3	-0.3	2.4	-0.8	2.1	-1.1	0.2	-1.2	1.5	-1.5	3.9	-3.9
CA	-2.8	0.2	3.3	-0.7	-0.2	-0.2	2.9	-2.5	-0.3	-1.2	4.2	-2.7
IL	-2.2	-1.3	3.3	-0.7	-0.2	-0.2	2.9	-2.5	2.0	-1.0	3.6	-4.7
PA	-2.3	1.7	2.4	-1.8	0.9	-0.2	3.0	-3.7	1.6	-1.6	3.3	-3.4
WV	-1.9	0.4	2.4	-0.9	0.4	2.7	2.7	-5.8	-0.5	0.1	3.4	-3.0
WI	-2.0	1.4	2.5	-2.0	0.6	-1.0	4.2	-3.8	0.2	-1.2	2.7	-1.8
Total	-2.0	0.4	2.7	-1.1	0.8	0.1	2.6	-3.5	0.9	-1.1	3.5	-3.3

The six states are most sharply divided over how to deal with school finance issues. As reported in the top part of table 4.3, the survey items contributing most to interstate differences are those drawn from the finance domain. Those who favor equalization of resources and an overall increase in the level of funding for education contrast most sharply with policy-makers who favor reducing restrictions on local budgets and are desirous of improving the use of tax dollars. That is, the discriminant function coefficients for fiscal choice and efficiency items are both negative, while those for items reflecting a commitment to fiscal equity and quality are positive. The value positions taken by policy-making groups from each of the six states in our study are indicated by the numbers presented in the middle section of table 4.3. The scores in this part of the table are called group 'centroids' and represent the overall view for each state's policy group. West Virginia respondents, for example, have the largest positive centroid score (.853), indicating that they strongly embrace the equity/quality perspective. Arizonans, by contrast, had the largest negative centroid (-.836), indicating that this group gave the greatest support to the choice/efficiency approach to school finance problems.

The second, weaker discriminant function is dominated by the items related to the organization and program policy domains. The governance item indicating support for strengthening community choice — 'Providing more choices for families and children' — had the largest coefficient (-.578). Disagreement over Choice is closely followed by the program equity item — 'Giving more attention to children with special needs'. One of the fiscal items appearing in the first discriminant function reappears as part of this one. That item, 'Increasing the level of funding for schools', indicates that the state decision-makers who favored greater Choice and more attention to students with special needs also favored increased funding for the schools. Contrasting with these items is the program choice item, 'More efficient school management'. This second function highlights a substantial disagreement between policy-makers who seek to emphasize traditional school improvement strategies — more money, special programs, and greater choice for families — and those who hold a more technical management approach rooted in program flexibility and better management. Illinois and Arizona tend to embrace the technical management approach, while Wisconsin respondents gave greatest support to the more traditional approach to school improvement.

The state centroids from table 4.3 are displayed graphically in figure 4.3. As shown in the figure, California and Pennsylvania policy-maker groups are at the center of the six state distribution. The other states are distinguished by the extent and nature of their differences from this California-Pennsylvania core group. West Virginia policy-makers, shown on the right side of the figure, were indifferent on the question of how to handle school improvement but gave singular emphasis to financial equity and quality. The Illinois group (in the upper right quadrant of the figure) share the West Virginia finance perspective, but add a technical management emphasis. Arizona (upper left quadrant) tends to share the Illinois management view, but gives strong support to local control over finances. Wisconsin, being neutral on the finance question and uniquely embracing the traditional school improvement strategies, is located at the bottom of the figure.

Figure 4.3   Policy Problem Perceptions: Preference Level in Each State

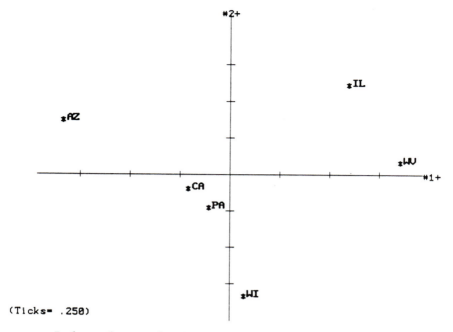

(Ticks= .250)

Independence of Policy Values and Political Cultures

Having found that cultural value preferences are reflected in state-by-state differences on specific policy issues as well as in an overall national consensus on school policy problems, two questions arise: (1) Are value preferences linked to the state political culture profiles identifed by Elazar and described in chapter 5; and (2) Are they linked to the amount of attention given by states to specific policy domains described in chapter 3, or to the competing approaches within each domain?

Political Culture and Value Preferences

Initially we expected a strong relationship between cultural value preferences and the three political culture orientations identified by Elazar. As will be seen in chapter 5, Elazar's theory of political culture led us to believe that different political cultures (traditionalistic, individualistic, and moralistic) evoke different value orientations. To our surprise, however, there was almost no relationship between the value preference and political culture perspectives of the respondents. As shown in table 4.4, none of the forty-eight correlation coefficients generated when the three political culture indices were correlated with each of the twelve policy value items and with the four aggregate value preference scales is statistically significant. Apparently these two approaches to culture definition and analysis are completely distinct and independent ways of capturing policy-maker value orientations. While both the value preferences described in this chapter and the political culture variables discussed in chapter 5 effectively shape policy orientations and preferences, each source of influence arises in its own unique way. Apparently there is no link between a policy-maker's personal value systems and his or her sense of the moralistic, traditionalistic, or individualistic citizen orientations toward governments.

Table 4.4   Correlations between Political Culture and Public Values (Pearson Product Moment Correlations; all p-values exceed .10)

Public value		Cultural perspective		
		Individual	Traditional	Moral
Cost-effective programs	PGMEF	-0.007	-0.033	0.062
Attend to special needs	PGMEQ	0.136	-0.121	0.090
Higher academic standards	PGMQU	-0.094	0.110	-0.090
Increase flexibility	PGMCH	-0.039	0.048	-0.067
Improving tax use	FINEF	0.072	-0.038	-0.025
Greater equalization	FINEQ	-0.094	0.072	-0.013
Increasing funding	FINQU	0.056	-0.055	0.052
Reducing restrictions	FINCH	-0.035	0.023	-0.018
More efficient management	ORGEF	0.008	-0.073	0.084
Broader participation	ORGEQ	-0.023	0.078	-0.088
Quality leadership	ORGQU	-0.083	0.134	-0.112
Providing more choice	ORGCH	0.108	-0.148	0.121
Aggregate value scales:				
	Efficiency	0.033	-0.064	0.054
	Equity	0.008	0.013	-0.002
	Quality	-0.055	0.087	-0.069
	Choice	0.014	-0.035	0.015

Value Preferences and Attention to Policy Mechanisms

Individual value preferences are closely linked to policy-maker views regarding state-level interest in various policy mechanisms and approaches. That is, value preference scores are strongly correlated with reported levels of attention given to the state policy mechanisms and approaches described in chapter 3. When we asked policy-makers to rank the levels of attention given to each of seven policy domains, and to evaluate competing approaches within each domain, we found substantial interstate differences. As a result, we wondered whether these assessments were related to the policy value preferences described above.

The simplest way to get a measure of association between cultural value preferences and state policy mechanism rankings is to correlate the state mean scores on each set of variables. Table 4.5 shows the correlation coefficients of state mean scores on each of the value scales with the policy mechanism rankings for each of the seven domains described in chapter 3.[8]

Table 4.5   Correlations between State Policy Mechanisms and Education Policy Goals (only correlations greater than .30 are shown)

Policy Mechanism	Efficiency	Equity	Quality	Choice
Finance	0.666	—	-0.881	—
Personnel	-0.686	0.892	0.451	-0.639
Testing	-0.447	0.621	—	-0.334
Program	—	—	-0.398	0.576
Governance	—	—	-0.349	0.728
Curriculum	0.333	—	0.432	-0.547
Buildings	0.508	-0.785	—	0.472

As indicated in table 4.5, many strong relationships exist between the average value preference scores and the average state mechanism rankings. To interpret the data in this table it must be remembered that high ranking for a mechanism yields a low number (e.g., top ranked school finance had a grand mean of 1.555, while building policies ranked last with an overall mean of 5.894). By contrast, increasing preference for any of the four core cultural values yields a higher numerical score. Hence a negative correlation between a value preference and a policy mechanism indicates a positive relationship between the policy domain and the value preference; a positive correlation coefficient indicates the opposite.

While the sample of states is too small to be certain, the correlation coefficients shown in table 4.5 suggest a number of substantial relationships between state reliance on particular policy mechanisms and overall cultural value preference. For example, in states where Quality is most strongly embraced (Illinois and California) there is also a stronger than average tendency to rank school finance as the most prominent policy mechanism. The opposite is true for states scoring high on Efficiency (Arizona): they report the lowest relative ranking for finance. The relative ranking of the personnel certification and training policy mechanism is related to both Efficiency and Choice value preferences. Arizona with the highest Efficiency preference was also highest in attention to personnel issues. West Virginia, with the lowest Choice score, was lowest in personnel policy attention.

Testing policy follows the same pattern as personnel policy, but is much less strongly associated with value preferences. The only value to affect the ranking of student testing and assessment policy was Equity. West Virginia's very high sensitivity to equity questions following a recent court mandate was accompanied by the lowest ranking of the testing policy mechanism. Low interest in equity policy in Arizona was associated with intense attention to testing and assessment policy. Pennsylvania and Wisconsin were outliers on this scale. Policy-makers in these states gave the equity value a near-zero score, but still reported high levels of attention to testing and assessment policy questions.

Program definition, school governance, and curriculum materials policy mechanisms were all related to choice value preference scores. Interest in curriculum materials was positively associated with Choice, while the program definition and governance mechanisms were negatively affected by a Choice value preference.

Table 4.6   Correlations between Alternative Policy Approaches and Education Policy Goals (only correlations greater than .30 are shown)

Policy approach	Efficiency	Equity	Quality	Choice
Finance policy options:				
Equalize	—	-0.462	0.419	0.494
Fix amount	—	0.809	—	-0.580
Target	—	—	-0.437	0.321
Finance	0.826	-0.542	-0.531	—
Offset	-0.498	0.536	0.674	-0.623
Personnel policy options:				
Certification	—	—	-0.732	0.377
Professional development	—	-0.723	—	0.777
Accountability	-0.894	0.469	—	—
Job redefinition	—	0.624	—	-0.952
Testing policy options:				
Specify format	—	-0.319	0.671	—
Use to place students	-0.829	0.777	—	—
Use to evaluate	—	0.522	—	-0.641
Measure non-academics	0.767	-0.724	—	—
Mandate local use	—	0.480	-0.390	—
Program policy options:				
Specify time requirements	0.683	—	—	-0.677
Specify subjects	—	-0.384	—	0.933
Set standards	—	—	0.504	-0.610
Target special groups	-0.940	0.498	0.371	—
Governance policy options:				
Distribute state power	—	—	—	—
Increase state power	0.623	-0.831	—	—
Shift to site level	0.388	—	—	-0.527
Strengthen teachers	—	-0.354	—	0.850
Strengthen students	—	0.603	0.615	-0.905
Strengthen administrators	—	0.540	—	-0.777
Strengthen citizens	-0.718	0.356	0.864	-0.322
Strengthen districts	-0.304	—	-0.401	0.459
Curriculum policy options:				
Mandate local use	—	-0.447	0.427	0.525
Special scope and sequence	-0.363	—	0.508	—
Special materials	0.663	—	-0.917	—
Building policy options:				
Technical reviews	—	—	—	—
Long-range planning	0.480	-0.475	—	—
Remediate problems	-0.635	0.419	—	—
Build new capacity	—	—	0.403	-0.592

Building and facilities policy attention is positively related to an interest in Equity, but negatively related to Efficiency scores. This relationship was most strongly expressed in West Virginia where building policy was high-lighted in the court decision mandating equalization of school facilities in that state.

Values Preferences and Approaches to Policy Domains

Table 4.6 presents the correlations between the four public values and the alternative approaches to policy within each of the seven broad state policy domains. As with the policy mechanism rankings discussed above, this table has an array of impressively large correlation coefficients. A number of obvi-ously strong relationships between specific policy approaches and preference for particular cultural values exist across the six state sample. Figure 4.4 summarizes in non-statistical terms the relationships shown in table 4.6. The four value preferences are shown in the columns of the figure, and the seven state policy mechanisms make up the rows.

Entries in the cells of figure 4.4 indicate how value preferences are affected by policy approach choices among the states. Approaches positively associated with each public value are shown in the upper (pro) half of each row. Those negatively associated are listed in the lower (con) half. The *finance policy* domain provides a clear illustration of the relationships that develop between cultural values and policy approach priorities. Of the five alternative approaches to finance identified during field interviews and offered to respon-dents for comment, at least one is positively related and one negatively related to each of the four cultural value preferences. Efficiency oriented states embrace a finance policy approach that emphasizes offsetting burdensome costs (e.g., transportation or municipal overburden). At the same time policy-makers in these states reject financing particular school functions (e.g., text-books or teacher salaries).

As would be expected, Equity oriented states endorse equalization fund-ing. They also embrace the financing of particular school functions approach rejected by those with an Efficiency value preference, and oppose finance policy approaches emphasizing offsetting burdensome high cost items for particular districts. Finally, an Equity value preference leads to rejection of efforts to fix the total level of spending on education.

Two of the finance policy approaches show a strong positive correlation with the Quality value preference. States preferring the quality value embrace a finance approach focused on directing state revenues to particular school functions. At the same time the quality value preference is negatively associ-ated with the use of state funds to offset burdensome high costs occurring in some, but not all, districts. Such a view is quite reasonable where state policy-makers believe that educational quality problems spring primarily from the fact that local districts fail to identify the most important school functions. Where this is true, state policy-makers would wisely conclude that they must earmark funds for local expenditure. Local policy-makers, had they been surveyed in our study, might well have indicated that quality problems are caused by low school funding levels, by demographic and regional forces, or perhaps even by dislocations created by state and federal mandates that force locals to misallocate scarce resources.

Figure 4.4   Taxonomic Framework for Education Policy

	Efficiency	Equity	Quality	Choice
1 Finance	Offsetting	Financing and equalizing	Financing	Offsetting, fixing, or targeting
	—	—	—	—
(Quality; not efficiency)	not financing	not fixing or offsetting	not offsetting	not equalizing
2 Personnel	Accountability	Professional development	Training and certification	Job redefinition
	—	—	—	—
(efficiency; not choice)	not training and certification	not job redefinition	not accountability	not professional development
3 Testing	Placement	Non-academic	Evaluate	
	—	—	—	—
(not equity)	not non-academic	not placement, evaluate/mandate	not specify form or placement	not to evaluate
4 Program definition	Target special groups	Specify subjects	Specify subjects	Set time and standards
	—	—	—	—
(not choice)	not specific subjects	not target groups or specify time	not setting program standards	not specific subjects
5 Governance	Citizen influence district role	Increase state over locals		Site/student rights, administrative control
	—	—	—	—
(not choice)		not students or administrators	not citizens or students	not teachers
6 Curriculum materials	Specify scope and sequence	For special populations and mandate locals	For special populations	Specify scope and sequence
	—	—	—	—
(choice)	not for special populations	not specify scope and sequence	not specify scope and sequence	
7 Building facilities	Remediation of problems	Long-range planning	Remediation of problems	New capacity
	—	—	—	—
(equity; not efficiency)	not technical reviews		not new capacity	

Three of the five fiscal policy alternatives identified for study are strongly correlated with an emphasis on the value of Choice. As Choice preference increases (though it is never very high), states increasingly reject equalization funding, and accept finance approaches that embrace fixing the total amount of funding and offsetting burdensome high costs for particular school services or functions.

It is especially important to recognize the existence of a strong and symmetrical disagreement between Efficiency and Quality oriented value preferences, and another between Equity and Choice perspectives. The policy-makers in this study equate Quality with directing state funds toward particularly critical school functions such as improved teacher salaries, better testing programs, or text materials. States emphasizing the value Efficiency, by contrast, view these approaches as much less attractive. They emphasize instead using state resources to offset costs that threaten the fiscal integrity of local districts. Efficiency oriented states tend, therefore, to leave the decision about how best to allocate fiscal resources among competing program elements in the hands of local educators. No doubt this broad disagreement on fiscal approach springs from the fact that policy reform efforts in the early 1980s are motivated largely by strong concerns about school Quality. Efficiency preferences (which fifty years ago were the central issue in school reform) are likely to be strongest, therefore, in states where reform is not a prime consideration.

The tension between Equity and Choice oriented state policies is quite different. These two value positions are directly opposed to each other on the issue of per pupil expenditure equalization. They also disagree about the virtues of fixing total school district expenditures and using state policy to direct funds to particularly burdensome high cost items. Equity oriented finance policy appears to be defined in terms of combining per pupil expenditure equalization with targeting state funds on state-defined policy goals, while rejecting attempts to fix the overall level of expenditure. The choice value perspective is directed towards fixed total expenditures and policies aimed at offsetting burdensome costs and opposed to equalizing the per pupil expenditures.

As important as the Efficiency vs. Quality and Equity vs. Choice patterns of symmetrical disagreement are, it may be even more important to recognize that the specific basis for disagreement differs sharply between them. Policy-makers whose primary concern is Quality, for example, while directly opposed by efficiency advocates, are likely to be seen as 'out of touch' or 'irresponsible' by those whose primary interests emphasize Choice or Equity. While school finance is a matter of great concern to most decision-makers, differences in value orientation lead to very different concepts of how to approach the issue. As a result, advocates of the various value positions are in danger of 'talking past' each other — framing arguments and proposals to deal with policy actors who either share their views or directly oppose them, while failing to consider the views of those whose interests lead them to endorse one value in the other pair of competing public values. Since victory for one value position does not always mean defeat for those holding different value preferences, these opportunities for misunderstanding offer marvelous opportunities for compromise and coalition-building within the policy system. However, they also create the optimum conditions for confusion and feelings of betrayal.

A quick review of the entries in the other rows of figure 4.4 will confirm that lines of disagreement like those found in the finance policy domain are quite strong, but not consistent, across the other policy arenas. The links between value preferences and the various *personnel policy* approaches generally follow the finance pattern. As with finance, Equity and Choice value preferences are accompanied by a strong symmetrical disagreement over personnel policy approaches. Disagreement is focused on whether professional development or changes in teacher job definitions are given the highest priority. Those who give highest emphasis to Equity favor professional development and oppose approaches involving adjustment of teacher work roles. Those who set a priority for choice will favor adjusting teacher work roles but oppose professional development. Efficiency and Quality values also lead to divergent personnel policy approaches (though without the direct opposition found in the finance domain). Where policy-makers set priority on Efficiency, one finds support for approaches using personnel accountability systems. Those wanting Quality, by contrast, will emphasize a pre-service certification and training approach.

In the *student testing* policy domain symmetrical disagreement is more sharply seen in the contrasting views of the Efficiency and Equity value positions than in differences between Efficiency and Quality. An equity orientation leads to support for non-academic testing, and to rejection of testing for placement of students. An Efficiency value preference reverses these approach priorities. Quality oriented states reject the importance of specifying the form and content of tests, but had no other strong views about assessment policy alternatives. Increasing concern with Choice was positively associated with giving greater attention to using tests to evaluate staff and/or programs.

In the *program definition* area Equity and Efficiency value preferences are in opposition on the question of whether states should target programs on specific groups of children. Surprisingly the Equity value position opposes this targeting approach. Perhaps this finding is the result of the fact that a largely white group of policy-makers rather than community leaders was surveyed. To our surprise states with higher interest in Quality showed lower attention to program standards. Those with a Choice orientation, however, supported policies for setting state standards for program definition.

In the area of *governance* a Quality value preference did not lead to positive attention being focused on any particular policy approach. Those who wanted to pursue Quality did, however, reject policies for enhanced citizen influence and policies that emphasize students' rights and responsibilities. It appears that these democratizing approaches were viewed as having potential for watering down standards. Enhanced teacher authority was rejected in states embracing a Choice value position. As might be expected, Equity value preferences lead to greater interest in expanding state over local authority. Traditionally centralization is used to alleviate local inequities. Efficiency value preferences lead to traditional lines of policy emphasis — increased citizen influence while rejecting centralization of power in the hands of state agencies.

In the *curriculum materials* domain symmetrical disagreements are similar to those in finance and personnel domains, but are weaker. State mandates for local curriculum usage, an approach preferred by equity oriented states, is rejected by choice enthusiasts. Curriculum mandates are often used to introduce Equity state-wide but they take away local educators' options. Special materials development, seen as a source of quality enhancement in states so oriented, is viewed as an impediment to Efficiency. Presumably those concerned with Efficiency believe that a range of specialized materials is unnecessary and non-cost-effective.

Building policy options are subject to divergent, but not contradictory, attention as policy value preferences change. Where states place great value on efficiency, remedial attention to architectural problems is of special importance. Where states place great value on Equity, they use the approach of long-range planning. Policy-makers give the policy approach of expanding building capacity a higher priority if they see Choice as a more important value preference.

How Cultural Values Shape Policy

This chapter has examined the role of cultural value preferences in shaping state-level education policies. Data on value preferences among policy-makers in six states were gathered by means of a semantic differential type questionnaire pairing policy problems related to educational program definition, finance, and school organization and governance. Scales of relative preference for the cultural values of Quality, Efficiency, Equity, and Choice were constructed within each policy domain.

Analysis of the value preference data indicates that in the 1980s educational Quality considerations substantially outweigh all other values. Attention has definitely shifted away from the equity considerations that dominated policy during most of the last quarter of a century. Across the six sample states significant differences were found in value orientation. These value orientation differences are unrelated to the political cultures identified by Daniel Elazar (discussed in chapter 5). Nevertheless, substantial links exist between the cultural value orientations characteristic of each state and the tendency for policy-makers to report high levels of attention being paid to particular policy mechanisms and frequent adoption of specific approaches to policy-making within each domain.

Chapter 1 framed the cultural approach to state policy research as the persistent question: which values predominate? This chapter, using data reflecting overall philosophical orientations among key policy-makers, developed a method for assessing dominant values. The resulting analysis demonstrates the importance of an overall national culture in shaping core values as well as individual state differences that veer from the national norms.

Notes

1 Significant portions of the material presented in this chapter were previously published under the title, 'The Structure of State Education Policy', in Lotto, L. and Thurston, P., *Recent Advances in Administration Theory and Research*.

2 The complete instrument is shown in Appendix B.

3 The complete instructions to all respondents read: 'Indicate your views by placing an 'x' on the line nearer to the phrase in each pair that you feel is more important. Mark the space closest to the end of the line if that item is *much* more important than the other; mark the next space if it is *somewhat* more important; and mark the space close to the center of the line if it is *only a little* more important.'

4 To do so, we simply compare the variance of the total group mean scores for each policy domain with the average item variance for the same items. The group means in the organization/governance domain have the largest variance (6.31). That represents about 48 per cent of the 13.16 average variance for each of the four items in this domain.

5 The variance of 5.01 for the group means represents only about 30 per cent of the average item variance of 16.63. Value consensus was weakest of all in the program policy domain. (The variance of the means was only 3.17, about 21 per cent of the 15.06 average for the variance of the individual items.)

6 When scores for all three subscales within the survey instrument (organization/governance, finance, and school programs) are averaged, shared variance increases across the entire policy-maker sample. That is, the 35.29 variance in the combined mean scores shown in table 4.1 is about 57 per cent of the average individual variance in the four basic values — a substantial improvement over the 48 per cent agreement within the organization/governance subscale, and an even greater improvement over the amount of shared variance in the finance and program domains (30 and 21 per cent respectively).

7 As shown in the table, one very powerful discriminant function is generated (the multiple R of .50 means that it accounts for about 25 per cent of the group member variance). Of the remaining variance, an additional 18 per cent (multiple R = .43) is explained by a second function whose low statistical reliability (p = .1) requires that we interpret it with caution.

8 With only six state means to correlate, it takes a coefficient of .729 or greater to produce statistical significance (at the .10 level). For our purposes, however, this technical requirement is not too important. Our sample of policy-makers is small and could easily be biased, hence the correlations could be spurious. The mean score for each state was produced by averaging over the entire state sample, however, making the score used to calculate this correlation much more reliable than the single measure assumed in establishing the .729 minimum value for significance.

Chapter 5

Political Culture and Policy Patterns among the States

Mobile Americans have noticed a different 'feel' as they travel to a new state or region. People in Wisconsin seem to expect a certain level of public concern for fairness and government intervention but that expectation is not there when they travel to West Virginia or Tennessee. What causes these cultural differences? Can they be identified, defined, and measured? What effect do they have on education policy? This chapter answers these questions, guided by theories of politics and culture. Culture has a significant dual nature; it creates values and choices and it is created by values and choices. In the cultural theory of Aaron Wildavsky, events in human experience become values in a context of social relations:

> Always in cultural theory, shared values and social relations go together; there are no disembodied values apart from the social relations they rationalize. . . . [People] construct their culture in the process of decision making. Their continuing reinforcement, modification, and rejection of existing power relationships teaches them what to prefer. Preferences in regard to political objects are not external to political life; on the contrary, they constitute the very internal essence, the quintessence of politics: the construction and reconstruction of our lives together (1987b, p. 5).

A cultural framework promises to provide instruments to explore explanation. 'By classifying people, their strategies, and their social contexts into cultural biases that form their preferences, cultural theory attempts to explain and predict recurrent regularities and transitions in their behavior' (Wildavsky, 1987b, p. 5). It is possible to predict political results from cultural theory by: (1) coding persons or groups into cultural categories, (2) using cultures to predict how their adherents would behave, and (3) comparing that result with alternative explanations (*ibid.*). We use this framework in this chapter; we group states, try out measures to test these cultural groupings, then identify the predictable connections between cultural type and behavior, and, finally, check for alternative explanations.

Political Culture in America

Connecting the cultural context and the policy world in our six state capitals is a 'political culture' — a link of ideas that we will use in this chapter to explain major policy differences among the states. We examine the connection between policy and 'political culture', defined by Pye as 'the set of attitudes, beliefs, and sentiments which give order and meaning, to a political process and which provide the underlying assumptions and rules that govern behavior in the political system' (1968, p. 218). Political scientists have earlier sought out these 'underlying assumptions and rules' to explain policy differences among states and regions. Key (1949) had noted how the South's cultural emphasis upon race had produced its distinctive policies and politics. Later Patterson (1968) pointed out evidence that regional cultures reflected attitudinal differences on political polls. This interest and exploration of this subnational culture dimension in America were most developed in the work of Elazar (1984, 1970), who viewed a state's political culture as 'the particular pattern of orientation to political action in which each political system is embedded' (Elazar, 1984, p. 109). He identified three cultures — discussed later — whose origins lay in different migrant streams. Their local institutions reflected differing values through succeeding generations (Elazar and Zikmund, 1975).

Elazar's cultural 'orientation' consisted of three related factors:

(1) the set of perceptions of what politics is and what can be expected from government, held by both the general public and the politicians; (2) the kinds of people who become active in government and politics, as holders of elective office, members of the bureaucracy, and active political workers; and (3) the actual way in which the art of government is practiced by citizens, politicians, and public officials in the light of their perceptions (1984, p. 112).

He inferred from regional, religious, and political beliefs that citizens would differ in these three ways over the purposes of the political system. Great diversity of political culture would be expected, he argued, from major contradictions in our values about the proper role of government and about its relationship to leaders and citizens. Some would expect government to protect the existing social order, others for it to help the community to enjoy a better life, and yet others for it to help individuals to succeed. These core beliefs lie at the heart of the three political cultures: Traditionalistic (TPC), Moralistic (MPC), and Individualistic (IPC). Each manifested different attitudes toward various objects in the political world, as table 5.1 summarizes and as will be tested shortly.

A second research tradition in political science points out the policy relevance of this cultural approach. Understanding policy differences among the American states has a vigorous research tradition in the last quarter-century. It first focused upon the debate of whether economic or political factors more likely shaped states' policies (Dye, 1966). But other policy

Table 5.1   *Characteristics of Three Political Cultures*

Concepts	Individualistic	Moralistic	Traditionalistic
Government			
How viewed	As a *marketplace* [means to respond efficiently to demands]	As a *commonwealth* [means to achieve the good community through positive action]	As a means of maintaining the *existing order*
Appropriate spheres of activity	Largely economic [encourages private initiative and access to the marketplace] Economic development favored	Any area that will enhance the community although non-governmental action preferred Social as well as economic regulation considered legitimate	Those that maintain traditional patterns
New programs	Will not initiate unless demanded by public opinion	Will initiate without public pressure if believed to be in public interest	Will initiate if program serves the interest of the governing élite
Bureaucracy			
How viewed	Ambivalently [undesirable because it limits favors and patronage, but good because it enhances efficiency]	Positively [brings desirable political neutrality]	[Negatively depersonalizes government]
Kind of merit system favored	Loosely implemented	Strong	None [should be controlled by political élite]
Politics			
Patterns of Belief			
How viewed	Dirty [left to those who soil themselves engaging in it]	Healthy [every citizen's responsibility]	A privilege [only those with legitimate claim to office should participate]
Patterns of Participation			
Who should participate	Professionals	Everyone	The appropriate élite
Role of parties	Act as business organizations [dole out favors and responsibility]	Vehicles to attain goals believed to be in the public interest [third parties popular]	Vehicle of recruitment of people to offices not desired by established power holders
Party cohesiveness	Strong	Subordinate to principles and issues	Highly personal [based on family and social ties]

Concepts	Individualistic	Moralistic	Traditionalistic
	Patterns of Competition		
How viewed	Between parties; not over issues	Over issues	Between élite-dominated factions within a dominant party
Orientation	Toward winning office for tangible rewards	Toward winning office for greater opportunity to implement policies and programs	Dependent on political values of the élite

Source: Elazar (1984), pp. 120–1.

influences, more subjective in nature, have been explored more recently. For example, a religious factor underlay political cultures, and religion has been strongly correlated with state policy outputs (Fairbanks, 1977; Hutcheson and Taylor, 1973; Sweet, 1952).

Moreover, Elazar's three cultures are directly associated with policy differences. When this concept is operationalized (Sharkansky, 1969), it becomes an independent variable in multivariate analyses of state attitudes and policies. Such analyses regularly report that the three cultures can, with some significance, explain differences in: party competition and citizen efficacy (Hanson, 1980); state intervention in the society (Joslyn, 1980); state senators' attitudes towards social and economic welfare issues, as well as toward corruption (Welch and Peters, 1980); the extent of state control of local schools (Wirt, 1980); the quality of urban life in metropolitan areas (Kincaid, 1980); teacher-pupil ratios, the volume of government employment, and local income taxes among Indiana countries (Lovrich, Daynes and Ginger, 1980); and state spending and innovation (Johnson, 1976). Indeed, when tested against the influence of economic development, the cultural explanation has also held up in path and regression analyses.

Designing Research into Political Culture

If political culture can explain policy differences, then its attitudes, held by citizens, should also be shared by their representatives, and both groups should agree, even if roughly, on policy decisions. Our central question is: can Elazar's political culture differentiate the attitudes of state policy élites, and can such differences also explain their different policy views? Such analysis moves us into the cognitive world of these élites and away from the documentary-based evidence about finances and demography that is traditionally employed to explain state policy differences. It enables us to map policy élites' understandings of how the citizenry view the role of government, bureaucracy, and politics. Later we will determine whether cultural differences are associated with policy differences.

We require several very demanding tests of the influence of political culture on state policy élites in any given policy area.[1] If we are to assert that political culture theory explains and predicts behavior in our state culture, we must demonstrate the following:

1 that élites can perceive the broad understanding of general objects in the political world that is held by their constituents, as representational theory holds;

2 that élite perceptions of constituents' political culture will cluster distinctively within and between states in the directions that Elazar's ideas would predict; and

3 that élite policy judgments and élite perceptions will cluster distinctively among the states congruent with Elazar's political cultures.

The requirements for these tests were threefold. We had to select states with the three political cultures, devise questions that tap these cultures, and test the results against the élites' judgments of current policy matters.

Measuring Political Culture

In this project two states in each of Elazar's three political cultures were employed in order to avoid possible idiosyncratic influences. The states were Wisconsin and California — MPC; Illinois and Pennsylvania — IPC; Arizona and West Virginia — TPC. Other criteria were adopted to ensure we were not examining only extreme cases. Only one state (Pennsylvania) was the most central to its own cultural category (Elazar, 1984; Sharkansky, 1969); also all but Arizona had about the same degree of state control over local schooling (Wirt, 1980). Consequently our design for testing cultural influence was conservative in the sense that easy cases were not picked.

In each state the education policy élite, interviewed in two waves, were elected officials, appointed executives, and group representatives selected by the positional method.[2] These were the 'state policy élite'.

Operationalizing Political Culture

To tap political culture, the élite were asked to provide a *perception of how people in the state generally saw or felt about a cultural object* (e.g., party competition), but not their own perception. We assumed that political experience had enabled the élite to sense roughly their citizens' cognition and affect about major aspects of the political world. Such knowledge had high survival value for the élite's representational role. We also assumed that citizens hold both cognitive and affective perceptions of these political events and objects, and that these assumptions could be tapped by a generally expressed sentence. Linguistic theory justifies this assumption (Chomsky, 1968), and has been employed recently in explaining political culture aspects of urban fiscal stress

(Clark and Ferguson, 1983). Consequently we devised eleven questions that focused upon common political events and objects, pretested with college students. Each question had three answers, each of which tapped one of the three political cultures and each closely following Elazar's characterizations (see table 5.1). The combined question and the answer that a respondent selected constituted a statement about one of the political cultures; the full set appears in Appendix F.

For clarity we provide an example (code in brackets not in original):

2   *The most appropriate sphere of government activity is seen by citizens in this state as*:
—   economic, i.e., support for private initiative, guaranteeing contracts, economic development, etc. [IPC].
—   community enhancement, i.e., public services, community development, social and economic regulation, etc. [MPC].
—   maintenance of traditional social patterns and norms, i.e., setting social standards, enforcing separation of private and public sector activity, etc. [TPC].

In states that Elazar had labelled, for example, MPC, most policy élites should mark the MPC answer above. However, the policy élite in the IPC and TPC states would select, respectively, the first and third alternatives above. Then, across eleven events and objects of political culture, the MPC answers should cluster within states that Elazar had designated MPC, IPC answers within IPC states, and TPC answers within TPC states. If this happens, then cultural responses can serve as an independent variable for analysis of policy choices. To determine clusters in the appropriate cultural category, we employed multiple discriminant analysis (a multivariate extension of one-way ANOVA).[3]

Do Élites Recognize Political Culture?

The preliminary objective in this analysis was to determine whether élite perceptions of their constituents' political cognitions and affects consistently clustered within the political culture of a designated state. If they do, then culture can be used to determine differences in élite policy judgments.

State Élites' Responses

Do the responses cluster within each state in a culturally distinct fashion? Table 5.2 reports the mean cultural answers for each state. Here a lower number signifies a higher ranking on that answer, because respondents could mark a '1' if they believed it most fit their citizens' perception, and a '3' if it least fit it (see Appendix F).

Table 5.2   Group Means of Élite-perceived Political Culture (by states)

	IPC	MPC	TPC	NÉlites
AZ	19.8	25.03	22.0	18
CA	19.50	23.29	23.21	14
IL	17.82	26.73	21.45	11
PA	17.33	25.50	23.17	23
WV	19.00	25.00	22.00	17
WI	20.91	19.86	25.36	22
Total	18.99	23.99	23.07	105
Wilk's				
Lambda	.76	.72	.84	
F	6.77	8.49	4.25	
Sign.	.000	.000	.001	

The table shows that the answers do fit rather closely within Elazar's historically-based designations. California and Wisconsin, designated MPC, load most heavily upon MPC answers and least upon IPC answers. IPC-designated Illinois and Pennsylvania load most heavily on IPC answers and least upon MPC answers. Finally, TPC-designated Arizona and West Virginia are among the three states loading most heavily upon the TPC answers; only Illinois surpassed them (a state noted for a southern region where traditionalism has dominated — Jensen, 1978; Power, 1953). These differences are not only significant statistically, but as table 5.3 shows the MPC vs. IPC/TPC difference accounts for most of the variance among the responses, and the TPC vs. IPC/MPC for a little.[4] Figure 5.1 displays the state's separation on these two dimensions. The summed scores of each state's respondents are

Table 5.3   Canonical Discriminant Functions

		Part A			
Function	Eigenvalue	Percentage variance	Percentage cumulative	Canonical correlation	Significance
1★	.436	81.0	81.0	.551	.000
2★	.080	14.9	95.9	.272	.199NS
3	.021	3.6	100.0	.142	—

★marks the two canonical discriminant functions to be used in the remaining analysis

	Part B	
	Structure matrix and group centroids	
Cultures	Function 1	Function 2
Moralistic	-.924★	.356
Individualistic	.805★	.500
Traditionalistic	.563	-.813

★significant

Figure 5.1   State Centroids of Political Culture on Two Functions

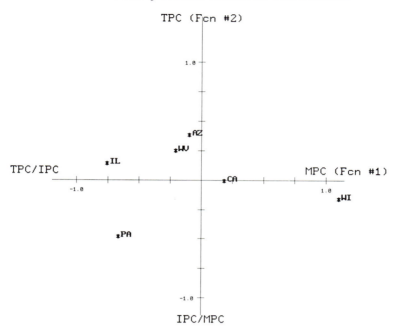

located on each. Note also the gap that separates élite perceptions in bordering states which, like Wisconsin and Illinois, had different settlement streams with contrasting values (Elazar, 1970; Wyman, 1984).

In short, our first test of the validity of Elazar's political culture was met. Our élites do see the political world in ways that discriminate among the three cultures in the direction that his historical analysis reported. We can safely assume that when we tap into political culture, we are looking at something that exists in the cognitive systems of élites and that varies from state to state.

The Fit of History to Élite Judgments

For those unfamiliar with the cultural history of our six states, a brief review will demonstrate that our findings on their political cultures fit historical accounts (Peirce and Hagstrom, 1983; Elazar, 1970, 1984; Wyman, 1984; Monroe, 1977).

Illinois is seen here as having the most IPC and TPC and least MPC perceptions of all six states. The IPC views the political system as a marketplace where individuals compete for rewards, business and politics are indistinguishable, rewards are group-based, and party loyalty binds like-minded persons. Such thinking has been well documented in Chicago whose party machine was the last to die among our big cities. But IPC also strongly influences the central areas of the state. In addition, TPC influences its southern half, and MPC influences its northern border; both trace to migrants from the South and New England respectively. These different origins shaped differences in regional economics, expression, architecture — and politics; sectional rivalry has been and remains a constant of politics, despite evidence of increasing similarity of the public's policy views in Illinois (Nardulli, 1989).

Wisconsin has provided here the most MPC and the least IPC and TPC outlooks of all six states. Its Scandinavian culture has dominated its past and is central to its Moralistic culture. Even the strong Milwaukee party system operated differently from Chicago's. The MPC underlay the state's early twentieth-century reputation for political reforms which other states have adopted. In the turn-of-the-century Progressive movement, led by Governor Robert LaFollette and university scholars, Wisconsin pioneered many non-partisan changes in local governance and the party system which swept the nation. These ultimately undermined the once-pervasive strength of the American party system, machine politics, and patronage. Its populist emphasis on initiative, referenda, and recall elections emphasizes the Moralistic insistence on citizen involvement in politics and policy-making. That historical record accords with the idea of using government for the good of the community, for addressing problems of maldistribution and inequity in human resources, and for encouraging citizen participation.

Arizona and *West Virginia* reflect a strong TPC outlook, emphasizing the leading role of economic élites in shaping public decisions, with a consequent fusing of private and public sectors and a limitation on citizen participation. Both states have known élite control of their major economic activities (extraction and agriculture) and of their parties and government. In Arizona mining industries and cotton had dominated both the economic system and state governance; in West Virginia coal mine operators' influences permeated not merely the state capitol but had literally controlled local county governments and sheriffs. In both states traditionalist élites had resisted taxing and spending for social needs, and with much violence had blocked the spread of trade unions. External forces may be breaking that up, which may account for the lack of TPC significance in table 5.2. Arizona's one-party Democratic control faded after World War II when the middle-class, professionals, and retirees from the east created a strong Republican party and new industries and commerce. Control by élites continued, but the élite were newcomers. West Virginia has known control by the coal industry state-wide and by one-party machines in the counties with attendant corruption; the state continues to hold this élite reputation, along with little change in the population.

California predominates in MPC élite cognitions over all states but Wisconsin. While eastern party systems had adapted to non-partisanship by maintaining party control until recently, in California non-partisanship has long dominated in local elections. But the state — as always — is in transition, as in-migration and economic changes have brought political changes. TPC exists in the dominance of agribusiness in the valleys, and IPC appears in the ethnic-racial conflict of the bigger cities. Those influences account for the MPC-IPC classification of Elazar and its lesser MPC location in our tables.

In sum, history (greatly condensed here) has had consequences for the kinds of political systems that evolve in our states. Religious and ethnic strains have generated differences that can be separated by only a state border, for example, with Illinois and Wisconsin, California and Arizona, and West Virginia and Pennsylvania. For our purposes these historically-rooted differences which led to Elazar's classification also match (with some looseness) contemporary élites' perceptions of their constituents' attitudes about objects in the political world. Both measures and our constraining tests suggest that there do exist varying state political cultures, namely, 'the set of perceptions of what politics is and what can be expected from government, held by both the general public and the politicians' (Elazar, 1984, p. 112).

Other Explanations: Testing for Spuriousness

However, the coherence of these responses about political culture might be spurious, concealing some other explanation. In keeping with Wildavsky's earlier noted test for validity, we needed to search for other explanations. For example, the force of urbanization — often identified with modernization — might explain the different perceptions revealed here. However, within each of the three culture types there is variation in this force. For our sample states chosen with a range of rates of urbanization the two TPC states exhibit both low and high urbanization, while within each of the other two types there is both medium and high urbanization. Consequently whatever gross demographic influence might arise within these states, urbanization does not capture it here.

We also wondered whether the personal and ideological qualities of these élites could account better for the observed differences in the answers. For example, younger élites might have a more moralistic view of changing society for the common good, or conservatives might hold more traditionalistic views of the role of government. If that did not occur, however, and élite views clustered regardless of age or ideology, then the cultural explanation would be strengthened. Consequently we selected as explanation qualities of status, partisanship, and ideology qualities which other and familiar research has shown might account for differences in social and political outlook. These variables included age, sex, occupation, party identification, self-reported degree of liberalism vs. conservatism, and income.[5] Education data were secured but omitted in the analysis because the variation was so small; most of the élite were college educated.

Do élites' personal backgrounds cause differences in their answers? The results of our analysis were striking for the absence of effect upon the answers. Six step-wise regression equations using these personal quality variables were run, three for each of the sets of cultural responses, both controlling and not controlling for influence of the state itself. However, *not one of the variables had enough significance to enter the analysis for even one equation*. In short, élite's personal qualities did *not* account for variations in their political culture perceptions. Even though élites were different in their age, sex, income, party, literalism, etc., their élite judgments were consistent across and within the six states. There was no pattern of differences that corresponded with differences in age, sex, political party, and so on. The results of this test for spuriousness further reinforce the validity of cultural responses seen in earlier tables. This finding clearly answers affirmatively Wildavsky's test 'about relative adequacy: How well does cultural theory compare in power to alternative explanations?' (1987b, p. 29).

Researching Linkages among National-Peripheral Cultures

These findings are interesting empirically, but of greater theoretical interest is whether élite perceptions actually influence their policy judgments. For this determination we need a theoretical framework to test cultural influences.

National-Peripheral Tensions within Federalism

As mentioned in chapter 1, there has been a historical debate over the influence of the national government and the national culture in the management of education. Our guiding theory is rooted in the tensions of a federal system that are generated by diversity in group values and histories. Federalism allows peripheral subsystems some freedom to express these differences in cultural forms. However, federalism also enables a national culture to develop which, under our constitutional system, can subordinate the periphery cultures. So the periphery cannot have sole and insulated influence in a society where a national culture dominates.

Consequently any peripheral government is subject to two major policy currents. First, it must generate distinctive policy currents to meet its special needs. Thus Florida needs no budget for snow removal, but nothing could move in Minnesota without it. There results great national diversity, a multi-eddied current of peripheral systems and policy sets; each eddy is roiled by its own views of government and politics. For example, we know that the states differ greatly in their openness to policy innovation (Walker, 1969), and in their policies and politics (Grey, Jacob, and Vines 1983). These realities illustrate the periphery's capacity to diffract changes sweeping through the nation.

A second policy current working upon the periphery arises from national, systemic influences that are imposed on it externally. For example, urban places must respond to external influences, to mandates of higher governments, to constraints from market oligopoly, and to the uniform impulses of professionalism (Wirt, 1985). Especially in education states also have had to respond to these three external influences, and national influences cannot be ignored. Over the last quarter-century states have responded to federal mandates in compensatory, bilingual, and handicapped schooling policies (Ravitch, 1983). Over just the last decade they have responded to a shift in emphasis from equality to excellence and choice (Boyd and Kerchner, 1988), a shift in which the Reagan administration has played a major part (Clark and Astuto, 1986). In the economy a few publishers determine textbook content for all states based on demands from just three large purchasing states. Further, for a century university professionals have set the norms of service, trained the personnel, and determined the method and content of instruction (Tyack and Hansot, 1982).

Theoretically we can understand how a state policy field will show the marks of these peripheral and national currents. Indeed, some external influences can be so effective and pervasive that peripheral cultures are swept aside across the nation. The literature of policy implementation (Ravitch, 1983) has often found this to be the case of the most publicized school policy — desegregation. On the other hand, a state's culture may challenge — even hold off — these national influences on policy, illustrated by the resistance to desegregation. In chapter 3 we determined what educational policies legislatures were adopting as a result of national and local currents. Those findings now allow us to examine the question of national versus peripheral influences. They provide the dependent variable against which to test the influence of political culture.

Testing Connections between Political Culture and Policy

The domains and alternative program approaches of our taxonomy provided a logical way to operationalize policy choices. We wished first to examine the connections between élites' political culture and the policy priorities in their states.

Élite evaluation of policy domains and approaches was derived in two forms. We asked them to rank the legislative *attention* or priority given these domains recently (last two to three years), as well as their own *preferences* for such attention. The same techniques were used to rank the program approaches for such attention. In either case this attention-ranking device provided a collective judgment by élites of legislative priorities in educational policy. A preference ranking, on the other hand, provided the élites' personal judgments of that program's importance. From these two scales of policy judgments we could ask questions about national versus peripheral influences and subsequently the influence of élites' culture perceptions.

What differences exist in élite rankings of educational domains and of program approaches? Is there evidence of national and peripheral influences upon policy? Do interstate differences exist? Does political culture explain these differences?

Findings: Domains and Approaches

Table 5.4 sets out the priorities in legislative attention given to the seven policy domains and the significance of interstate variations among them. The means of the priorities for the domains demonstrate the national and local cultures both have influence. For example, on two domains where reform currents have been working (finance and program definition) the élites' agreement was not significantly different among the states because both were being given much attention. Obviously a state political culture cannot explain much policy variation since little actual variation exists.

Table 5.4   Univariate Tests of Interstate Differences in Ranking of Seven School Policy Domains

Domain	Mean	SD	F	Significance*
Finance	1.58	1.15	2.20	.059
Personnel	3.32	1.47	5.00	.00
Student testing	3.36	1.49	18.45	.00
Program definition	3.51	1.55	1.22	.31
Governance	5.05	1.45	6.62	.00
Curriculum materials	5.12	1.46	6.26	.00
Buildings and facilities	5.91	1.54	16.25	.00

Note: ★ One-way ANOVA.

Such national agreement can result from reforms that spasmodically sweep across the states, and education has seen much of this recently because of fiscal and program dissatisfaction (Wirt and Kirst, 1989; Shinn and Van Der Slik, 1985). Not surprisingly table 5.4 reports that élites in six states consistently gave their highest attention to the school finance domain; it had the highest mean, lowest standard deviation, and insignificant interstate differences. A second reform — program definition — has also developed recently, with new course and graduation requirements (the mean was intermediate, and interstate differences were not significant). Since the national culture influences finance and personnel policy, we looked among the other five domains for the effects of peripheral culture. We wanted to examine whether state political cultures created distinctive policy choices.[6]

The thirty-three program approaches were also used to explore these nation-wide and state influences. Table 5.5 sets out the interstate variations in legislative attention to these programs. The means are a rough measure of the priorities of legislative attention, ranging from setting more program standards (highest priority) to altering the role of local districts (lowest priority). Where no significant interstate differences exist, then interstate agreements on legislative priorities can be inferred. These may result from recent national reform currents (e.g., targeting school funds on special groups, installing accountability systems, evaluating teachers and their programs, or

Table 5.5   *Interstate Differences in Legislative Attention to Thirty-three Program Approaches*

Program approaches	Mean★	Significance★★
Finance:		
Equalizing amount per child	2.21	★
Fixing total amount spent	2.35	★
Targeting on special groups	2.92★	.07
Offsetting burdensome costs	3.69★	.07
Financing particular functions	3.85	★
Personnel:		
Pre-service certification or training	1.78	.07
Professional development programs	2.32★	
Accountability systems	2.67	
Changing teacher job definitions	3.23★	★
Student testing:		
Specifying test format or content	1.47	★
Using tests for student placement	2.74★	
Mandating local test development	3.05	★
Using tests to evaluate teachers/programs	3.59★	
Measuring non-academic outcomes	4.12★	★
Program definition:		
Setting higher standards	1.42	
Mandating particular subjects	2.67★	.051
Developing programs for special groups	2.90	
Changing time requirements (day or year)	3.08	★
Governance:		
Increasing state-level control	4.10	
Strengthening administrative control	4.10	
Increasing site-level control	4.18	
Strengthening teacher influence	4.29	★
Redistributing power at state-level	4.37	★
Specifying student rights/responsibilities	4.60	★
Expanding citizen influence	4.64	
Altering role of local districts	5.02	★
Curriculum materials:		
Specifying scope and sequence of materials	1.49	
Developing specialized materials	1.91★	
Mandating local use of materials	2.58★	
Building and facilities:		
Remediation of building problems	1.63	
Technical review of plans	2.29★	
Long-range planning for change	2.70	★
Development of new capacities	3.34★	

Notes: ★ T-test of differences between means (range 1–7) on all pairs. Asterisk shows significance at the .05 level or better between group mean and the next closest group.
★★ One-way ANOVA test. Asterisked items significant at .05 level or better. Numbered items are near .05.

setting higher standards). Agreement can also result when élites do not want to consider certain policy alternatives (e.g., increasing site-level control, expanding citizen influence, or all the curriculum approaches). They may agree that it is wise to avoid such policies or that such policies do not provide leverage for changing schools.

Linking Culture to Policy Judgments: Examining Differences

If political culture can explain little policy variation where the states agree, it may where there *are* significant interstate differences. We can examine the school policy domains and program approaches in table 5.6 to see if there are interstate differences associated with such culture. Where national reform currents had been active recently — finance and personnel domains — correlations of the MPC dimension were especially weak.[7] Apparently the national goals override the state political culture. But in the other five domains stronger correlations suggest that state cultural influence may be at work.

Table 5.6   Political Culture Functions and Legislative Attention Rankings Among Seven Policy Domains

Function 1 (MPC)	R	R_2
Curriculum	-.69	.47
Governing	.47	.22
Function 2 (TPC)		
Testing	.61	.37
Buildings and Facilities	.44	.19
Program Definition	.43	.18

For example, we should expect the MPC emphasis upon the citizen's role in public life would cause these states' legislatures to give school governance *more* emphasis than in other cultures; the .47 coefficient strongly suggests that does take place. Moreover, out of deference to local participation (e.g., in devising curriculum materials) we should expect the state role in the MPC to be given *less* attention than in other cultures; the -.69 coefficient strongly suggests that is the case. Also the TPC emphasis upon élite dominance and distrust of 'liberal' school professionals should mean that their legislatures would give *more* attention to the domains of student testing and school program definition, where state mandates could override professional judgments. Both cultural inferences are supported by the strong coefficients of these two domains with the TPC dimension (.61 and .43 respectively). So in some instances political culture does explain and predict the kinds of education policy priorities.

This interstate analysis leads us to understand a major limitation on the power of political culture. It can have an effect only when nation-wide currents of policy reform do not. Nevertheless, the data permit a preliminary judgment that there is some connection between how state élites see their citizens' political world and judge educational policy.

Within-State Differences of Culture and Policy Judgments

A second method for analyzing the linkage between perceptions of state culture and policy judgments lies in sorting out differences within the states. In any state élite members may see their constituents differently. Those seeing in them, say, MPC may make policy judgments differently from other élite members in that state who see IPC or TPC in their constituents. To examine that possibility we shift from the state to the individual level of analysis. Are those individuals' differences in perceptions linked to different policy judgments by them? To answer that question, we employed within each state a multiple regression analysis of each set of cultural perceptions upon policy domains and approaches, using the legislative attention and personal preference scales noted earlier. In short, culture was the independent variable and policy judgments the dependent variable. The results appear in table 5.7.

Table 5.7   Within-State Regression Coefficients of Political Culture on Legislative Attention and on Élite Preferences in Programs

Predicting	Political culture	Beta	Significance
Legislative attention			
A. Strengthening state agencies	M	.439	.000
A. Strengthening teacher influence	M	-.297	.032
B. Long-range planning for school construction	M	.640	.000
C. Professional development programs	T	-.291	.028
Élite preferences			
D. Equity via targeting funds	M	.242	.039
A. Strengthening state agencies	M	.617	.000
A. Strengthening teacher influence locally	M	-.494	.001
A. Student control via discipline	T	.311	.037
A. Strengthening administrative control	T	.308	.034
A. Expanding parent/citizen influence	T	.324	.024
B. Long-range planning for school construction	I	-.464	.004
C. Remediation of existing building problems	I	.350	.009

Note: Letters refer to domains as follows: A=governing and organization; B=buildings and facilities; C=personnel; and D=finance.

As before, all state élites agree about priorities for legislative attention on certain domains and approaches, regardless of culture; again this agreement seems traceable to national reform currents. For example, the domains of finance and program definition were seen everywhere as getting first attention, and so do not appear in table 5.7 except in one program approach (achieving equity through funds). However, we find that there was *least* élite agreement in ranking the programs for the domain of governing schools; it is here that we would expect to find cultural differences as political cultures should have contrasting views about governing. Indeed, seven of the twelve significant differences in table 5.7 did fall within this governance domain.

Predicting Culture and Policy Judgments

Besides finding merely that there are observed differences, could culture predict policy judgments? From what we know about these cultures we would predict, first, that *MPC élites* would favor strengthening state authority to pursue common goals, that concern for equity in meeting educational needs would dominate spending, and that rationality would operate where most feasible. Some support for these predictions appears in table 5.7, where the MPC élite saw their legislatures emphasizing:

1 a financial approach that targeted funds on children with special needs (and élite preferences also agree on this priority);
2 a governing approach that favored strengthening state agencies but not strengthening the influence of local teachers (and élite preferences also agree on this priority); and
3 a buildings and facilities approach that featured rational, long-range planning for school construction (including allocation of state funds for this purpose).

Such findings are in keeping with a cultural view that governmental powers should be used centrally for equitable and rational purposes. This is direct evidence that the broad cultural dimensions that Elazar had inferred from historical data are indeed linked to the policy judgments of quite contemporary élites.

Second, *TPC élites* should be concerned about challenges to their political authority, especially from outsiders, such as the professionals who administer education. Table 5.7 shows that TPC élites:

1 opposed the strengthening of local administrators' control by giving them more discretion, by reorganizing their districts, and by mandating their evaluation and employee discipline programs;
2 favored more control of students by mandating their discipline and modifying their suspension or expulsion regulations; and
3 expanded the influence of parents and citizens over student assignment or transfer and favored tuition tax credits or educational vouchers which professional public educators oppose.

Put another way, TPC élites were significantly agreed on policies that would weaken the traditional influence in education that is exercised by the state government and by local school professionals, thereby strengthening local élite power. The first two approach preferences suggest a TPC suspicion of any power-sharing with administrators or students. In the third approach educational vouchers would weaken professionals' authority and its support is often seen as a traditionally 'conservative' program. Finally, empowering citizens to assign students to schools may reflect a traditional fear of federal intervention in desegregation.

IPC élites, driven by the desire to optimize freedom, should have a policy preference for the independence of local school authorities, preferring to keep the state's hands out of local matters. But we should also expect to find a policy diversity inherent in the term 'individualism', and that is indeed seen in table 5.7 in the absence within these states of an IPC view on *any* of the seven policy domains. However, some agreement among this élite does exist in:

1 opposing long-range planning for school construction; and
2 favoring remediation or the 'fixing up' of existing building problems (i.e., incrementalism) by removing asbestos and measures for earth-quake safety, and energy conservation.

These views support a local–control orientation but little else. State plan-ning is obviously inconsistent with a marketplace outlook that is at the heart of IPC. Also an incrementalist remediation approach to buildings would leave construction problems to local units to solve as their resources and preferences would dictate. But more importantly the IPC élite could not agree on anything at all in matters of school governance. This absence of any ideological orien-tation to the specific purposes of governing is quite unlike the outlook of the MPC. Rather the IPC élite seem to adopt consistently only one view on this range of domains and approaches : let locals handle it.

An Inductive Test of Culture-Policy Congruence

The twelve statistically significant findings in table 5.7 may seem meager results when one is testing three cultures' effects on seven domains and thirty-three programs. The most demanding test of the association between culture and policy would be that culture should predict élite preferences for all thirty-three programs. However, the small numbers of this study and the over .75 coefficient needed for confidence levels render that goal unlikely. But a meas-ure less demanding than this does point to the existence of a real linkage between élite perceptions of political culture and policy judgments.

The coefficients between each culture and the thirty-three program approaches should exist in a patterned way, even if not high enough for statistical significance. For our measure of culture we used the two MPC and TPC dimensions derived earlier, each a rough measure of its cultural views. Do these correlate consistently with how élites saw their legislatures treating the thirty-three program approaches? Does each broad dimension relate posi-tively with its central culture, that is, MPC dimension with MPC, and TPC dimension with TPC? Do their coefficient signs consistently differ, that is, TPC responses versus MPC? Table 5.8 provides the data for answers. To illustrate the measure, the first row shows a policy approach (its content is

Table 5.8   Predicted and Actual Coefficients of Culture with Program Approaches

Domain	Approach	Function I	M	Cultures T	I	Correct prediction
Program	1	.5	.4	−	−.6	
	2	−.6	−.6	+	.7	
	3	.8	.8	.6	.8	
	4	.5	.5	+	.6	
Finance	1	+	+	+	+	★
	2	−	−	+	+	
	3	+	+	−.6	+	★★
	4	−	−	+	+	
	5	−	−	+	+	
Building	1	+	+	+	−	★
	2	−.5	−	+	+	
	3	+	+	−	+	★★
	4	.7	.8	−.7	−.7	
Curriculum	1	−.9	−.9	.8	.8	
	2	−.5	+	−	−.6	★
	3	+	.5	−.7	−	
Governance	1	+	+	−.7	−	
	2	+	+	+	−	★
	3	+	−	+·	−	★★
	4	−.7	−.7	.6	.7	
	5	.5	.5	−	−.5	
	6	−	−	+	+	
	7	−	−	+	+	
	8	−	−	+	+	
Testing	1	+	+	−	−	
	2	−	−	+	+	
	3	−	−	+	+	
	4	−	−	+	−	★★
	5	+	+	−	−	
Personnel	1	−	−	−	.6	★
	2	−	−	+	+	
	3	−.6	−.6	.5	.7	
	4	+	+	−	−.5	

Notes: + = positively correlated with this program approach.
− = negatively correlated with this program approach.
(If blank, in last column, all three cultures have signs that culture would predict.)
★ = only polar types, MPC and IPC, have the predicted opposing signs.
★★ = predicted and actual coefficients were mismatched.

irrelevant here) in which the MPC dimension related positively to the MPC (that is, the two were congruent) and negatively to the other two cultures — as one would predict if cultures influenced policy choices.

As table 5.8 shows, there is indeed much consistency. Of the thirty-three programs:

1 the predictions in twenty-four cases are met for all three cultures; meaning that the MPC and TPC answers opposed one another in all these cases;

2 in five other cases the predictions are met, but only for the most polar cultures;

3 ultimately only four cases failed to predict;

4 overall, thirty-one cases have the MPC sign correctly matching the MPC dimension sign (both measures had the same signs for the thirty-one programs), and twenty-nine cases have the IPC sign opposing the other (that is, the cultural dimension nicely discriminates on program approaches);

5 some policy domains (e.g., school programs, curriculum materials) demonstrate high — even significant — correlations among the cultures.

Consequently these inductive findings strengthen the possibility that political culture is working *even amid these numerous and detailed program choices*. Moreover, the results suggest that in a study involving even more states the number of significant coefficients would increase. Employing our instrument (see Appendix F) for élites at other levels and with other policies would determine whether the inference of the political culture effect is valid.

Summary: The Explanatory Power of Political Culture

We have sought to validate the concept that political culture, especially the moralistic-individualistic dimension, appears to be structured within élite perceptions of citizens' views among six states. These cultural perceptions are independent of social context (or at least urbanism as a measure of modernism) and independent also of such personal qualities of élites as their status, partisanship, or ideology. These clustered perceptions discriminate among our states and in patterns that Elazar had inferred from historical research. Further, these perceptual clusters discriminate, albeit roughly, among a wide variety of policy domains and programs in education.

However, the explanatory power of peripheral culture is limited when all states are swept by specific policy reforms — such as finance — that arise out of currents that are national (Boyd and Kerchner, 1988) and indeed international (Wirt and Harman, 1986). Also political culture is limited when most élites regard a policy domain as unimportant, as in the case of buildings and facilities. But where peripheral cultures are free to work, we find that the legislature's attention and élites' preferences in some policy areas are patterned in ways consistent with each culture's policy orientations. This is particularly so for MPC and TPC, which Elazar had also claimed were the two prime cultures in American politics.

Validating political culture is important for any further state policy research because political culture provides a set of cognitive and affective screens that mediate between environmental and structural variables and state policy outputs. That is, this additional approach to policy élites helps us understand the important personal element in policy-making. That importance has been widely reported at the micro-level of policy research, for example, in case studies of the singular or comparative type (Peterson, 1981; Browning, Marshall, and Tabb, 1984). Our own micro-analysis of leadership in chapter 2 shows how implicit rules and attitudes are crucial in policy-making. At the macro-level, where one uses multiple case studies under the same research design, political culture is a strong candidate for explaining the variety of political systems, procedures, and policies. All of this is comprehensive evidence that 'cultures may be conceived of as grand theories, paradigms if you will, programs if you prefer, from whose few initial premises many consequences applicable to a wide variety of circumstances may be deduced' (Wildavsky, 1987b, p. 6).

Notes

1 These tests for validating political culture are very demanding for three reasons. For culture to affect élite judgment the test requires combining both élite opinion data and historical population data, it requires élites actually to be able to perceive their constituents' values, and it requires a congruence between élites' perception and their policy judgments. A difficult problem also arises in devising a measure of élites' perception of political culture without using just Elazar's general designation of their state as moralistic, traditionalistic, or individualistic. If élites' opinions of their state culture also fitted Elazar's historically-based designation, the latter concept would be validated. However, validation would fail if élites within any state disagreed about their constituent's cultural views, or if they did agree but in a direction designation. In short, a strong test of the presence of political culture must demonstrate both intra-state consistency of official views as well as congruence with the historical designation. If validated, political culture as perceived by élites can become an independent variable. But it must distinguish élites' judgment on current policy issues independently of other explanations, such as élites' personal and ideological qualities.

2 There were seventeen to thirty respondents from each state, totaling about 140, whose responses on various scales were used in subsequent multivariate analysis; however, the full set used on the political culture for this chapter totalled 105.

3 This technique distinguishes between groups (in this case policy élites) by a particular criterion variable (i.e., ways one might expect those groups to differ); the latter are the responses to the questions explained above and found in Appendix F. The technique combines the answers to make the policy élites' answers as widely and as statistically distinct as possible by constructing functions, that is, clusters of answers that are similar among

the states. The operation also generates a score for each group which can then be used in regression analysis. These functions are rotated to provide optimal separation among the groups, with the first function always providing the best discrimination possible. As axes of a geometric space, these functions can also demonstrate the spatial relationship among the groups studied.

4 In table 5.2 differences in mean scores are significant, IPC and MPC at the .000 level and TPC at the .001 level; rho coefficient = -.89. In table 5.3A these differences cluster into distinguishable clusters. The first function accounts for 81 per cent of the variance among this group of states, and was highly significant (.000). However, the second function has only 15 per cent variance and contains much sampling error, but it is used for the following analysis, while the third is dropped. Table 5.3B further reveals the specific components of the two functions that undergird the text statement.

5 Respondents were asked to rank order the alternative domains or approaches, with a 1 for the alternative receiving the most attention from the legislature and 7 the least. But respondents did not rank all alternatives, as they were asked to identify only the three domains with which they felt most knowledgeable; if time permitted, they would rank on other domains. The number of evaluators ranged from 37 (buildings) to 114 (finance). The average respondent provided data on 3.5 domains.

6 States were entered first as a block before introducing élites' cultural perceptions; this process took out any state effects which would have confounded the effect of culture.

7 With but six states, statistical theory requires a quite high coefficient (.75) for associations to be regarded as significant; most coefficients did not reach that level.

Chapter 6

Cultural Values Embedded in Statutes

The newcomer to Wisconsin's school systems is told to 'get with the program' when he persists in trying to give students and parents choices in curriculum. Citizens of Illinois are comfortable and accustomed to a focus on trying to make schools run efficiently and make them accountable. Within states there are understandings about the directions for policy. Where do the understandings come from? Can we identify and measure them? What do they show about policy directions for schools? These questions are answered in this chapter by an examination of cultural artifacts — the education codes. The codes are evidence (just as pottery shards are) of social relationships and understandings of previous times. They are the residue of the cultural values that prevailed.

Social and political realms of culture are interwoven. The culture shapes the value preferences and guides the behavior and choices. In this chapter we wish to explain how culture has implications for value preferences and how variations in those values are influenced by differing political histories that shape political culture. We need, first, to understand how we will use the term 'culture' before we can understand how its variation has shaped differing value choices over education policy.

Culture as Theories of Preference and Program

At the core of the meaning of culture are two phenomena: social relationships and common values. Sharing in these relationships and commonalities has great utility in helping people make their way with few cues through the ambiguities and uncertainties of life. As Wildavsky has noted:

> Cultures may be conceived of as grand theories, paradigms if you will, programs if you prefer, from whose few initial premises many consequences applicable to a wide variety of circumstances may be deduced. Think of cultures as rival theories; they organize experience [and] tell

us what to take for granted (the assumptions) and what to test (the consequences) (1987b, p. 6).

But we must understand that at the core of such interactions lie values or preferences for action and belief. That understanding is crucial for also understanding the educational policies among a set of governing units. Equally important is understanding the diverse value choices that citizens may make. Certainly no aspect of life available to the senses is free of differing preferences about what is being seen and valued. This variety in cognition and affect is not infinite, but even the dissensus that can exist about the commonest object in experience has consequence for the political world. Mundane matters — for example, whether the state policy is allocated to dictate the number of books in elementary school libraries — can create intense political battles.

For the political system everywhere is engaged centrally in allocating resources among competing preferences for their use. It is our contention that a major explanation of how such policy-making transpires lies with cultural variations over social relationships. According to Wildavsky:

> Any strategy or policy, therefore, has to be justified by beliefs concerning what people are about and how the world is — a particular idea of justice and a particular idea of nature. Such pairing of beliefs and their sustained values is visible in all societies. . . . In cultural analysis, context is critical. . . . Thus, in this theory, cultures are not embedded in something else; they are the thing-in-itself, social structure, if you will, that needs to be explained and that, once known, helps explain such phenomena as political preference (1987b, pp. 25–6).

What is the range of variation in these beliefs and value preferences about education, how may these values be detected, and how does cultural variation explain value variation? We began by defining and detecting the variation in values.

Specifying Values in State Education Policy

Values are important to study because they represent 'one of those stable units for understanding human nature in its political, as well as in many of its other aspects' (Easton, 1965, p. 11). But using them for empirical analysis in policy-making has always been hard because so often they are seen simply as some 'soft' notion of what policy-makers are attempting, something to be inferred from behavior. After an iterative process in which we reviewed the various ways to analyze values, we determined to attempt the task of empirical analysis of values by defining values in terms which permit their analysis behaviorally, that is, by revealing what policy behavior is to be rewarded or penalized. One record of such behavior lies in the education statutes among our six states; these are authoritative documents, allocating resources among preferred ends. The analytical method we use is content analysis of these documents, usually called 'codes', for their implicit values.

In Chapter 4 we noted that Garms and associates (1978) have argued that just three values could encompass all of this policy-making — Quality, Efficiency, and Equity — to which we added Choice. Our tasks were, first, to define behaviorally a set of values in state educational policy; second, to draw out the internal logic of these values so as to suggest that they stimulate certain tensions in the policy world that are treated differently by political cultures; and third, to determine if these values possess an historical sequence. Reducing multiple experiences to limited categories in this fashion has great utility in building social theory. It helps identify and clarify for analysis relevant referents in social action, such as the value preferences that are sought by political authorities when they make policy.

Procedures for Content Analysis

We reached our definitions of four basic values by an iterative process among the three authors. First, our discussions started with generalized notions of what a given value might mean when inferred from the behavior of those political actors pursuing it. This process eschewed those 'carousel' definitions beloved by dictionaries, wherein one vague term is defined by another just as vague. Rather *we sought to define values by the behavior required in law.* Next we employed these behavioral definitions in a preliminary review of whether they did indeed match the statutes' wordings — or codes — of the six states. That review then led us to specify in more behavioral detail what a given value meant when public resources were expended in law. A behavioral definition, then, requires that a value's meaning rests upon *the observed presence of specified program actions that educational authorities take in order to affect educational clients* — pupils, parents, teachers, and so on.

Four excerpts from the Illinois code for 1983 serve to illustrate how we approached the problem of trying to understand the values incorporated in the education code. These involve practices familiar in all states and fall under the general policy domain (as defined in chapter 3) of personnel training and certification:

1. [Teachers and supervisors must] be of good character, good health, a citizen of the United States [and hold] a certificate of qualification granted by the State Board of Education or by the State Certification Board . . . [Sec. 21–1].
2. [Each teacher must] keep daily registers . . . of each pupil [to be returned] to the clerk or secretary of the school board. [If not, no teacher] shall be paid any part of the school funds . . . [24–18].
3. [Forbids a ban against certification, training, or teaching] because of a physical handicap including but not limited to visual and hearing handicaps. [21–1]
4. [School boards may, but need not,] examine teachers by examinations supplemental to any other examinations . . . [10–21.1].

These references all focus upon behavior, and the wording uses mandatory terms (shall, must), as well as permissive terms (may). The behavior in the wording is manifest, e.g., teachers must keep daily registers of students' attendance.

These four selections also display different values, and four broad types of values behavior underlie these four items. Item 1 infers that certain *qualities* of behavior are important in teachers; Item 2, that a specified method is required to keep records *efficiently*; Item 3, that no one class of citizens can be denied *equity* of access to something of value; and Item 4, that public authorities may *choose* or not to employ other testing means. This code analysis, then, focused on operational definitions of values, since codes are written with values implicit in behavioral terms.

Behavioral definitions of four values. After arriving at detailed behavioral definitions of four broad categories of values, we refined these definitions by testing them against the language of state codes, and finally concluded that our value categories had matched all the behaviors prescribed in these codes. However, other values do exist that could be subsumed under these four. For example, in Item 2 a desire for *honesty* in governmental performance is subsumed, but honesty is only instrumental to achieving a more basic value — Efficiency. This illustration indicates the inextricable linkage of values, which can only be clarified by more precise definition and analysis of their highly political qualities. The next sections provide such a definition and analysis.

Choice. Normally Choice means the presence of a range of options for action, as well as the ability to select a preferred option. Here Choice means a state mandate that offers a school clientele the opportunity either to make policy decisions or to reject them (see essays in Boyd and Kerchner, 1988). Note the contradiction in terms: a mandate is a 'must' term, but in this case it permits someone to exercise power if desired. Note further that Choice exists for clients in a district even if no state law exists on a given matter. For example, some states, like Pennsylvania, have a code allowing individual school districts to implement anything not mandated or proscribed; and so a special course for honor seniors may be offered by a school without any state law.

The presence of Choice in codes can be indicated by several rules:

1 explicit granting of policy options, for example, a law granting districts their choice of textbooks for a given course;
2 use of permissive verbs like 'may' or 'can' in reference to a district's options, for example, a parental advisory board for a particular program may be adopted locally if wished;
3 selection of an option by non-professionals in the district (voters, parents, students), even though professional administrators and teachers would have to carry out that policy option; for example, voters may vote a bond issue up or down.

It is important to look behind the presence of Choice for the substructure of other values which generate it. In this case the underlying value is the key political value of democracy, popular sovereignty; this is the constitutional, and hence legitimate, authority of citizens over public officials in their policy actions. Choice becomes an instrumental value, a means for citizens to exercise their sovereignty.

Efficiency. Efficiency is widely used as a standard in many aspects of American public and private life, but it is also a very complex value. Its classic definition is that of a ratio of work to energy expended, a totally machine-like approach. But in referring to human actions Efficiency is popularly seen as a goal, as in 'We intend to make this program the most efficient in the country.' In reality this value is less ends oriented than means oriented. That is seen in state codes where Efficiency appears in two forms:

1   Efficiency has an *economic* form, as seen in the effort to minimize costs while maximizing gains in order to optimize program performance. This usage is an economic surrogate for the ratio of work-to-energy definition. In state codes economic Efficiency may appear as a state mandate to determine local compliance with a policy goal by specifying the resources that will be needed to accomplish specified units of work. Most often this appears as a ratio of services to be provided for a given number of persons, the familiar pupil-teacher ratio.

2   Efficiency also has an *accountability* form. This is the mandating of those means by which superiors in an authority system can oversee and hence control their subordinates' exercise of power and responsibility. This form of Efficiency is manifest in the detailing of procedures that school authorities must follow in many matters, especially in the budgetary process. Such procedures ensure that those affected by the exercise of power can judge its wisdom, honesty, and effectiveness.

We saw earlier that underlying Choice is the political value of popular sovereignty that asserts the necessity for those who use power to be responsible to those who authorize its use, a fundamental principle in any democratic nation. Efficiency is an instrumental value — a means to an end. Its values put in place the economic and accountability methods to make the exercise of popular sovereignty work well.

Equity. In the policy world Equity usually means the use of public resources to redistribute public resources for the purpose of satisfying disparities in human needs. In behavioral terms this value involves two stages. In the first, a disadvantage, deficiency, or other measure of the gap between the norms of social life and the needs of citizens is found to exist in some public services. Moral and political conflicts thereupon arise over this gap, and always the same questions arise (Wirt, 1983). Which groups should be listened to about their needs? How should those needs be addressed programmatically? How should programs be financed? What level of government should address the problem? In the second stage of Equity policy-making, public resources are applied through programs designed to close the gap between norm and need. It should be noted that public resources are not needed by those already advantaged by their own private resources. Unlike other values, then, Equity is a distinctly *private* value — what one needs — treated by *public* policy — government action to meet one's need.

Equity is most familiarly seen in education in compensatory or handicapped educational programs. Typically both define a norm-need gap, and both then employ public resources in the form of mandates to close that gap. Quite often such state mandates are designed to implement similar federal programs. Such equity requirements appear in codes as detailed guidelines for ensuring the distribution of school resources for particular pupils.

Implied in Equity are other political values, however, such as the worth of every individual in society and the responsibility of society to realize that worth. These values are also aspects of the democratic ideal which emerges in modern life as programs of social democracy. In brief, realizing individual worth requires its enhancement and protection by public and private institutions. Equity policy thus reflects an instrumental value for realizing this more basic value of the individual's worth and society's responsibility.

Quality. Popularly Quality means 'the best', and in this case public policy matches the public view. Again a two-stage behavior operates in the application of this value. First, the state will mandate the need for certain standards of 'excellence', 'proficiency', or 'superior ability'. However, policy actors can seldom find widely acceptable definitions of Quality performance. Quite often Quality is designated simply by statements of minimum standards that have been redefined over time; in the 1980s we are at the back side of such a reform wave following *The Nation at Risk* call. A second stage of Quality requires that, in order to achieve these standards, public resources are applied across districts, or within a district across schools, with their typically uneven distribution of resources (see essays in Boyd and Kerchner, 1988). Quality is evident in such educational policy areas as training, use of instructional resources, and performance by school professionals or pupils. This history of education has been driven by this search for Quality, whether in curriculum, teaching methods, teacher and administrator training, or other attributes of the professional model of education (Cremin, 1964). In state codes this search is seen most commonly in the certification procedures for teachers or in school program definitions.

Quality is instrumental for another and more basic social and political value, namely, the belief in the crucial importance of education for the future citizen's life chances. As means, Quality policies can provide the norms and resources to improve those life chances by preparing the citizen for a complex world.

Summary

The crucial significance of these four values in the educational policy world cannot be overstated. They are major normative references for this policy in any nation, although priorities will differ with the system. Even an authoritarian system has rulers who must be concerned about Quality and Efficiency in education. They also need to provide Equity remedies to close gaps between public norms and private needs; but they will ignore Choice by others when they believe they know best. In democratic systems, on the other hand, all four values are pursued, although, as we will see shortly, not with an even hand. How these values are distributed by the priorities of policy-makers is an issue of interest to which we now turn.

Codes as Reflections of Cultures

Laws are ultimately statements about the particular values that dominate within a political system. Such values reflect cultures. In any democratic system different cultures are commonly found, each emphasizing particular values that their members pursue in their behaviors and interactions and in their public policy preferences. In this section we demonstrate the presence of such cultures as a means for understanding state policy-making. We also show how the analysis of codes identifies the value priorities of cultures.

Testing these propositions was made possible through content analysis of state codes for the emphases given our four values.[1] Rarely undertaken (but see Henning *et al.*, 1979; Wirt, 1977), content analysis demonstrates which behaviors are preferred and which are not. Our analysis rests upon a tally and analysis of all 'items' of the codes of education for Illinois and Wisconsin in 1980. These two states were chosen for their contrasting political cultures based on historical studies (Elazar, 1979, 1984; Peirce and Hagstrom, 1983), a distinction more fully substantiated in chapter 5. Furthermore, we examined seven broad policy domains (explored more fully in chapter 3) for the frequency of the four values in their state codes.

The Cultures of Merit, Democracy, and Equity

In chapter 1 we noted the almost continuous conflict over the issue of who should govern in education policy. We posited that this conflict, often viewed as one between levels of government, could also be viewed as one between cultures, and that state codes and statutes reflect prevailing cultural views. We suggest that three broad subcultures interact with values. A meritocratic culture is implicit in bureaucratic, organizational norms that are a hallmark of modern civilization, and amid these norms the professions serve increasingly to influence policy ideas. Their influence has become so great that one close observer finds that we now have in this country 'the professional state' (Mosher, 1982). Its value emphasis would be Quality and Efficiency. However, this meritocratic cultural theme can run counter to two other cultures: the egalitarian and democratic. Proponents of egalitarian themes seek special resources to remedy deficiencies imposed by the economic or political orders, an idea developed in chapter 4. Its value emphasis would be Equity. Adherents to democratic cultural themes, on the other hand, seek to exercise authority over meritocratic policy-making, so its value emphasis should be choice. Consequently actors within meritocratic, egalitarian, and democratic cultures pursue in public policy their respective values of Quality and Efficiency, Equity, and Choice, and their claims often conflict. We have noted how value priorities shifted quite dramatically among these cultures since the 1970s from Equity to Quality in federal policy (Clark and Astuto, 1986), and a parallel state reform shift toward Quality (see essays in Mueller and McKeown, 1985).

What can we discover about the presence and conflict of these cultures in the state codes? An analysis of cultural assumptions and of the decisions of state policy-makers led us to believe that a comparison among cultures would show that:

1 The culture of professionalism would be evidenced in code references to the Quality and Efficiency values, as defined earlier. A full literature has attested to the profession's efforts to create and maintain professional norms of this kind (Callahan, 1962; Cremin, 1964; Tyack and Hansot, 1982). This culture features an élite group who sets standards of service, qualifies the approved personnel, and evaluates its own work — in the pursuit of Quality. Also Efficiency values involve the control of implementation by higher over lower authorities; in this way professionals seek responsiveness to their standards of Quality at district levels.

2 This professional culture, however, would exhibit some conflict with the culture of democratic control, as evidenced by code references to Choice. Thus non-professional control of schooling policy through board elections and referenda is a distinctive feature of American education, but one that professionals have systematically sought to deflect to support their goals. However, in this country and elsewhere a popular challenge to professional decision-making has increased in recent decades (Wirt, 1981, 1988), an assertion of the Choice value.

3 Another culture would exist in the egalitarian impulse as made evident by Equity values in the code references, those that seek to redress the maldistribution of schooling resources. The meanings of Equity are many, of course, and a federal system augments such differences as reflected in its varied state policies (see essays in Gray *et al.*, 1983). But the 1960s witnessed national ventures — thereby stimulating state support — that sought Equity in legal, financial, and substantive policies (Iannaccone, 1988).

4 Different configurations of these four values would mark broad differences in state cultures, although we suspected that Quality references would dominate because they define so many aspects of the school program.

5 Different configurations would appear where different political histories have generated different expectations about the social and political relationships of citizen to government, i.e., different political cultures.

In this fashion an analysis of codes within states can provide insight into past effects upon policy actors. To test this linkage, we selected two states of strongly different political cultures that the preceding chapter substantiated. These were the MPC of Wisconsin and the IPC of Illinois. A content analysis performed as noted earlier provided the distribution of the four values, as table 6.1 shows. The N represents the total of all code references in each state, and the percentages report the proportion of that total represented by each of the four values derived from our content analysis.

Table 6.1   Cumulative Distribution of Values in Code References by States

	N★	Quality	Equity	Efficiency	Choice	
IL	1190	19.3	19.0	48.2	13.5	=100%
WI	401	18.4	27.2	36.2	18.2	=100%

Note: ★ The numbers represent the total of all items in each state's education code, with an item defined as in footnote 1.

Common Cultures and Patterns of Value

The presence of the meritocratic culture in these codes is spread across both states in the dominance of Efficiency and Quality values. In particular the dominance of Efficiency in both states suggests that previous policy-makers were less motivated by Quality than by the need to control the implementation of their authority. These code references are replete with reporting and accounting procedures for the implementation of substantive policies. This dominance makes sense because it flows first from the constitutional pre-eminence of state authority in education, but it is also evidence of meritocratic influence by the professionals in defining those procedural requirements. Policy-makers assumed that good accounting systems run by the professional educators would result in good schools.

This meritocratic dominance is striking in the light of the few signs of the democratic culture in Choice references; these turned up the least of all four values in both states' codes. They cover election, referenda, and representational requirement. However, this small frequency is not necessarily directly equivalent to small importance in policy-making. After all, Choice can generate powerful policies. The decisions made under such values can significantly affect distribution of resources and values at every district in a state. That is especially evident when all tax overrides or increases must be brought to the voters for acceptance.

As for the fourth value, strong evidence of the egalitarian culture appeared in Equity provisions, such as for equal educational opportunity, desegregation, special education, and other redistributive programs. Again smaller numbers need not mean smaller influence on those affected; after all, Equity provisions, through their redistribution of resources, must have some importance for those whose deficiencies are being addressed.

Differences among State Cultural Values

This distribution by values in table 6.1 shows also differences between the states. Aside from the predominance of Efficiency in both states, two configurations emerge.

In Illinois the other three values are distributed about equally; another analysis (not shown here) found that Efficiency consists mostly of accountability provisions that are designed to control the use of power. These provisions ensure that for any responsibility granted, school authorities will be held accountable by those over whom it was exercised. In Illinois power granted has meant power checked.

Political history helps explain this configuration (summarized from Peirce and Hagstrom, 1983). Illinois is characterized by fragmentation of state power, political corruption in Chicago and some rural counties, a citizen sense of politics as 'dirty', and high conflict between parties and regions (see essays in Nardulli, 1989). Consequently making grants of authority accountable reflects the reformist reaction against these practices; reformers sought control in reporting, accounting, and publicizing requirements for decision-making by local authorities. By 1988 the same effort was undertaken to institute accountability for alleged incompetence in the Chicago schools. Another element of this state's political culture is considerable localism, a preference for local control paired with a suspicion of state control (Wirt, 1977). As described in Chapter 5, Elazar (1970, 1984) has characterized Illinois' political culture as 'Individualistic', one where the political system is seen as a marketplace in which one seeks to maximize individual preferences, regardless of legal, moral, or other constraints.

It is clear from the data of table 6.1 that Illinois is different from Wisconsin in the configuration of its code values. While Efficiency is most evident in Wisconsin, it is closely rivalled by Equity values, substantially more than in Illinois. While both states give about the same attention to Quality, Wisconsin gives substantially more to Choice. Wisconsin's configuration shows the marks of both the meritocratic as well as the egalitarian cultures in its educational policies, with also comparatively more attention to the democratic culture.

The Wisconsin findings are not surprising in view of its history, culture, and policies. The political history of Wisconsin differs from that of its neighbor. As noted in chapter 5, the Scandinavian influence among its founders generated a view of government as a positive instrument for improving the common good. Consequently Wisconsin has been a leader in social, political, and economic reforms, a laboratory of policy change. In this culture the citizen plays a positive role with more activity expected in governmental operations; hence its politics have a healthy affirmation of that citizen role. For example, the initiative and referendum were pioneered in this state, both measures that enable the citizen to vote directly on public policy. In short, political power here has been used positively to improve citizens' lives but still within a web of democratic control. This is the political culture labeled 'Moralistic' by Elazar.

In the value configuration of Wisconsin, then, while the political culture is important, other cultures have a larger place. The meritocrats' Efficiency values reflect that state's need to ensure that policies are created and administered in an accountable fashion. The egalitarians' Equity values respond to a special theme in this state's culture, a positive use of authority to improve the common weal by reducing inequitable distributions of resources. Moreover, a strong democrats' belief exists that citizens should have policy choices to vote upon, hence the larger share of Choice values. All this proceeds within a moral orientation to the political system; its 'squeaky clean' reputation noted by others (Peirce and Hagstrom, 1983) was evident in our own field work.

Political cultures affect the degree to which professionals, bureaucracies, and politicians are allowed by the codes to exercise control. Codes, history, institutions, and societal relationships are built upon such cultural assumptions. For example, Wisconsin's political culture means that Efficiency values are directed to protecting against the abuse of power — the accountability aspect — but this culture can also be built into Quality educational programs, special concern for redistribution programs for Equity, and into effective citizen involvement in decision-making. Thus these diverse cultures intermix within each state in response to historical influences which continue to shape contemporary institutions. This is evidence that state preferences have become realized in their societal relationships, in short, that culture affects policy decisions. As Wildavsky (1987b) has noted in the title of his path-breaking classification of cultures, this is a case of 'choosing preferences by constructing institutions'.

Political Culture and Program Choices

This thesis can be tested further by looking closely at these states' educational programs in order to determine whether cultural influences reach even to the detail of program choice. For this and other purposes we distinguished among seven domains of school programs; as earlier noted, each is a policy mechanism for the authorization of resource choices. The distribution of code references for these seven broad policy areas among our two states (table 6.2) shows that some policies receive little attention, others have much, and yet others are intermediate. But there are differences in how states treat these policy matters. Two areas received over half of the references, but different pairs account for this — governance and finance in Illinois (60 per cent) and program definition and governance in Wisconsin (66 per cent). Greatest priority for the most important policy area also differs, that is, organization and governance in Illinois and program definition in Wisconsin.

How each state configures these seven policy areas should be influenced by the meritocratic, democratic, and egalitarian cultures, as well as by the

Table 6.2   Distribution of Code References by State Policy Mechanisms and States*

Policies	Illinois	Wisconsin
Finance	22	17
Personnel	12	8
Testing and assessment	2	2
Program definition	15	36
Organization and governance	38	30
Curriculum materials	3	1
Buildings and facilities	9	6
Total	101%	100%
N	1190	401

* All percentages are rounded to the next higher whole number.

overreaching political cultures set out above. In short, policy decisions should be influenced by value preferences which arise out of differing combinations of cultures in the states. Table 6.3 presents the distribution of the four values by these seven state policy mechanisms in the two states. For example, the first column shows how all Quality values were distributed among these policy areas, first in Illinois and second in Wisconsin.

Table 6.3   Distribution of Code References to Values by SPMs and States*

SPM	Quality		Equity		Efficiency		Choice	
	IL	WI	IL	WI	IL	WI	IL	WI
Finance	7	9	12	93	31	17	*27*	18
Personnel	*30*	12	14	8	6	8	6	1
Testing and assessment	4	—	4	3	—	2	1	—
Program definition	26	*53*	22	*40*	5	23	22	*38*
Organization and governance	19	15	*34*	19	51	43	25	33
Curriculum materials	3	1	5	—	1	—	3	3
Buildings and facilities	*12*	9	10	6	*5*	6	16	6
Total	100%	99	101	93	100	99	100	99

* All percentages are rounded to the next higher number.

Some policies demonstrate little of these four values (e.g., curriculum materials), while other policies cluster with particular values, but the interstate differences are noteworthy. The differing frequency distributions in table 6.3 can be seen by our italicizing in each value column of the largest share that it received in each state policy mechanism. The result shows that for three of the four values the two states contrast in their value distributions. This lack of an equal distribution in any column suggests that a differentiating factor is at work, which indicates the likely influence of these state political cultures upon the codes.

That is, even among the same policy areas states use value choices in

different ways. Illinois spreads its Quality values among personnel and program definition mechanisms, while Wisconsin concentrates its Quality in
program definition. Equity values concentrate in organization and governance
policy nearly evenly among three policy mechanisms in Illinois, but they
focus more upon program definition in Wisconsin. Only for the value of
Efficiency do parallel frequencies emerge; here both states concentrate on
detailed control procedures. The priority given this value in organization and
governance policies is suggestive of the meritocratic culture's emphasis on
accountability. A similar priority for finance policies is suggestive of the
democratic culture's emphasis on the control of authority by means of elections, referenda, and budgetary procedures. However, when each policy area
is viewed across the rows, similar percentages between states are not common
(i.e., those within 5 per cent). That clearest finding points to the differentiating
effect of political cultures whose educational laws reflect different mixes of
values within the state mosaic of American federalism.

The Educational Value of Illinois and Wisconsin

A clearer picture of how each state culture reflects these four values is also
found across the seven domains of policy. In each case we sketch a portrait
of its policy profile excluding the two policies which had very few provisions
(testing and assessment, curriculum materials).

In Illinois over half of the Quality values appear in just two policies:
personnel and program definition. However, the distribution for Equity differs, concentrating mostly on program definition. Also Efficiency, which
accounts for almost half of all code references, loads heavily on organization
and governance, and the rest load on finance. In sum, one-quarter of all
Illinois code references fall into the category of Efficiency in organization and
governance policies. That finding reinforces the perception by the authors
and other observers of the pervasive distrust of political authority in Illinois.
Amid the snarl of procedural details in governance and finance provisions,
designed to protect against abuse of authority, we detect the basic fear of
political power rooted in a long history which has realistically justified that
fear.

Another Illinois concern arises in the Choice column of table 6.3. Motivated by this same fear of corrupt power, Choice provisions extend across as
many as three state policy mechanisms and in large amounts — finance,
organization and governance, and program definition — while the buildings
and facilities percentage is not far behind. These provisions ensure local
control which, after all, is partly a fear of state authority. Typical provisions
require that certain groups be represented on local boards (governance), that
taxes or bonds may be used to raise money to support federal programs
(finance), and that special curricula or schools may be a local option (program
definition). It is noteworthy that little curriculum has been mandated by this
state (until 1985 only physical education), which meant that this matter was

regularly one for local control. Of course, in 1985 new state curriculum requirements were added in the wake of national reform currents (the state leads in little). Finally, while Choice accounted for the fewest references, its absence tells us much about the influence of the meritocratic culture. This interpretation is substantiated by the findings in chapter 2 showing the relatively larger influence of locals in keeping state mandates away from them until quite recently.

Crossing this state's border to the north takes one to a strikingly different policy culture, Wisconsin, whose values are more concentrated in one state policy mechanism rather than spread among them. The Quality value fixes on program definition (unlike Illinois), suggesting the much larger role of state mandates in school programs and reflecting the influence of Wisconsin's chief state school officer and school lobbies in policy-making. But professional influence does not extend to dictating curriculum materials, either here or elsewhere.

A related element of this political culture appears in its reflections of Equity values. Providing more than Illinois, this value preference concentrates on an area — program definition — where resources are characteristically used for those who fall below educational norms. Also more than in Illinois Equity looms large in Wisconsin's finance provisions, usually providing funding for programs designed to raise students up to the norm. So both program definition and finance policy areas show signs of policy-makers motivated to use authority to serve a widely perceived common good — better education.

In Wisconsin as in Illinois Efficiency values were concentrated on organization and governance, thereby facilitating citizen participation as well as protecting against abuse of authority. This state also infuses its program definition policies with the Efficiency value. These are efforts to ensure that staff-mandated programs and formula-based resources are implemented effectively through reporting requirements. Finally, Wisconsin has half again as many provisions for Choice as Illinois. Characteristic of this culture, these are spread among the policy areas much more. Typically Choice is provided for pupils in some curricula (program definition), and for voters in referenda (finance) and board elections (organization and governance). All three are linked to Wisconsin's cultural emphasis upon citizen participation.

Summary

Clarifying the role of cultural values in school policy-making can take many routes, as this book will attest, and this chapter's route follows the trail of the set of preferences, associated with distinctive political relations, shaped by the historical framework of the states. The statutes of our two states, while passed at different times in their histories, combine to represent the accumulated record of those policy preferences. What we have found in them have been four major value preferences which differ not simply in behavioral meaning, but in their distribution across seven policy areas. This variation can be partially explained by different kinds of culture — meritocratic, egalitarian, democratic — as well as by different histories, as the political cultures of Illinois and Wisconsin demonstrate. In addition there are common approaches to these values. Thus both states use Efficiency to reflect their meritocratic and democratic cultures and also a similar degree of attention to the same policy set. We will return in the next chapter to these political cultures and their influence on policy élites' perceptions and policy references. We need next to look closer at these four values to gain insight into how value conflict underlies all policy-making.

Dimensions of Values

How do these four policy values relate conceptually to each other? Do they possess some internal logic which connect them? Do they oppose or reinforce one another? Are they hierarchical? Can one value be selected by policy-makers while ignoring the others? Answers are important because they provide insight into the value conflict underlying all policy-making.

Conceptualizing Values in Conflict and Support

That values do conflict is illustrated by the American political ideology itself, where the different requirements of equality and liberty have regularly driven citizens into confrontation. For example, enforcing programs of equal opportunity works against the inequalities which necessarily result from citizens when they freely pursue disparate ends. In education current controversies over desegregation and affirmative action are most illustrative of this basic opposition of American values.

On the other hand, different values can also reinforce one another, and then they may be mutually served in a policy-making atmosphere of cooperation. For example, both rationality in policy-making and due process of law are reinforcing values because both rest on adherence to fundamental procedures that are designed to serve a major value — fairness in the actions of government. Observers of American bureaucracy have noted since World War II the incorporation of due process into standard bureaucratic procedures, for example, in the requirements of notice, hearings, and appeals.

We may think of these possibilities of conflict and reinforcement of values as conceptual dimensions along which values that reinforce one another are close together, while those that are opposed are more removed. On these dimensions the intersection of our four major values may be conceptualized *a priori* as follows:

Choice	Quality	Equity	Efficiency
Quality	N.A.		
Equity	Oppose	N.A.	
Efficiency	Reinforce	Reinforce	N.A.
Choice	Oppose	Oppose	Oppose

Our reasoning, developed below, will show that Choice inherently opposes all values, Efficiency reinforces all but Choice, and Quality opposes all but Efficiency.

The Quality-Equity Dimension

When viewed operationally, Quality and Equity are in opposition because the first seeks *uniform* minimum standards and services applied to *all* clients of schools, while the second seeks *special* services or standards to meet needs of *particular* clients. Quality resources seek to serve all students' needs, Equity resources serve the needs of some. If educational resources were fully expansible, there might be no conflict here; more funds for educating or rewarding special clientele would not cut into funds for all other pupils. But except in boom periods expenditures at all governmental levels tend to be near zero–sum (either for steady-state or declining economic eras); consequently demands for Equity services are often opposed by those who would not benefit. Equity supporters claim, properly enough, that their efforts are designed to achieve Quality standards for their clients. But out of economic, racial, ethnic, or status fears, supporters of Quality will view redistribution programs for Equity as a loss to them and so will oppose them. Many major disputes within educational services — over desegregation, affirmative action, bilingual and handicapped education — are basically rooted in the opposing position of these two values.

The Quality-Efficiency Dimension

On the other hand, Quality and Efficiency illustrate the reinforcing connection. Protagonists of the uniform minimum standards that underlie the thrust of Quality must rely upon both the economic and accountable forms of Efficiency to achieve their purposes. Consequently formula–based laws and regulations, rooted in rationality, as well as elaborate reporting procedures, are consciously designed by policy-makers to ensure that their legislative goals of Quality are effectively implemented. At the state level the large Quality bureaucratic apparatus may be seen as Efficiency in search of Quality.

The two values' necessary linkage also accounts for the political conflict that always accompanies implementation of Quality goals. Implementors seek both efficient and effective means of realizing legislative purposes. Politically sophisticated groups know, however, that decisions at the implementation stage can enhance or protect their particular goals, and so they convert the search for rationality into a political contest to preserve their goals. In this contest all groups may agree on the Quality goals and even on the need for efficient and effective means of realizing them. So they fall into dispute over defining the efficient and the effective; however, they do not quarrel over the Efficiency goal itself.

The Quality-Choice Dimension

Quality and Choice are opposed because the operation of Choice leads often to different definitions of Quality in educational programs. In the past only one definition of Quality has been authoritative, that of meritocratic professionals in education. The practical effect of their involvement in policy-making for a century or more has been the dominance of their views of Quality, especially in matters of personnel training and school program. Control of one's personnel is a major hallmark of any profession, and so state codes reflect much professional control, but very little evidence of Choice in personnel training matters.

Control of school program does show more Choice code references in these codes, but they are still few. There is an opposition in the Quality-Choice dimension because of the moral lessons that curricula can provide. The current struggle over teaching creationism versus evolution is only the latest skirmish in a long war over the values our children should learn. The dominance of the state role in selecting those values varies; generally there is tight state control over textbook selection in the South, but a larger local role elsewhere (Henning *et al.*, 1979; Wirt, 1977). Parental involvement in curriculum appears only when matters occasionally become heated. It is clear that the meritocratic influence in determining Quality — arising from academia, teachers, and state bureaucracy — has played a much larger role over far more issues than Choice.

The Choice-Equity Dimension

The opposition between Choice and Equity arises because the first provides options from which districts and clients *may* choose, while the second mandates requirements that districts and clients *must* choose. This opposition is evident in the wording of codes. The 'shall' and 'must' terms of Equity provisions stand sharply opposed to the 'may' provisions of Choice.

That opposition in concept has also been evident in the record of history. The historic unwillingness of a decentralized education system to redistribute resources to those with special schooling needs has generated the drive for Equity-based state law. The poor, minority, handicapped, and gifted pupils have each known a similar history in which local districts gave their needs only inattention, discrimination, and underfunding. Each disadvantaged group also went through a similar process of seeking political mobilization in courts and legislatures at higher levels of government. Finally, these two values especially exemplify the generic contradiction between equality and freedom in our nation's political ideology. (As noted earlier, that clash is a recurring theme in the excellence and choice efforts of the 1980s — see essays in Boyd and Kerchner, 1988).

The Choice-Efficiency Dimension

Choice and Efficiency are opposed values because providing a range of options for decisions must intrinsically run against the 'one best way' orientation of achieving educational goals that is favored by meritocrats. In one sense the means orientation of Efficiency policies is at odds with the self-fulfillment purposes inherent in Choice policies. The first seeks a single set of economic or accountable procedures for optimizing the chances for achieving educational goals; the second provides plural paths to these goals.

In a larger sense the Choice-Efficiency opposition epitomizes the enduring tension in democracies between two political forces. One force might be termed the 'participatory', that is, citizens' desires to participate in those decisions about services which affect their lives. 'Local control' has been so important for so long in American education because it so well reflects this participatory impulse. That does not mean that all, or even a majority of, citizens do participate, or that the control is even effective. But there has been a socialized expectation that we should have some say over choice of officials and of public policy.

The opposing force in democracy — indeed, in all nation states — has been the 'rational-technical' influence on policy-making of meritocrats. This is the effort to make rational choices with limited resources between policies that expand those resources; here 'rational' means a clear fit between means (plan for using resources) and social goals. In its crudest sense this force is seen in the fascination of the Reagan administration with choice-benefit models for policy-making. These participatory and rational forces arise from different segments of society, from lay citizens versus the professional managers of service systems. That conflict is manifest in many policy areas, and it is clearly evident in the Choice-Efficiency values of the state education codes.

The Efficiency-Equity Dimension

Finally, Efficiency and Equity are reinforcing values because the goals of the second employ the means of the first to be realized. That is, the redressing of unequal distributions of education resources cannot be accomplished without formula-based goals or without accountability procedures to ensure goal compliance. However, the two values are often conceived as being opposed.

Certainly that is suggested by the complaints over new Equity programs that upset established (i.e., efficiently administered) norms of school services. However, Equity programs, once authorized, require means for administering them in both the economic and accountability forms of Efficiency.

Desegregation exemplifies this conceptual linkage between means and ends. The familiar disparities of resources in segregated school systems required, first, the will to seek a political solution; second, the technical knowledge to devise means which would redistribute resources within a school system; and third, the will to enforce it through oversight of implementation (that is, an accountability form of Efficiency). There have been other Equity policies in education — vocational education, bilingual education — and each has been accompanied by much protest over that goal and its efficient accomplishment; the protest came from those not benefited by this goal and its methods in a reflection of other values.

This review of four values in six dimensions is unified by conceptualizing them as influences in the policy-making process. In four of the six dimensions we suggest that these values are in conflict, both conceptually and historically.

Priority of Values in Policy-making

Do these major values enter law in a particular order? Or do all values emerge simultaneously? Does the policy-making process shape the order in which values arise? These questions of policy sequence are important in broadening our theoretical grasp of the role of values in policy-making. In causal terms why do certain values dominate different stages of policy? It would be important first to conceptualize the most characteristic interactions that would affect a policy sequence. What follows is only a sketch of a very complex and interactive process.

Major policy change begins in perceived crisis. More political effort is needed, however, to get into the agenda of governmental policy-making. This act takes place amid an inchoate set of forces — political streams of ideas, sudden windows of opportunity for policy advocates, and knowledge bases rooted in expert advocates (Kingdom, 1984). Such forces become crystallized by 'triggering events' erupting from societal stress that may affect all of society (e.g., wars and depressions) or only some groups (e.g., urban riots in the 1960s) (Cobb and Elder, 1983). Amid the clashes of crisis, leaders serve to direct onto the agenda policy responses to this stress. In education policy they have a pivotal role in building administration (Tyack and Hansot, 1982), in constructing professional control (Cremin, 1964) and even earlier in urging adoption of free, public education.

Such a model of policy origins, much condensed here, is clearly evident in the societal stress that is often channelled into public schools. We all know how successive generations have laid changing requirements upon the curriculum, professional training, financing, student testing, and organization of our schools (Ravitch, 1983).

Why Quality Comes First

This historical analysis makes evident that the first efforts to build such a service were premised on some groups' and their leaders' belief in Quality. The reaction against the machine control of schooling in the late nineteenth century was rooted in the convictions that it created poor education, and that more quality would come from transforming teaching and administration into a profession. It was argued that the policy ideas of this profession — both professors and practitioners alike — were the best source for improving educational quality. This primary orientation to quality is manifest in the writings of these planners who sought 'one best system' (Tyack, 1974) run by 'managers of virtue' (Tyack and Hansot, 1982). In short, transforming schools (Cremin, 1964) was premised on first bringing Quality into schooling.

A broader perspective on professions in general will illuminate what happened here. In any service that is profession-driven (unlike, say, auto repair), the attendant profession seeks to dominate four basic policy domains. What is good service? How much of it should be provided? How is a competent practitioner defined and trained? Who shall evaluate the results? (Wirt, 1981). Ultimately these are political questions, and in answering them, professionals have usually dominated, although recurrent challenge from their clients can alter them, as chief education officers in English-speaking nations are now finding (Wirt, 1988). But all four questions center on defining Quality in service, in quantity, in personnel, and in evaluation.

We need not look back too far to understand why Quality is the first value concern of policy-makers. In the effort to reform educational services among the states in the mid-1980s, much of the discussion centered on a central idea in *A Nation at Risk*, that pervasive deficiencies in the delivery of educational service have produced poor quality results. This and later reports accepted this premise and then turned to different remedies to improve Quality. The resulting state reforms dealt mostly with adding more courses to the curriculum, to increasing in-school time, and to improving instruction. All of these have in common a concern about Quality — as some professionals defined it (Boyd and Kerchner, 1988).

Why Efficiency Comes Second

Goals of Quality, once proclaimed, are not automatically self-executing; like all good aims in life, they must be worked at to be realized. That is, the creation of any Quality goal next requires that it be effectively implemented. That requirement necessitates some rational estimation of the procedures and resources that will be needed to meet goals, all set in a framework of decisional rules. Implementation also calls for oversight of these rules in order to ensure compliance (Nakamura and Smallwood, 1980). We conceive this process as Efficiency-based, which is why it follows, not precedes, the setting of Quality goals. This two-step sequence of values makes conceptual sense. If the

Efficiency value generates means-like actions, those must be directed to some end which must predate the means. Otherwise we would have means floating around in human action without a direction, a behavior that is usually termed non-rational; or it may be dressed up as the 'garbage can' model of decision-making (Cohen *et al.*, 1972).

The large amount of Efficiency in laws is striking in tables 6.1 and 6.2 earlier. That is because, both conceptually and empirically, legislating one policy goal necessitates creating more than one Efficiency method to achieve it. The latter value must necessarily infuse all policy domains. That may be why the Golden Rule required only ten commandments, but human regulations without number must implement it.

Why Equity Comes Third

The provisions of a Quality program, followed by Efficiency-based methods to implement it, lead to a familiar pattern in results — maldistribution of public services. Whatever the policy, some clients get more than others, and not merely because of a simple Marxian notion of class power. For example, in studies of how a range of urban services are distributed in many cities, we find that the poor need more public welfare and housing services than do the middle and high income citizens, and they need more protection against violent crime (but not against white-collar crime, a middle-class problem) than do the others (Lineberry and Sharkansky, 1978). These findings make the point that differential service delivery arises because of differential social needs.

Differing needs have been a constant in education as well. We know that basing school funding upon a single, locally-based tax makes the resulting quality of a child's education a function of district wealth. State funding reforms, implemented in the 1920s via 'foundation' programs and in the 1970s via redistributive programs, testify to that (Garms *et al.*, 1978). It is also clear that students' educational achievements differ dramatically, although the argument continues whether the differences are a function of status, race, or resources.

Let us make an even larger point, that *any educational service is bound to be maldistributed among all clientele to whom it is directed*. Even in a classroom of wealthy students, backed by reinforcing parents and a resource-filled school, there is still a grading curve; not even here is learning equally received, instilled, and rewarded. Consequently, when any Quality goal is sought through Efficiency means, those who do not benefit are likely to seek additions to existing resources and procedures which will assist them. Another point important to understand is that *not all inequities are pursued in the policy world*. Many inequities are not visible to clients; or if visible, citizens may feel alienated from participating in that world; or if they indeed perceive inequities and do desire action, they may still lack the maze-wisdom of how to succeed in it. In short, barriers of perception, will, and knowledge act to depress political reaction against objectively evident inequities. But in our sequence model Equity concerns must follow the creation of Quality goal and of Efficiency means.

Why Choice Pervades the Sequence

While linear, this model must yield to the fact that Choice operates at every step. Logically Choice arises even *before* laws exist on a matter. Without laws, there would be the 'state of nature' beloved of seventeenth-century philosophers, with its maximum Choice to do anything. However, that kind of Choice without law would leave power in the hands of the few who controlled superior resources. Under these conditions a world of full Choice would end up badly for most people, a life that, as Hobbes wrote, was 'mean, nasty, brutish, and short'. While the coming of government and its law in a 'social contract' would limit Choice for some, it would nevertheless expand freedom from violence for most.

That insight helps us understand the place of Choice in the policy sequence. The citizen-participatory influence noted earlier has always entered into decisions about the other three values. Choice was present even before Quality goals for education were established. After all, people could choose *not* to be educated, and many did, as Census Bureau data on illiteracy continue to testify.

More significantly Choice entered at the founding of our educational system, because free public education was an idea which gained wide public acceptance among Protestants; Peterson (1985) has shown how its founding rested on a broad base of workers and trade unions. Further, Choice was maintained after creation of the public school system in the operations of school boards and in referenda on financial decisions designed to implement Quality decisions (Wirt and Kirst, 1989). Also Choice has episodic impact on Efficiency, as seen in the socialization of professionals to anticipate the public's 'zone of tolerance' of their actions (Boyd, 1976). It is evident also in the necessity of professionals to manage conflict that has been generated by the public (Zeigler *et al.*, 1985; Wirt and Christovich, 1989). Finally, the recent struggle for Equity has generated much pressure, with its group litigation and legislative initiatives at state and Federal levels (Ravitch, 1983). These political actions mean that many citizens were exercising Choice in order to alter maldistributions of resources for special pupils.

A recent consideration of the role of choice in schooling policy has put the pervasive nature of Choice concisely:

> Should parents and students be empowered to choose among schools, or among programs within schools? Should educators be empowered to organize and manage schools, to design educational programs, to recruit and select students, and to receive public funds for providing education to those students? These are the two fundamental questions of education

choice [that] go to the very roots of the finance, organization, and political control of American public education (Elmore, 1988, p. 79).

In short, democratic principles have made Choice an active ingredient of educational policy that has affected the other three values. Its potential for challenging professional decisions about Quality and Efficiency makes it an ever-present consideration of educational policy-making.

Cultural Values Embedded in Codes

In this chapter we sought to clarify one of the major concepts in policy analysis — values. We posited that four major values permeate the structure of state educational policy, each of which represents underlying political values in the policy system. Empirically we found these values distributed unevenly among the statutes of two states of contrasting political cultures, a distribution associated with these cultures.

Conceptual analysis led to the conclusion that these four values exist in no hierarchical fashion, but rather reinforce or oppose one another. In many policy choices resting on these values, the weight of professionals has been of key importance, although episodic influences from the participatory force of democracy also played a role; the latter's influences are most visible in the accountability form of Efficiency and in Choice. Furthermore, there is a logical sequence by which three of these values enter the policy system: Quality begets Efficiency which begets Equity; Choice, however, begets all three values.

The political basis of all educational policy-making rests upon the necessity of leaders and citizens to select which values will be reinforced by public resources and which will not. In a democratic nation policy-making is infused with the possibilities, not always realized, for citizens to choose which values will be reflected in their policy services.

Note

1 We read the whole of a numbered sub-heading in the volumes of statutes ('codes') in order to infer the presence of one or more of the values defined above. By inferring a value(s) from a sub-heading, we avoided the problem of making innumerable decisions if the basic item of analysis were only a word or sentence.

This tally process was applied to four categories of values, and then summarized by value for each state and for each policy domain within a state. The tallying was supervised by the three project faculty who trained research assistants and sampled their work. Others undertaking this process should be aware of problems — changing research assistants, uncertainties about how codes should be interpreted, misunderstandings of instructions.

However, we concluded that in two states — Illinois and Wisconsin — the inter-coder agreement was very high because the same assistant read all codes with continuous reference to the senior author.

The authors express appreciation to Elizabeth Wirt for the code analysis performed for these two states.

Chapter 7

Understanding Cultural Influences on Educational Policy

The committed policy analyst reads voraciously, trying to understand American politics. Having got to this point in the book, the reader quite correctly asks, 'What do I know about the American culture — what does the politics of education show?' This chapter explains some of our major findings within a larger sense of cultural influences than our separate chapters have employed. This larger cultural paradigm will bring understanding of our often complex, if not contradictory, reports. Both complexity and contradictions are important parts of the cultural explanation.

Our opening chapter set out to address the major queries. The cultural paradigm, we promised, would encourage reconceptualization of old research questions and dilemmas about education policy. It would set out ways one might describe, track, explain, and predict, however roughly, policy choices that certain states make. It would also enable both practitioner and researcher to understand the mosaic of the policy world of state education. If we could do even some of these things, it should assist in better analysis by providing an understanding of the forces that constrain and stimulate policy-making in the American states. We need to summarize what we found in that state policy world in the mid-1980s as all fifty states struggled with economic limits and quality concerns in increasingly politicized and centralized educational systems. Then we can confront the contradictions as they emerge from a national culture which itself is a mosaic of differences and commonalities. In this chapter we are like the cultural anthropologist emerging from the jungle of a primitive civilization, sitting at a desk and trying to make larger sense of the totems and taboos that the field notes contain. The civilization of the world of state education that we report on is not so primitive, of course, but more parallels will be noted than one might first think.

What We Now Know: A Propositional Inventory

Previous chapters were filled with detailed findings and explanations, employing methods that ran from the qualitative to the quantitative, and we do not wish to repeat much of that here. But it seems useful for practitioner and scholar alike to understand our main findings about the role of values in state education policy — our primary analytical focus.

Élites' Assumptive Worlds

Culture deals with social relations and preferences about them, and we found those relationships and preferences in the assumptive worlds of state education policy élites. These élites are elected or appointed to reinforce a preferred way of organizing schooling. Acculturated to their state's history and to the values it has delivered, they become socialized to a distinctive assumptive world with its particular understanding of power and processes. This world is a mix of historically given political cultures, informal processes within formal structures, and key actor values strained through partisan politics.

There are surprising similarities in these assumptive worlds. First, a perceived hierarchy of power and influence emerges from élites' cognitions. Ranging from insiders (the legislature and its leaders) to remote players often forgotten, policy influence is stratified in a fashion that filters policy demands from external constituencies. Their names, accents, and politics may differ from California to West Virginia, but education committee leaders are still perceived in the same deferential way, and the private sector has rare influence on them.

A second similarity in these élites' assumptive worlds is an operational code for policy-making that rests on the same set of driving questions. From Arizona to Wisconsin state policy élites determine who initiates policy action, what ideas are acceptable, what activity is fit, and what special conditions will affect the policy process. These domains and their subcategories have major utilities for the decisional system; they maintain its power, give it predictability, and promote its cohesion.

Policy Mechanisms as Cultural Products

That culturally shaped policy system also influences the values embedded in education policy. In our analysis we viewed policies as structures embodying these state governments' value-laden intentions. Policy can be seen as a system of controls (fiscal, regulatory, contractual, ideological) designed to shape and limit schools' behaviour in ways that reflect culturally-based values. Differences in states of control reflect underlying differences in values.

To classify these differences we developed a theoretically consistent and operationally powerful taxonomy of these mechanisms of control, each an expression of cultural intent. We could derive seven policy mechanisms: finance, personnel training, student testing and assessment, program definition, organization and governance, curriculum materials, buildings and facilities — as well as thirty-three program approaches. Underlying all these were just four basic values employed to achieve policy control: Choice, Quality, Efficiency, and Equity — each rooted in complex political theories that permeate our national history.

Value preferences clearly made a difference in the policy emphasized. Thus we found bias in every state for Quality oriented definitions of education policy issues. That finding confirmed others' analysis that the Quality theme had replaced the Equity theme in recent years, just as Efficiency had dominated even earlier. Moreover, value preferences carried with them policy mechanism preferences. Where Quality preference was high, it was the finance policy mechanism that received most attention from these élites; but where Choice preference was high, then program definition, governance, and curriculum materials received élite attention. Even amid the numerous program approaches there were still some links between value and action. Thus states emphasizing the Efficiency value most often selected the finance policy approach of offsetting burdensome high costs (like transportation), while rejecting the approach of financing some school operations (like textbooks).

Codes as Cultural Artifacts

Another indicator of culture other than élites' cognitions and affect was the codified legislation — the instrument of their action. These codes demonstrated the presence of the four values and the imprint on them of different cultural histories. Content analysis of such codes for two states found them the depository of policy conflict resolution from the past, and all show how the legislative intent to control school behavior varies with the respective value. Those values formed no complementary set but rather contained both opposing as well as reinforcing components; indeed, their contradictions have generated policy tensions over time. We argue that three values — Quality, Efficiency, Equity — were historically sequential, although the Choice value sought to affect them at every stage.

In these codes evidence emerges of different cultures. The meritocratic culture is seen in the dominance of Efficiency-based code references, the democratic culture in the Choice references, and the egalitarian culture in the Equity provisions. Moreover, differing political histories have generated different political cultures that had impact on these values and their related policy mechanisms and program approaches. Thus value distributions in the codes of Illinois and Wisconsin contrasted sharply, as did the priorities given to the seven policy mechanisms. These code differences were consonant with differences in the historical cultures that these states have known. So another way of viewing culture is as a history that shapes such cultural indicators as legislative codes.

Political Culture and Policy Choices

Political cultures are not only latent in the perceptions of state policy élites but they can roughly distinguish which state policy mechanisms and program approaches are selected. Three political cultures — Moralistic, Individualistic, Traditionalistic — have been drawn from historical and demographic analysis by others. The presence of these three was confirmed in our work from judgments that our élites made about their constituents' preferences for different objects and events in the political world. In short, élite perceptions clustered significantly in patterns that were much like the historical designations.

Those perceptions were roughly associated with some, but not all, differences among policies. The fit is loose because the limited number of states employed limited statistical significance. On the one hand, the political cultural judgments and four-value preferences of these élites showed no significant correlation. On the other hand, code analysis showed Equity and Choice policies were of greater interest in a Moralistic Wisconsin, and Efficiency-based policies in an Individualistic Illinois. Indeed, across six states and the full range of thirty-three program approaches there was substantial (but not statistically significant) correlation with these three political cultures; the differences could not be explained by personal qualities of the élites.

What the data suggest is that the political institutions we create shape the value choices in public policy in a way consistent with a state's history. Thus history reaches through the cultural institutions that it established to shape the present. That is just as true for the cognitive maps of policy-makers' assumptive worlds as it is for the basic values that they choose, with their attendant policies. All this operates in a surprisingly consistent way.

Empirical Contrasts in the State Policy World

This summary overview of state education policy glosses over a set of quite contrasting patterns. Whether we explain policy values and their cultural historically rooted political cultures, or the actual choices of policy-makers, each explanation reports contrasting findings in its separate approach. Any cultural paradigm must encompass such contradictions, so it is to the latter that we next turn.

The first puzzling contrasts were manifest in the findings that while there was a small set of *operational principles* with their action guides that formed élites' assumptive worlds, their application was quite diverse among the states. Indeed, their stories about their operations at first threw up a smoke screen of such contrasts that no pattern seemed evident. Only an anthropological approach could find the common threads among these contrasts, and even then much careful deduction about principles and guidelines had to take place. How could such contrasts in application be incorporated within an overarching cultural paradigm?

Second, while just *four values* dominate state laws on education, most of them oppose one another. For example, we have a nation of states in each of which some groups seek Equitable allocation of education resources, while other groups seek Quality in that allocation. Inherent in such value contradictions is the potential for group conflict that inevitably gets hammered out in the policy arena. Because in this set of values no neat complementarity of belief exists, intrinsically or experientially, education policy must always be conflictual and hence political. But what cultural paradigm could encompass such contrasts?

Third, while at a given time there is inter state agreement on *policy mechanisms* (e.g. school finance in the 1980s), there is also much dissensus about them. As we demonstrated amply, there were great contrasts in what our set of states preferred and did about most policy domains and programs. What cultural paradigm could explain both agreed and differing policy choices?

A fourth set of contrasts arises with the presence of distinct subcultures having their own policy influences. We noted these influences in the three political cultures of Individualism, Moralism, and Traditionalism, as well as in the democratic, meritocratic, and egalitarian cultures; all were demonstrated in our data about state codes and élites' understanding of political culture and values. State political culture analysts have pointed out in great detail the striking policy differences that result from these contrasting cultural judgments about the purpose of the political system and its parts. Further, historians of education have shown the meritocratic vs. democratic tensions clashing in the course of developing our schools; the same contrasts are manifest in the quality egalitarian tensions arising over school policy, especially in recent decades.

A final set of contrasts arises in the clash between national influences and state preferences in the education policy world. During and after the 1960s national influences were driven by Equity concerns which often ran counter to local preferences on use of school resources; desegregation is just the most publicized example. Those national influences shifted in the 1980s to an emphasis upon quality concerns and to deregulating the Equity concerns of the past. That shift, however, clashed with many local districts where Equity in allocation was necessary to cope with huge educational problems. Note that in both periods the national influences sought standardizing, and the local influences sought differentiating, the delivery of this service. How could a cultural paradigm hold together such center-periphery tensions?

Culture and Polarities

The preceding observations remind us that the American states are such a complex of empirical contrasts that no conceptualization could encompass, much less explain, them. But it is upon this very obvious point of contrasts that we propose to build a cultural paradigm of explanation.

The Tensions of Polarities

The challenge is to explain how a cultural paradigm can provide meaning to the political part of social relations as these affect the values of education policy. As Mary Douglas (1978) has noted, at the center of culture is the individual engaged in transactions with others, and some transactions are disputes about standards and values which have deep roots. These disputes take place in the culture which is:

> a deposit from myriads of individual decisions made in the past, creating the cost-structure and the distribution of advantages which are the context of present-day decisions. . . . [The] action is this afternoon, the context was made afresh this morning, but some of its effects are long, low fibres reaching from years back (p. 6).

So the meaning of culture comes from understanding the behavior of individuals as they operate within a social context. Social context and cultural meanings are abstractions, of course, certainly not the thing one would meet walking in the schoolroom door. Properly constructed, however, such conceptualizations permit us to perceive and understand behavior that seems unrelated. Structural anthropologists, most notably Claude Levi-Strauss, have emphasized focusing upon 'the relations among phenomena, rather than the nature of the phenomena themselves, and the systems into which these relations enter' (1963, p. x). Such an analysis makes possible the construction of models that encompass and explain often seemingly disparate human phenomena. For example, Levi-Strauss (1963) has shown how stories from one culture can be abstracted to derive myths whose internal structure can then be compared to equivalent myths across cultures.

Invariably, though, if we think of culture as social relations patterned around values, we have to expect polarities or contradictions in values. These must be reconciled, however, and the dialectic process of reconciliation provides powerful meaning for its members. Meaning-making centers of culture are structures where conflict occurs and where the dialectic process that leads to value consensus occurs. Any model of culture should have this conflict-dialectic-consensus at its center. Levi-Strauss has pointed to the 'dual (and at first sight almost contradictory) nature of structural studies' (1963, p. 285). Other social anthropologists point to the presence and importance of 'contrasted patterns', 'binary antitheses', 'unconscious paradoxes' (Leach, 1970, pp. 67–71). Such polarities mean that one set of values *must have* an opposing set in order to clarify and distinguish the cultural meaning of either set. There can be no God without devil, no creation without chaos, no ying without yang — one must be the mirror image of the other in order to have meaning. In short, any model of culture must encompass contrasts and conflicts.

Such polarities have consequences as well for general theories of political culture; we will note briefly only the most recent use of this concept. Mary Douglas (1978) finds cultures biased by special emphases they give to individualism versus group influences. Laponce (1981) shows how attitudes about space cause us to use terms like 'left and right' or 'up and down' to carry powerful value loadings and shape political action in Western democracies. 'We use space', he summarizes, 'to give shape to our thoughts, and in turn these shapes generate and constrain new ideas' (p. 3). The tensions between group strength and the number of prescriptions as they work upon individuals form two dimensions of cultural theory for Douglas and Wildavsky (1982); Wildavsky's 'cultural theory of preference' (1987b) focuses on the opposite values of hierarchy versus equality as reflections of those two dimensions.

Such ways of thinking about political culture have consequences for the American system. We have noted some of this specifically in earlier chapters using Daniel Elazar's three political cultures. These rest upon 'two contrasting conceptions of the American political order', i.e., 'the marketplace' versus 'the commonwealth' (1984, p. 112). Similarly Merelman (1984) believes our culture has lost much of its 'boundedness' because of the failure of three 'political visions' which once helped Americans explain and give meaning to social relations. Each of these three — Puritan, democratic, and class visions — contains a dualism of opposite values and experiences: 'Puritans vs. nonbelievers; democrats vs. nondemocrats . . . workers vs. capitalists' (p. 23). The failure of these, as Merelman demonstrates incisively, leaves a body politic not bounded by any cohesive culture that can control and channel value polarities. What remains is a 'loose boundedness' that is a weak substitute for Americans who seek meaning in, and reflect, television, advertising, schooling in political values, and so on.

These sketches of analyses of extremely complex social relations suggest the importance of understanding culture as sets of polarities. At the core of the cultural paradigm are polarities of preference and social relations that give meaning to the whole. Intuitively, as well as analytically, such a view of culture seems to fit — to describe, explain, and predict — the political activity in the American states. The next section demonstrates the viability of this framework of polarities.

State Education Policy Contrasts and Cultural Polarities

The cultural paradigm of policy contrasts and cultural polarities guides us to focus again on earlier chapters, examining each of a set of contrasts in value and experience and noting their role in policy-making. We found contrasts in the assumptive worlds of influential actors, values, policies, political cultures, and national-localistic influences. These contrasts should provide material for explanation within a cultural paradigm of polarities. Analyzing the cultural dynamics within states (as in table 7.1), we see the polarities, where conflicts lie, and we see the forces that bring stability, cohesion, and predictability in states.

Assumptive Worlds of State Policy Élites

The subcultures of influence among state policy élites exist in constant tension over the allocation of public resources, as reported in chapter 2. Their assumptive worlds necessarily operate at the focus of interactions with past and present features of the political system. Not all those features exert common influences, as they reflect conflicting interests and values in the civil community of each state. Illustrative of this intrastate context is the cluster of perceived influence that ranked sub-élites; from Insiders to Often-Forgotten Players, each cohort exists in continuous, but not continuing competition and opposition to others.

Table 7.1 Cultural Dynamics within States

Forces for cohesion, stability, and predictability	*Polarities*
Tradition (in codes and institutions)	Conflicts among four values
Political culture	Democratic-meritocratic conflicts
Assumptive worlds	Power and influence hierarchy
National culture	Power and justice
policy issue networks	
redistributive policies	Localism and nationalism
national reform	

To encompass the regular conflict within a policy-making system, there must be something binding élites to it, or else the whole would fall into chaos and inaction. Common interests cannot bind its members on all matters. The hallmark of contemporary policy-making for education in the states has been a pattern of fragmentation of interests that succeeded in earlier monolithic pattern incorporating all interest groups. The umbrella cohort of teachers, administrators, school boards, and their rubber-stamping by legislative and executive branches, is no longer the norm — maybe now only the exception. The policy system has become more open to needs of smaller components of the educational system.

Several features of the assumptive worlds provide cultural meaning to how these empirical contrasts are handled. The reality of policy conflict drives participants to set out implicit agreed upon ways of ordering conflict in the form of decisional rules — even before decisions are confronted. These are implicit in the cultural paradigm underlying, first, the influence clusters (figure 2.1) and, second, the action guides and operational principles (figure 2.9) of these state policy élites.

First, a democratic policy-making culture generates the understanding that while all votes may be equal, influence is not. Deference to those with more power and expertise, or more commitment and interest, necessarily results when skills are differentiated in a complex organization. This deference in influence translates operationally into knowing whose voice will be heard when decisions must be made amid the clamour of demands and complaints. In the education policy system of the American states this clarion voice is that of the key legislators and the legislature — Insiders and Near Circle; they are the pivots about which the policy system revolves. Even more basic than these understandings is the influence of the culture of democracy. That is, those deferred to have been legitimated by their election under the rules of democracy, and subsequently their policy decisions are authorized by the democratically supported state constitution. In short, what the culture of democracy calls for is more or less what was found.

Second, while democracy assumes all policy demands are equal, decisional rules must be created to sort out what is politically feasible. In these terms 'feasible' means what decisions the policy élite think most likely to pass through the complex negotiations of the policy subculture and through their assumptive worlds. We drew from our élites accounts of their policy actions underneath which lay a consistent culture of determining feasibility that gave policy power to 'feasible' demands. Thus some have the accepted right and responsibility to initiate demands that will most likely be acted on. Some policy ideas are broadly agreed as unacceptable. Some uses of power in making policy are widely regarded as improper. Some special conditions in the state's culture, geography, or demography affect both the process and the substance of policy-making. Each of these domains contained operational principles that drove the system's response to policy demands. Because not all demands are regarded as feasible, but some are, the result must be bias in the political system's output.

This drive toward feasibility that ends up in bias reflected an underlying culture of organizations. Thus these elements of feasibility focus upon two internally consistent functions of the policy system: maintaining power and predictability and promoting cohesion. Those functions underlie any organizational system, whether democratic or authoritarian, public or private. Moreover, the influence clusters and operational principles are reinforced, because the latter have produced the structured and guiding power of the former. Employing these principles rewards most those with greatest deference. As a result, the policy system reflects considerable cohesion in dealing with the flood of demands, permits its élite considerable predictability in shaping their own political futures — and necessarily is biased to some demands.

In short, focusing specifically upon empirical contrasts permits the analyst to understand the underlying cultural considerations that shape behavior. Both democratic and organizational cultures help us understand contradictions, like the contradiction of the culture of democracy pursued within a political reality of élites, the contradiction when we assume that all demands are equal, but we end up with biased outputs from the policy system. Obviously there are different applications of these democratic and organizational cultures from state to state, but it is underlying structure that provides understanding of how diverse citizens and experiences can still reflect basic unities.

The Four Values

Within this larger framework of understanding we can better understand the clash within the policy system that is generated by contrasting values. We explored in chapter 5 how four values emerged as the source of education policy conflict, how they both reinforced and opposed one another, how they could be detected in state statutes, and how they were affected by contrasting political histories of different states. Our emphasis upon a cultural paradigm of empirical contrasts provides an even larger understanding of these values.

The distribution of statutory values can be explained by noting the opposing influences of egalitarian and meritocratic ideas which have swirled within the larger American political culture (table 5.1). Of course, there exists no neat compartmentalization of such ideas because these are merely different directions taken by the driving culture of democracy. That is, as long as a democratic system encourages its citizens to register their differing value preferences in public policy, even if indirectly through elected representatives and pressure groups, differing policy thrusts will result. These will seek Choice on some educational matters, and on yet others they pursue Quality goals to guide schooling, redistribution of resources to create Equity, and instruments of Efficiency to implement the other three values. In short, democratic culture presumes no agreement on specific policy values but rather encourages the pursuit of many; what the culture presumes, our analysis of élites' preferences and state codes demonstrates.

Clearly then, all cannot be unanimous among the states in policy values. After all, differing histories of state resources and group demands created different experiences; these gave differing shapes to these values, so consequently differences in educational policy should be expected. We know of the striking contrasts of such policies in the fifty-state system, starting with the differences in states' share of local costs and running on to other input and output measures. Underlying these policy differences are sharply contrasting preferences about the role of the individual and the community in society, shortly to be noted.

But the main point is that no culture here or elsewhere is about simply one value. Our culture must deal with contrasting experiences and conflicting values, and hence diversity in policy must be expected. There will necessarily be some contradiction in both belief and behaviors across and within the states. The policy-making arenas must be designed to accommodate such diversity and contradiction. Finally, over time the resulting policy profile should reflect a patchwork of values. Again the democratic culture, properly understood, demonstrates that such complexity is necessary and proper.

Policy Domains and Programs

Our effort to provide meaning to the mass of educational policies in any state through use of a taxonomy returns us to the importance of structure in understanding complex phenomena. Like structural anthropology, structural policy analysis rests on discovering the patterns of order and contrast in policy in order to derive an abstract meaning that encompasses both the order and the contrast. This approach permits us to examine parts of a whole policy set and their effects on other attributes of the set; this approach differs sharply from policy analysis that examines the intent of those who made policies or are affected by them.

In our case the structural approach was designed to give insight into policy as a control mechanism, that is, how school program and practice are controlled through state policy. A systematic understanding of public policy flows from understanding this underlying structure of control (rather than just understanding a policy's utility for an educational problem). Classification of controls permits distinguishing like and unlike mechanisms and the attendant regularities within each class. Use of a taxonomy presumes that all policy is neither unique nor identical, but that there are classes of regularities which can explain what states are attempting to do.

The cultural focus on control arises because that is an imperative in each state's constitutional system; education in a highly decentralized system generates a pervasive need to control the locality from the center. But this effort is resisted by the cultural force of localism that is endemic in our history here and elsewhere. This center-periphery tussle arises in any organization, public or private, and the bigger it is, the greater is the need for the center to control it.

Consequently states must originate and administer their own policy goals through control mechanisms and program approaches of great value diversity. We believed that this diversity could be encompassed within a structural approach that focused upon a taxonomy of education policy. Our élites' assessment gave us data to identify a taxonomy of seven control mechanisms, thirty-three program approaches, and four values. Differences within these sets should not confuse the fact of the common structure of internally logical connections between units of analysis. This structure and its subsets could be used for similar policy analysis yesterday and tomorrow; only the distributions of actual policies within each set would alter with time. The structure of the taxonomy should remain.

Underlying these commonalities is a deeper understanding of states' selection of policies within this taxonomy. First, there was an interplay between basic values and selected mechanisms and approaches that emerges within the calls of the taxonomy, as detailed in chapters 3 and 4. Note that there was nothing about the force of a basic value, say Quality, which made it determine the content of any policy. The reason for this indeterminacy lies in a second understanding about this taxonomy. It is the product of a conflict between two deep cultural thrusts in any policy system — the meritocratic vs. democratic demands. In a crude sense the policy decisions reported in the interstices of this taxonomy provide a kind of scoreboard of which cultural force won out. There is not always a conflict between these two cultures in making policy decisions; when they share complementary goals or when the citizens are indifferent, then the meritocratic view usually dominates.

But there also exists a latent tension between the two cultures because their interests and values can conflict; there then emerges the bureaucratic-participatory tension typical of democracies. For example, a meritocratic thrust for a policy with Quality content (say, certification), which invariably requires more revenue, may confront citizens who are reluctant to increase their taxes to pay for it (especially in an era of economic constraints). Or a meritocratic commitment to providing Equity in a schooling service (say, spending to target special groups) may confront a majority who sees that it will not benefit them but just a minority. In both cases by pursuing Choice values the majority restricts professional power through their elected officials. This is a major reason why egalitarian policy of all kinds has consistently originated and been carried out by higher, not lower, governments in American federalism, as discussed later.

In short, the contrasts of value and reality found in the structure of our taxonomy are products of the meritocratic and democratic cultures that have shaped them. The cultural paradigm enables us to understand that state policy-makers deal with these polarities not simply in a structured way — hence the taxonomy — but they also must operate strategically by satisfying the four major values at the same time.

Historical Political Cultures

There is much evidence that the historical movement of populations, with their baggage of political ideas, could be differentiated among regions. We sought in chapter 5 to find such ideas within élite perceptions of their constituents' views of the political world; then we could determine the structural relationships of these views, and estimate their effects on policy choices in education. These methods did permit our mapping élites' understanding of how citizens viewed certain political objects and events in consistent, internally cohesive patterns. These patterns, termed 'political culture', were found in three types that also fitted states where others had found political behavior based on similar cultures.

Using political culture to explain policy decisions among the states was not as clearcut as identifying it. First, agreement across the nation about some kinds of policy limited any difference traceable to state cultures (e.g., the preoccupation with finance policy everywhere in an era of economic constraints, or with program definition in an era of program reform). Such national agreement on some policies will always be a systematic limitation on local cultures. A second problem was that the few states we used precluded significant statistical results when testing for the influence of political culture; in some cases the results were not even close to significance.

Nevertheless, some results were congruent with the prediction that political cultures would be associated with policy differences. Thus certain large differences existed in élites' policy judgments, not only between states, but between members within states, and these were structured by the three political cultures. These culturally-based judgments dealt with legislative priorities for control mechanisms and program approaches. Particularly strong was the cultural disagreement on matters of governance and organization — where we would expect political cultures to differ most sharply. Even among the numerous program approaches, where structure would seem unlikely, their political cultures affected most of our élites' perceptions of legislative priorities. In addition there were differences in how these political cultures shaped the value basis of state education codes in two states, and they did so in a manner consonant with their political histories.

These contrasts in the states' political cultures reflect a more basic underlying aspect of the American national culture as it addresses the nature of a good political order. That effort wrestles with two political concerns that drive every society: power and justice. Recall that the first major treatise on government, Plato's *The Republic*, focused on the meaning of justice and how power should be used to achieve it. Power means resources that optimize achieving of one's own values against the opposition of others ('who gets what, when, and how'). Justice is meant here in the classical or Platonic sense, that is, the creation of a good social order.

The three political cultures revealed in our élites' judgments contain different solutions of this power-justice polarity, about which Daniel Elazar (1984) has noted:

> The major continuing task of every civil society is to shape an immediately practical relationship between the two poles in a manner that best fits its situation. Indeed, the character of any civil society is in large measure determined by the relationship between power and justice that shapes its political order. Consequently, a particular civil society's concepts of the uses of power and the nature of justice are important aspects of its political culture (p. 113).

Our interest here is not to trace how three cultures are derived from this polarity but rather to comment on their contrasts. The focus in our cultural paradigm has been how society handles its contrasting experiences and values through certain strategies; that conceptualization is particularly sharpened in these political cultures. That is, each is a structured but contrasting response to deeper — often conflicting — concerns about using power either to promote the individual (the 'marketplace' response) or the community (the 'commonwealth' response). The first use of power, when pursued pervasively, creates one kind of political system in which society rewards individual effort and the rewards are distributed unevenly. The second use of power creates another political system in which members are rewarded collectively and rewards are distributed somewhat more evenly.

Past and present are merged in these contrasting cultural responses. The dual concerns for power and justice have generated contrasting cultural responses because they were shaped by contrasting histories, demographies, and resources among the nation's regions. Their contemporary results appear in our élites' data as significantly different 'sets of perceptions of what politics is and what can be expected from government, held by both the general public and the politicians', one of the components of political culture (Elazar, 1984, p. 112). The differences also appear both in how these states structured their education laws and values in the past, and in how their élites structure their legislative priorities in the present.

What holds together such polar cultural types in a workable relationship? First, the fact that those of a given culture will cluster within civil communities means that their control mechanisms will reflect appropriate policy demands; these differ across communities. So the problem of a political system facing polarities is reduced when they are disaggregated to those civil communities. However, that is not possible when such communities contain mixtures of these political cultures, or when the community is the nation as a whole — 'a nation of nations', as Walt Whitman noted.

So a second way that such polarities are contained lies in their adherents sharing a common belief which will enable them to work together. This is the function of believing in a democratic culture. That belief is also supported by a constitutional tradition that goes far to compel differing true believers to work together in the policy process. Of course, there still remains a wide area for conflict over such policy. Such is the nature of politics anytime, and its clamor can disguise the underlying cultural unity that permits opposites to work out their policy goals separated by their political cultures. Ironically, then, cultural unity relies on letting states produce distinctive policies when their polar political culture is a heavy influence. But also, where cultures mix, those sites suppress the potential for harsher conflict by substituting the democratic albeit rancorous political process to which all members subscribe. Our cultural paradigm thus allows for both diversity on the power–justice polarity and consensus on the nature of the democratic process.

National and Local Experiences

The diversity of American federalism means not simply differences among civil communities, but differences between levels of government that encompass these sites. These intergovernmental linkages involve much cooperation (a regional bus system or police network), but they also stimulate differences (state competition to attract industry). One of these major differences lies in a differing orientation to basic public policies (Peterson, 1980). Thus policies designed to provide essential public services or to develop business have traditionally been the province of state and particularly local governments. This passion for service and developmental activities is standard across cities of all sizes.

However, these units cannot easily redistribute public resources to overcome their citizens' income and status disparities imposed by the economic and social structure. Rather it has required action by higher governments to achieve such Equity policy. The lower governments' inability lies in their reluctant power systems or their lack of resources to redress such inequities. That is, either the dominant group and its representatives in community or state do not wish Equity, or, even if willing, these levels lack the resources to do the job. Consequently it has become the task of state and national governments (Wright, 1988).

This brief sketch helps us to understand that civil communities create multiple arenas in which citizens have pursued their economic and social goals, and in each the result has been the same. The pursuit of freedom has created a structure of rewards in which some do not share, whether for economic, social, political, ethnic, or racial reasons. Efforts to change this allocation pattern from inside each community or state have been very difficult, not often attempted, and rarely successful. Rather it has been in escalating this Equity effort to higher governments that resource redistribution does take place. For example, over time the higher levels of government have provided its citizens with comprehensive public education, regulation of unfair trade practices, welfare assistance to the poor, the franchise for different groups, due process in law enforcement, and so on. It has been regulation and subsidy issuing from legislatures and courts that have accomplished this top-down implementation of Equity.

A nation that encompasses such contrasting values as freedom and Equity provides another example of our cultural paradigm about polarities. The last two decades have witnessed educational policy pivoting between these two values. Great Society reforms of the 1960s, designed for educational equity, generated a bureaucracy at every level committed to that goal. However, as close observers noted, the Reagan administration of the 1980s has meant that 'the landscape of American educational politics has been transformed [and] that there has been a marked shift in the fundamental values guiding [it]. The pursuit of excellence has replaced equity as the leading goal of American schooling [which some believe] is driving out attention to equity and social justice' (Boyd and Kerchner, 1988, p. 1).

Our own chapters have noted the state education policy élite response to this top-down stimulus causing the states to shift from Equity and Quality. Thus, while finance policy tops state legislative priorities in the 1980s, within that control mechanism there was much less attention to Equity-driven programs. Similarly improvements in school program and teacher qualifications have accompanied the Quality-driven thrust from *The Nation at Risk* and like reports. So powerful has been that nation-wide reform current that differentiating political cultures of the states can explain little difference in what happened. Our field studies also reported this reform preoccupation filtering through the assumptive worlds of policy makers (even West Virginia).

We can analyze value polarities by focusing upon one at a time over a period of time. While the civil communities and political cultures of a large nation seem separated, in reality their borders are open to being seized by a policy idea. Familiar cases are the adoption of free public education after 1850, of the professional model of schooling and of political party reforms after 1900, of state foundation tax systems during the 1920s, and of other reforms among these civil communities even more recently. There are impressive evidences of James Madison's contention in *The Federalist Papers* that fruitful change can cross state borders; we see it even in the policy issue networks that transcend state lines (Kirst, 1981).

This pattern of alternating waves of education policy change may look random and inefficient. But the waves are really evidence that policy-makers are responding to competing values, that they understand not all values can be given enough resources at a given time, and that varying pressures can cause them to alter policy thrusts. The result is policy change stemming from alternating passions for a few values.

The Cultural Paradigm: Strategic Implications

We return to the larger understanding of our cultural paradigm, namely, that value polarities can be handled by policy-makers through several strategies. That is, they can:

1 mute their inherent conflict by adherence to a fundamental belief in a policy process, as shown in the assumptive worlds and political culture chapters;
2 provide for all of them, as seen in the state codes and taxonomy chapters;
3 swing back and forth over time in satisfying them, as reported in national vs. localistic influences throughout the book.

Consequently what the observer understands of the value context of a policy system depends upon when and where one looks at it. One perspective can be a snapshot. That is, at any one time policy-makers may be intent on some value-based reform sweeping the nation, such as federal programs for Equity in the 1960s. At another time they may shift their focus to another value-based policy, as in the 1980s emphasis on state policies for Quality and Choice. But viewed over time these snapshot perspectives yield to a second, that of a motion picture chronicling changes in state control mechanisms. A third perspective is analytical, rather like an x-ray; that is, the focus is upon the deep structure of the total policy system at any given time in order to understand the relationship of parts. As we did with assumptive worlds, statute content analysis, the control mechanism taxonomy, and political culture, the whole relationship can be analyzed in different ways. The purpose is to uncover the enduring structures of behavior and belief that constitute cultural bases for ongoing institutions and for the policies they generate.

The Utilities of Cultural Analysis

This book has sought to introduce to policy analysis how one approach — the cultural — may provide new insights into a policy world that is conceptually and empirically extremely messy; that is because we are in a nation of cultures and no single culture binds us to one value set. Nevertheless, the policy world is organized in structured ways, and a cultural approach permits finding those basic structures. For that reason alone, if not others, using culture for conceptual understanding should be explored.

Thinking Like the Anthropologists

The cultural anthropologist describes the variations of basic beliefs and behaviors of a few tribes for the purpose of identifying common structures in order to build theory from comparative analysis. So too we have compared values, rules, roles, cognitions, rituals, and policies across six different states in order to discover underlying principles about how values are incorporated into their policy systems. Along the way we have used concepts and methods from political science, policy analysis, politics of education, and linguistics — all for the purpose of exploring a cultural paradigm about strategies for handling polarities. The result has been a political anthropology of state education policy, crude but workable.

All of these activities center on the necessity in all political systems to make policy as a response to value preferences. Again, as Aaron Wildavsky noted, 'Put plainly, people . . . construct their culture in the process of decision making. . . . Preferences in regard to political objects are . . . the quintessence of politics: the construction and reconstruction of our lives together' (1987b, p. 5). At the center of our effort has been understanding and employing the concept of culture as applied to the policy systems that result from this necessity.

Culture turns out to provide diverse ways of understanding, even though we have primarily used a structural approach across these chapters. Thus assumptive worlds research demonstrates the latent and functional meanings of rituals, like silence for new legislators, or of symbolism, like the status significance of personal staff. Content analysis of state codes reveals both how the same basic values underlie education policy cultures, often in conflict, and how history's differing impact on culture can shape differently the education laws between adjoining states like Illinois and Wisconsin. Moreover, a taxonomy provides insight into the culture of centrally controlling local districts. It also permits the comparative tracking of education policy across place and time in a fashion that may be transferrable to other policies. Further, historically-based state cultures, like Elazar's three types, suggest fundamentally different ways for citizens to imbue the political world with meanings that can shape education policy.

The Uses of Cultural Analysis

These are not minor utilities for a paradigm that can give new meaning to the disparate data on the politics of education in the American states. We presented a model that would frame the policy through cultural lenses, an effort different from, although built upon, previous theory and research. We began the book suggesting that the cultural paradigm would enable us to organize data in different ways, to raise new questions about familiar data, and to reconceptualize old questions and dilemmas in understanding the policy world. In the chapters that followed we further demonstrated how this paradigm would enable us to carry out fresh research. We think the exercise provided us with better policy analysis because it was more grounded in the realities of the political world while still possessing theoretical importance. At the very least the cultural approach to policy analysis requires both scholar and practitioner to step back and search for deeper meaning to the contemporary events of policy-making. This is the meaning rooted in basic values whose differentiated pursuits constitute cultures that drive policy directions. Both the practitioner trying to influence the policy process and its products, and the policy researcher trying to get one's work used, should benefit from this search for deeper meaning.

Readers may judge how well any of these tasks or promises were fulfilled. But we hope this cultural approach causes some rethinking about the dizzying variety of data on education policy, and that some may explore the theoretical field of political anthropology. But most of all we hope that some will employ this or related thinking about culture to sharpen or invalidate our own uses of the approach. We promise that such an effort will be more thought-provoking — even more frustrating — than some of the paradigms that have dominated policy studies in the past. Indeed, the result may lead some to think about a larger but related topic — the nature of the American culture in which education policy is but one part.

State Policy Systems and 'Loosely Bounded' Culture

Some thinking along those lines leads us to the end of our joint effort. Behind the set of polarities we have discussed lies a more seminal question which can cast our work in even larger conceptual terms. What is there about the American culture which creates so many tensions and so much value diversity, which makes very difficult much national agreement on values in education — or anything else for that matter? We find most useful the comprehensive view of that question that Richard Merelman (1984) has provided, from which we can deduce the case for state education policy.

As noted earlier, Merelman finds no single, unifying culture or encompassing myth which binds the American people, but rather only a 'loose boundedness'. At one time or another we could be held together by a culture of, first, Puritanism, then later a vision of democracy, and finally a class vision. Each vision shared much: linking the individual closely to society, providing one with an understood identity that was opposed by a particular enemy, stimulating the growth of encompassing organizations, and creating cooperative mechanisms to control power in society. 'The ultimate appeal of these visions', Merelman explains (p. 22), 'lies in the fact that each is a kind of cultural blueprint or a suggestive road map of American society. They exemplify what structural anthropologists call cultural codes, systems of meaning akin to language which schematize the main features of a given society.' But each of these in turn was challenged and then adulterated. The result in time led to fragmented, often highly personal or individualized, views of what society means, hence the 'looseness' of the binding of culture in the contemporary scene.

Turning to the world of state educational policy, we note the absence in our élites of any 'cultural vision' except the necessity to possess and use power. Note this element in our chapters. Maintaining power is a basic purpose of the assumptive worlds of these policy-makers; the taxonomy we derived is a set of control mechanisms; the values underlying policies are often contradictory but their constituencies seek power to realize them; and visions of the purpose of the political system, or political cultures, drive different kinds of power systems. All these manifest the absence of a single unifying culture. Rather it is in the structure of subcultures that we have been able to draw out some — and not all — meanings of these behaviors and social relations.

Not even the dedication to educating children — 'Education Is a Good Thing' — can suffice as a binding culture because questions follow from that theme. These are questions of means and ends needed to implement that dedication, and over these questions reasonable people will differ reasonably in an open, unbounded society. For example, the way such questions are answered by Traditionalistic, Moralistic, and Individualistic cultures points directly to the absence of any cultural binding that might shape agreement on tough education policy questions. The same absence of binding is evident in differences over which control mechanism is to be stressed, or even in an agreed major mechanism — finance — whether Equity, Quality, or Efficiency or Choice will be served. Here are *not* the ties that bind.

This presents a messy picture for those who think that 'culture' can offer a single, encompassing explanation to policy life. What neatness exists lies in the multiple uses of the cultural approach that we have employed throughout this book. There is no simple way to describe how the policy game is played in fifty state arenas, but our use of subcultural concepts enabled us to find the different structures of meanings. Meaning depended upon what part of this elephant one touches, or on the kind of camera one uses for a snapshot or motion picture. Such an approach is fruitful for one who loves paradox, contradiction, myth, high deals and political scheming.

In short, the cultural approach to understanding education policy in the American states opens the scholar and practitioner to 'the relations among phenomena, rather than the nature of the phenomena themselves, and [to] the systems into which these relations enter' (Levi-Strauss, 1963, p. x). This approach also offers an understanding of the multifaceted wonder of an effective, but not always efficient, democratic political system.

References

ADAMS, K. (1982) *A Changing Federalism: The Condition of the States.* Denver, CO: Education Commission of the States.

ASTUTO, T. and CLARK, D. (1986) *The Effects of Federal Education Policy Changes on Policy and Program Development in State and Local Education Agencies.* Occasional paper, Policy Studies Center University Council for Educational Administration, Bloomington, Indiana, University of Indiana.

BAILEY, S. K., FROST, R. P., MARSH, P. E., and WOOD, R. C. (1962) *Schoolmen and Politics.* Syracuse, NY: Syracuse University Press.

BARBER, J. D. (1965) *The Lawmakers: Recruitment and Adaptation to Legislate Life.* New Haven, CN: Yale University Press.

BERMAN, P. (1981) *Improving School Improvement: A Policy Evaluation of the California School Improvement Program.* Berkeley, CA: Manifest International.

BOYD, W. (1976) 'The public, the professionals, and educational policy-making: Who governs?' *Teachers College Record,* 77: 539–77.

BOYD, W. L. (1987) 'Public education's last hurrah?: Schizophrenia, amnesia, and ignorance in school politics.' *Educational Evaluation Policy Analysis,* 9, 2: 85–100.

BOYD, W., and KERCHNER, C. (Eds.) (1988) *The Politics of Excellence and Choice of Education.* New York: Falmer.

BROWNING, R., MARSHALL, C., and TABB, D. (1984) *Protest Is Not Enough.* Berkeley, CA: University of California Press.

BURLINGAME, M. (1983) Stories and Local Level Politics and Education. Unpublished manuscript. Urbana, IL: University of Illinois.

BURLINGAME, M., and GESKE, T. (1979) 'State politics and education: An examination of selected multiple state case studies.' *Educational Administration Quarterly,* 15, 2: 51–75.

CALLAHAN, R. E. (1962) *Education and the Cult of Efficiency: A Study of the Social Forces that have shaped the Administration of the Public Schools.* Chicago, IL: University of Chicago Press.

CAMPBELL, R. F., and MAZZONI, T. L., Jr. (1976) *State Policy Making for the Public Schools.* Berkeley, CA: McCutcheon.

CHEIF, G. P. (1977) *Congress in the American System,* Chicago, Nelson-Hall.

CHOMSKY, N. (1968) *Language and Mind.* New York: Harcourt, Brace and World.

CLARK, D., and ASTUTO, T. (1986) 'The significance of permanence of changes in federal education policy.' *Educational Research*, October: 4–13.

CLARK, T., and FERGUSON, L. (1983) *City Money*. New York: Columbia University Press.

COBB, R., and ELDER, C. (1983) *Participation in American Politics*. 2nd ed. Baltimore, MD: Johns Hopkins University Press.

COHEN, M., MARCH, J., and OLSEN, J. (1972) 'A garbage can model of organizational choice.' *Administrative Science Quarterly*, 17: 1–25.

COHEN, M. (1985) 'Tracking education policies among the stars.' *State Education Policy Consortium*. Alexandria, VA: National Association of State Boards of Education.

COOMBS, F. S. (1980) *Opportunity in the Comparison of State Education Policy Systems*. Stanford, CA: Institute for Research on Educational Finance and Governance.

CREMIN, L. (1964) *The Transformation of the School*. New York: Random House.

DONMOYER, R. (1984a) 'Choosing from plausible alternatives in interpreting qualitative data.' Paper presented at the annual meeting of the American Educational Research Association, New Orleans, LA, April.

DONMOYER, R. (1984b) 'Cognitive anthropology and research on effective principals: Findings from a study and reflections on its methods.' Paper presented at the annual meeting of the American Educational Research Association, New Orleans, LA, April.

DOUGHERTY, V. (1983) *State Programs of School Improvement, 1983: A 50-State Survey*. Denver, CO: Education Commission of the States.

DOUGLAS, M. (1978) *Cultural Bias*. Occasional Paper No. 34, Royal Anthropological Institute of Great Britain and Ireland.

DOUGLAS, M., and WILDAVSKY, A. (1982) *Risk and Culture*. Berkeley, CA: University of California Press.

DOWNS, R. B. (1974) *Horace Mann: Champion of Public Schools*. New York: Twayne Publishers.

DYE, T. (1966) *Politics, Economics, and the Public*. Chicago, IL: Rand McNally.

EASTON, D. (1953) *The Political System*. New York: Alfred A. Knopf.

EASTON, D. (1965) *A System Analysis of Political Life*. New York: Wiley.

EDELMAN, M. (1977) *Political Language: Words That Succeed and Policies That Fail*. New York: Academic Press.

EDGERTON, R. B., and Langness, L. L. (1974) *Methods and Styles in the Study of Culture*. San Francisco, CA: Chandler and Sharp.

ELAZAR, D. (1970) *Cities on the Prairie*. New York: Basic Books.

ELAZAR, D. (1972) *American Federalism: A View from the States*. 2nd ed. New York: Crowell.

ELAZAR, D. (1984) *American Federalism*. 3rd ed. New York: Harper and Row.

ELAZAR, D., and ZIKMUND, J., II (1975) *The Ecology of American Political Culture*. New York: Cromwell.

ELMORE, R. (1988) 'Choice in public education.' In Boyd, W., and Kerchner, C. (Eds.) *The Politics of Excellence and Choice in Education*. Lewes: Falmer Press.

FAIRBANKS, D. (1977) 'Religious forces and "morality" politics in the American states.' *Western Political Quarterly*, 30: 411–17.

FENNO, R. F., Jr. (1973) *Congressmen in Committees*. Boston, MA: Little, Brown.

FENNO, R. F., Jr. (1978) *Home Style: House Members in Their Districts*. Boston, MA: Little, Brown.

FUHRMAN, S., and ROSENTHAL, A. (1981) *Shaping Education Policy in the States*. Washington, DC: Institute for Educational Leadership.

GARMS, W., GUTHRIE, J., and PIERCE, L. (1978) *School Finance: The Economics and Politics of Education*. Englewood Cliffs, NJ: Prentice Hall.

GINZBURG, A. L., NOELL, J., and PLISKO, V. W. (1988) 'Lessons from the wall chart.' *Educational Evaluation and Policy Analysis*, 10, 1: 1–12.

GLASER, B., and STRAUSS, A. (1967) *The Discovery of Grounded Theory*. Chicago, IL: Aldine.

GRAY, V., JACOB, H., and VINES, K. (Eds.) (1983) *Politics in the American States*. 4th ed. Boston, MA: Little Brown.

HANSON, R. (1980) 'Political culture, interparty competition and political efficacy in the American States.' *Publius: The Journal of Federalism*, 10, 2: 17–36.

HEDLUND, R. (1985) 'Organizational attributes of legislative institutions: structure, rules, norms, resources.' In Loewenberg, G., Patterson, S., and Jewell, M. (Eds.) *Handbook of Legislative Research*, Cambridge, MA: Harvard University Press.

HENNING, J., WHITE, C., SORGEN, J., and STELZER, L. (1979). *Mandate for Change*. Chicago, IL: American Bar Association.

HUTCHESON, J., and TAYLOR, C. (1973) 'Religious variables, political system characteristics, and policy outputs in the American states.' *American Journal of Political Science*, 17, 414–21.

IANNACCONE, L. (1967) *Politics in Education*. New York: Center for Applied Research in Education.

IANNACCONE, L. (1988) 'From equity to excellence: Political context and dynamics.' In Boyd, W., and Kerchner, C. (Eds.) *The Politics of Excellence and Choice in Education*. Lewes: Falmer Press.

JENSEN, R. (1978) *Illinois*. New York: Norton.

JOHNSON, C. (1976) 'Political culture in the American States: Elazar's formulation examined.' *American Journal of Political Science*, 20: 491–509.

JOSLYN, R. (1980) 'Manifestations of Elazar's political subcultures: State opinion and the content of political campaign advertising.' *Publius: The Journal of Federalism*, 10, 2: 37–58.

KATZ, M. B. (1971) *Class, Bureaucracy, and Schools: The Illusion of Educational Change in America*. New York: Praeger.

KAUFMAN, H. (1956) 'Emerging conflicts in the doctrines of public administration.' *American Political Science Review*, 50, 4: 1057–73.

KEY, V. C. (1949) *Southern Politics in State and Nation*. New York: Knopf.

KINCAID, J. (1980) 'Political culture and the quality of urban life.' *Publius: The Journal of Federalism*, 10, 2: 89–110.

KINGDOM, J. (1984) *Agendas, Alternatives, and Public Policies*. Boston, MA: Little, Brown.

KIRST, M. W. (1981) *The State Role in Education Policy Innovation*. Policy paper no. 81–C1. Stanford University, Institute for Research on Educational Finance and Governance, Stanford, CA, April.

KIRST, M., MEISTER, G., and ROWLEY, S. (1984) 'Policy issue networks: Their influence on state policymaking.' *Policy Studies Journal*, 13: 90–115.

LAPONCE, J. A. (1981) *Left and Right: The Topography of Political Perceptions*. Toronto: University of Toronto Press.

LASSWELL, H. D., LERNER, D., and ROTHWELL, C. W. (1952) *The Comparative Study of Elites*. Stanford, CA: Stanford University Press.

LEACH, E. (1970) *Levi-Strauss*. London: Fontana.

LEVI-STRAUSS, C. (1963) *Structural Anthropology*. New York: Basic Books.

LINEBERRY, R., and SHARKANSKY, I. (1978) *Urban Politics and Public Policy*. 3rd ed. New York: Harper and Row.

LITT, E. (1965) 'Education and political enlightenment in America.' *Annuals of the American Academy of Political and Social Sciences*, 361: 35–45.

LOWI, T. (1964) 'American business, public policy, case studies, and political theory.' *World Politics*, 16, 4: 617–715.

LOVRICH, N., Jr., DAYNES, B., and GINGER, L. (1980) 'Public policy and the effects of historical cultural phenomena: The case of Indiana.' *Publius: The Journal of Federalism*, 10, 2: 111–26.

LYNCH, K. (1986) *School Finance Policy Formulation in Pennsylvania*. Philadelphia, PA: University of Pennsylvania.

McCARTHY, M. M., and DEIGNAN, P. T. (1982) *What Legally Constitutes an Adequate Public Education: A Review of Constitutional, Legislative, and Judicial Mandates*. Bloomington, IN: Phi Delta Kappa Educational Foundation.

McLAUGHLIN, M. (1981) *State Involvement in Local Education Quality Issues*. Interim report prepared for the Policy Development Center for Equal Educational Opportunity for Disadvantaged Children. Santa Monica, CA: Rand Corporation.

MARSHALL, C. (1984) 'Elites, bureaucrats, ostriches and pussycats: Managing research in policy settings.' *Anthropology and Education Quarterly*, 15, 3: 194–201.

MARSHALL, C., MITCHELL, D., and WIRT, F. (1985) 'Influence, power and policy making.' *Peabody Journal of Education*, 62–64: 61–89.

MARSHALL, C., MITCHELL, D., and WIRT, F. (1986) 'The context of state level policy formulation.' *Educational Evaluation and Policy Analysis*, 8, 4: 347–78.

MARSHALL, C. (1989) 'Educational policy dilemmas: Can we have control and quality and choice and democracy and equity?' In Borman, K., Swami, B., and Wagstaff, L. (Eds.) *Contemporary Issues in US Education*. Norwood, NJ: Ablex Publishers.

MATTHEWS, D. R. (1960) *U.S. Senators and Their World*. Chapel Hill, NC: University of North Carolina Press.

MAYHEW, D. (1974) *Congress: The Electoral Connection*. New Haven, CN: Yale University Press.

MERELMAN, R. (1984) *Making Something of Ourselves*. Berkeley, CA: University of California Press.

MERRITT, R. L. (1970) *Systematic Approaches to Comparative Politics*. Chicago, IL: Rand McNally.

MILSTEIN, M., and JENNINGS, R. (1973) *Educational Policy-making and the State Legislature: The New York Experience*. New York: Praeger.

MITCHELL, D. (1981) *Shaping Legislative Decisions: Education Policy and the Social Sciences*. Lexington, MA: Lexington Books.

MITCHELL, D. (1985a) 'Education policy: The state of the art.' *Educational Administration Quarterly*, 20, 3: 129–60.

MITCHELL, D. (1985b) *Case Study of California Education Policy Making*. Unpublished manuscript. University of California, Riverside, CA.

MITCHELL, D., and ENCARNATION, J. (1984) 'Alternative state policy mechanisms for influencing school performance.' *Educational Researcher*, 13, 5: 4–11.

MITCHELL, D., and IANNACCONE, L. (1980) *The impact of California's Legislative Policy on Public School Performance*. Berkeley, CA: Institute of Governmental Studies, University of California.

MITCHELL, D., MARSHALL, C., and WIRT, F. (1986) 'The structure of state education policy making.' Paper presented at the meeting of the American Education on Research Association, San Francisco, CA, April.

MITCHELL, D., WIRT, F., and MARSHALL, C. (1986) 'Alternative state policy mechanisms for pursuing educational quality, equity, efficiency, and choice goals.' Final report to the National Institute of Education, October.

MONROE, A. (1977) 'Operationalizing political culture: The Illinois case.' *Publius: The Journal of Federalism*, 7, 1: 107–20.

MORGAN, E. (1977) *Inequality in Classroom Learning*. New York: Praeger.

MOSHER, F. (1982) *Democracy and the Public Service*. 2nd ed. New York: Oxford University Press.

MUELLER, V., and MCKEOWN, M. (Eds.) (1985) *The Fiscal, Legal, and Political Aspects of State Reform of Elementary and Secondary Education*. Yearbook of the American Education Finance Association. Cambridge, MA: Ballinger.

MUIR, W. K. (1982) *Legislature: California's School for Politics*. Chicago, IL: University of Chicago Press.

MURDOCK, G., FORD, C., HUDSON, A., KENNEDY, R., SIMMONS, L., and WHITING, J. (1971) *Outline of Cultural Materials*. New Haven, CN: Human Relations Area Files, Inc.

MURPHY, J. T. (1976) 'Title V of ESEA: The impact of discretionary funds of state educational bureaucracies.' In Williams, W., and Elmore, R. F. (Eds.) *Social Program Implementation*. New York: Academic Press.

MURPHY, T. (1980) *State Leadership in Education: On Being a Chief State School Officer*. Washington DC: Institute for Educational Leadership, George Washington University.

NAKAMURA, R., and SMALLWOOD, F. (1980) *The Politics of Policy Implementation*. New York: St Martin's Press.

NARDULLI, P. (1989) *Peoples, Cultures and Politics in Illinois*. Urbana, IL: University of Illinois Press.

ODDEN, A., and DOUGHERTY, V. (1982) *States Programs of School Improvement: A 50-State Survey*. Denver, CO: Education Commission of the States.

OSGOOD, C. E., SUCCI, G. J., and TANNENBAUM, P. H. (1957) *The Measurement of Meaning*. Urbana, IL: University of Illinois Press.

PATTERSON, S. (1968) 'The political cultures of the American states.' *Journal of Politics*, 30: 187–209.

PEIRCE, N., and Hagstrom, J. (1983) *The Book of America*. New York: Norton.

PETERSON, P. (1981) *City Limits*. Chicago, IL: University of Chicago Press.

PETERSON, P. (1984) 'Plowing the field of political theory.' *Politics of Education Bulletin*, 12, 1: 1–2.

PETERSON, P. (1985) *The Politics of School Reform*. Chicago, IL: University of Chicago Press.

PFEFFER, J. (1981a) 'Management as symbolic action.' The creation and maintenance of organizational paradigms. In Cummings, L., and Staw, B. M. (Eds.), *Research in Organizational Behavior*. Vol. 3, pp. 1–52. Greenwich, CI: JAI Press.

PFEFFER, J. (1981b) *Power in Organizations*. Marshfield, MA: Pittman Publishing.

POPKEWITZ, T. S. (1987) *Critical Studies in Teacher Education: Its Folklore, Theory and Practice*. Lewes: Falmer Press.

POWER, R. (1953) *Planting Corn Culture*. Indianapolis, IN: Indiana Historical Society.

PYE, L. (1968) 'Political culture.' In *Internationa Encyclopedia of the Social Society*. Vol. 12. New York: Crowell Collier and Macmillan.

RABE, B., and PETERSON, P. E. (1982) *Federalism, Education and Equity*. Paper presented at the annual conference of the American Educational Research Association, New York.

RAVITCH, D. (1983) *The Troubled Crusade: American Education 1945–1980.* New York: Basic Books.

ROSENTHAL, A. (1981) *Legislative Life: People, Processes, and Performances in the States.* New York: Harper and Row.

ROSENTHAL, A., and FUHRMAN, S. (1981) *Legislative Education Leadership in the States.* Washington DC: Institute for Educational Leadership.

SCHUTZ, W. C. (1958) *The Interpersonal Underworld.* Palo Alto, CA: Science and Behavior Books.

SHARKANSKY, I. (1969) 'The utility of Elazar's political culture.' *Polity,* 2, 1: 66–83.

SHARKANSKY, I. (1970) *The Routines of Politics.* New York: Van Nostrand.

SHINN, D., and VAN DER SLIK, J. (1985) 'Legislative efforts to improve the quality of public education in the American states: A comparative analysis.' Paper presented at the annual conference of the American Political Science Association, New Orleans, LA.

SMALLWOOD, F. (1976) *Free and Independent.* Brattleboro, VT: Greene Press.

SPRADLEY, J. (1979) *The Ethnographic Interview.* New York, Rinehart and Winston.

SWEET, W. (1952) *Religion in the Development of American Culture.* New York: Scribners.

TAYLOR, F. W. (1911) *Scientific Management.* New York: Harper and Row.

TILLICH, P. (1952) *The Courage to Be.* New Haven, CN: Yale University Press.

TYACK, D. B. (Ed.) (1967) *Turning Points in American Educational History.* Waltham, MA: Blaisdell.

TYACK, D. B. (1974) *The One Best System.* Cambridge, MA: Harvard University Press.

TYACK, D. B., and Hansot, E. (1982) *Managers of Virtue.* New York: Basic Books.

TYLER, S. A. (1969) *Cognitive Anthropology.* New York: Holt, Rinehart and Winston.

VERSTEGEN, D. (1988) *Fiscal Policy for Education in the Reagan Administration.* Occasional Paper No. 5. Policy Studies Center, University Council for Educational Administration, University of Virginia.

WAHLKE, E. H., EULAU, H., BUCHANAN, W., and FERGUSON, L. C. (1962) *The Legislative System.* New York: John Wiley Sons, Inc.

WALKER, J. (1969) 'The diffusion of innovation among the American states.' *American Political Science Review,* 63: 880–99.

WEATHERFORD, J. (1981) *Tribes on the Hill.* New York: Rawson, Wade.

WELCH, S., and PETERS, J. (1980) 'State political culture and the attitude of state senators toward social, economic welfare, and corruption issues.' *Publius: The Journal of Federalism,* 10, 2: 59–68.

WILDAVSKY, A. (1987a) 'Choosing preferences by constructing institutions: A cultural theory of preference formation.' *American Political Science Review,* 81: 3–21.

WILDAVSKY, A. (1987b) 'Frames of reference come from cultures: A predictive theory. Working Paper Series, Survey Research Center, University of California, Berkeley.

WIRT, F. (1977) 'State policy culture and state decentralization.' In Scribner, J. (Ed.) *Politics of Education Yearbook 1977.* Chicago, IL: National Society for the Study of Education.

WIRT, F. M. (1980) 'Does control follow the dollar? School policy, state-local linkages and political culture.' *Publius: The Journal of Federation,* 10, 2: 69–88.

WIRT, F. (1981) 'Professionalism and political conflict: A developmental model.' *Journal of Public Policy.* 1: 61–93.

WIRT, F. (1983) 'Institutionalization: Prison and Schools.' In Gray, V., Jacob, H., and Vines, K. (Eds.) *Politics in the American States,* 4th ed. Boston: Little, Brown.

WIRT, F. (1985) 'The dependent city? External influences upon local control.' *Journal of Politics*, 47: 83–112.

WIRT, F. (1988) 'The chief educational officer in comparative perspective.' *Comparative Education Review*. 32: 39–57.

WIRT, F., and CHRISTOVICH, L. (1989) 'Administrators' perceptions of policy influence: Conflict management styles and roles.' *Education Administration Quarterly*, forthcoming.

WIRT, F., and HARMAN, G. (Eds) (1986) *Educational Recession and the World Village.* Lewes: Falmer Press.

WIRT, F., and KIRST, M. (1989) *Schools in Conflict: The Politics of Education.* 2nd ed. Berkeley, CA: McCutcheon.

WRIGHT, D. (1988) *Understanding Intergovernmental Relations.* Monterey, CA: Brooks/Cole.

WYMAN, M. (1984) *Immigrants in the Valley.* Chicago, IL: Nielson Hall.

YOUNG, K. (1977 March) 'Values in the policy process.' *Policy and Politics*, 5, 3: 1–22.

ZEIGLER, H., KEHOE, E., and REISMAN, J. (1985) *City Managers and School Superintendents.* New York: Praeger.

Appendix A: Research Design and Methodology

The Nature of the Research

Using Easton's (1965) definition of politics as the authoritative allocation of values, our research focused on the values-translation function in state education policy-making. We wanted to know about where values originate, how they are transformed in response to the current dynamics of the state policy system, and how they can be identified in policy and organized by a taxonomy. Because there are different paths to understand the process of values embodiment, our research was designed with multiple data sets and analyses.

The research was conducted in six different states, using common data collection strategies, to allow comparative analysis. The comparative study allowed examination of differences in the common properties in the structure of state policy systems. The study focused entirely on the state level, with most data collected from key participants in education policy-making in the individual states. The data collection and analysis worked at two analytic levels: the individual policy-maker level and the state policy system level.

The rationale behind the focus on the individual as the unit of analysis came from the following propositions:

1 key policy-makers who occupy positions of influence have intimate knowledge of the values, interworkings, and the makings of actions in policy;
2 key policy-makers' values and preferences affect policy choice; and
3 key policy-makers work as sensors of problems, and as people who translate problems into policies, they have specialized information regarding policy choices.

Thus one analytic focus is on how individuals come to take up a position within the policy system and how individuals account for the transformation of beliefs and problems into policy choices.

The state policy system was another level of analysis. The system-level analysis was derived from pooling of individual data. Key policy actors gave their sense of policy priorities and choices, as well as the dynamics and background variables affecting policy-making in their states. The collectivity of their responses served as our 'best estimate' of the objective reality of policy-making in each state. Those estimates were the basis for description of the context of policy within each state and the basis for identifying the similarities and differences in the policy contexts among the six states.

Multiple sets of data, both qualitative and quantitative, were collected in each state. The design built upon the strength of qualitative data for discovering subjective meanings and perceptions about relationships. It also built upon the strength of statistical analysis for uncovering findings from data that were quantified responses to questions about perceptions and beliefs about policy.

The analysis of qualitative data provided the basis for the selection and design of instruments for collecting quantitative data, and in the analysis of findings the various sets and types of data were used to check validity, to search for deeper meaning and connections in interpretation, and to identify a model of the process of policy choice. We compiled case studies of the states using comparable data, and linked the descriptive case studies to statistical analyses whose questions and instrumentation were refined by the qualitative data.

The Conduct of the Research

The Research Design

The major data collection method of this research was through interviewing key participants in state education policy-making in the six states in two separate rounds of interviewing. Round One data were used to develop instruments for Round Two.

Round one The first interviewing of key policy actors was devised to elicit data regarding the 'overall framework' of a State Policy Mechanism (SPM), the major goals in that SPM, a recounting of any major changes in the last few years in that SPM, and that actor's sense of satisfaction with the way SPM policies were working. They were also asked to discuss sources of documents and their perception of who was most involved and knowledgeable in each of the policy areas.

First-round interviewees (described below in section on sample) responded to a list of SPMs using the Mitchell and Encarnation (1984) taxonomy and to protocol-based, open-ended questions. The protocol is presented in Appendix B.

The same procedures and questions were used with all interviewees, in all the sample states, to assure comparability. Interviewees were asked to focus on one policy area with which they were most involved and knowledgeable. Interviewees were encouraged to offer description and insights, focused only by the nature of the open-ended questions. These interviews were audiotaped and lasted approximately forty-five minutes. The audiotapes and field notes from Round One were important for refining the taxonomy, for developing research instruments for Round Two, and for discovering patterns in the context of policy-making.

Follow-up to round one Following Round One, the research team met to discuss similarities and differences among the sample states and to develop formal instruments for collection of quantifiable data during Round Two. Site summaries and other devices were useful for cross-case comparison of the states' policy-making processes and approaches in each SPM. From this analysis emerged the refinement of the seven SPMs and the identification of the general approaches within each SPM. Questions about rankings, knowledgeability, preferences and processes in the SPMs and their approaches were to be a major, refined focus in Round Two. The follow-up analysis of Round One data also showed the wide variation in context in the six states and, therefore, re-emphasized the importance of gathering more data on values, political culture, and relative power of the various groups and individuals involved in policy-making.

Round two In contrast to Round One's rather loosely structured interviewing, Round Two interviewing was more tightly structured. Round Two sample is described below. Interviewees were presented with outlines of the seven SPMs and were asked to provide their perceptions of education policy priorities (organized by SPM) in their state and then to discuss the alternative approaches to policy formation in the domains where they were most knowledgeable. The interview was organized and focused by a listing of SPMs and approaches, and the protocol is shown in Appendix C. Along with the interview respondents were asked to fill out five survey instruments. Round Two interviews were also audiotaped. The interviewers, while collecting quantifiable data regarding policy priorities, also took field notes, particularly where respondents offered detail and interpretation. Thus Round Two yielded quantitative and qualitative data on policy processes, priorities, and goals.

Additional data sets The education codes of each of the sample states were viewed as key documents that could be analyzed to identify patterns of past policy-making priorities. Therefore, a content analysis of the codes of each state was conducted, organized by the SPM framework.

In addition a compilation was made of all the fifty states providing baseline information on the political, economic, social, and educational conditions. Assertions about the special conditions or, on the other hand, the representativeness of the six sample states could be examined by comparing these states with the other forty-four on selected variables (see Mitchell, Wirt and Marshall, 1986).

Documents (e.g., agency annual reports on performance, policy proposals, budgets, memoranda, dissertations, and other previous research) were collected to be used to (1) prepare for interviewing, (2) check unclear data, and (3) establish historical conditions of policy-making in each state.

Instrument Construction

This research design required two different types of data and two different types of data collection instruments.

The qualitative instruments The interviewing procedures and instruments for this study were designed with recognition (based on the collective experience of the three researchers in policy settings) that policy-makers have their own language, meaning systems, and motivations (Marshall, 1984). The instruments and approaches had to be designed to motivate them to participate openly and to understand enough our intent so that their responses would be relevant to the research questions. The protocol for Round One interviewing was designed to ensure that interviewees had information about the purpose of the research and assurances of confidentiality, and that each interviewee in each state would be asked the same questions. Through this instrument (Appendix B), entry and receptivity of interviewees would be facilitated, and comparability of data would be assured. This interview was developed to be conducted as a 'conversation', so the interviewees were encouraged to expand on their responses.

In Round Two a two-part interview instrument was developed for the portion of the data collection that followed the interview format. The questions were framed by the taxonomy of refined SPMs and their approaches; the purpose was to collect individuals' perceptions of the priorities in their states' educational policy-making. The protocol focused on eight main questions, guided by the protocol shown in Appendix C. A notebook containing a listing and definitions of the SPMs and of the various approaches to the SPMs was prepared as a guide for the interviewee's responses as shown in Appendix D. A different notebook, containing forms to fill with the interviewee responses, was prepared for compiling the responses in a systematic and easily retrievable manner as shown in Appendix E. These instruments were designed to collect both qualitative interview data and quantitative data.

The Round Two interview protocols were pilot tested with five interviewees in Arizona by Mitchell, who trained Marshall and Wirt to ensure collection of comparable data, anticipate certain questions, and to provide standard responses to those questions.

Interviewees were told (or reminded) of the purpose and procedures of the study and were directed in the notebook to the list of the seven SPMs. The questioning centered on the following core information sought:

1 ranking of SPMs with regard to the amount of attention in the last few years;
2 perception of whether any SPM should be receiving more or less attention; and
3 ranking of the SPMs in order of individual's knowledgeability.

Responses were elicited verbally and recorded in the interviewer's notebook.

The instrument was designed so that interviewees were informed that, *within* the SPMs, there was a variety of approaches, displayed in their notebooks. They would respond to questions about the approaches in the three SPMs where they were most knowledgeable. The questioning centered on the following core questions:

1   Which approaches have been receiving the most attention? (An example of a specific policy incorporating the most popular approach was sought); and
2   What are personal preferences of the most promising approaches? How does the state incorporate his/her preferred way of approaching the SPM? What is the respondent's sense of whether the state would follow his/her preferences in the SPM in the next few years.

The quantitative instruments In order to compile quantitative data that would facilitate cross-case comparison on key variables, four structured instruments were devised to collect quantitative data in Round Two. Several were pilot tested in university classes and all were pilot tested in Arizona. They were presented to interviewees to be filled out as a second portion of the Round Two interview, with the interviewer present to direct and to answer questions, to continue the 'conversational' tone of interviewing, and to continue audiotaping.

One instrument was developed to uncover the individual's value system underlying education policy-making. The instrument was developed with a format similar to the semantic differential developed by Osgood, Suci, and Tannenbaum (1957) and refined by Mitchell (1981), and was called 'What Do You Feel Are the Important Policy Problems in Your State?' See Appendix F for full display of the instrument.

The instrument linked particular SPM-based options with fundamental values of Equity, Choice, Efficiency, or Quality. It consisted of eighteen pairs of phrases. Respondents were presented with the task of making choices between particular policy/value combinations, indicating which combination more closely fit with their values and policy preferences when paired with one other policy/value option.

A second instrument was developed to elicit individual respondents' perceptions of the relative influence of the various groups and key actors in state policy-making. This instrument (presented in Appendix G) was aimed at eliciting a numerical scale of the power ranking of policy groups — one way of creating individual models of the policy world of each state. It was developed from the experience of previous researchers, e.g., Fuhrman and Rosenthal, 1981; Campbell and Mazzoni, 1976; Mitchell, 1981, on state policy systems as well as from Round One findings.

The third instrument was developed to elicit the individual respondents' perceptions of the political culture of their states. The Political Culture Instrument was a questionnaire devised to test the cultural labels of our states assigned by Elazar (1984a) against the judgment of educational policy-makers in the states. The cultural objects explored were those set out and then described by Elazar (see chapter 5) — government, political parties, bureaucracy — employing Elazar's words as closely as possible. This measurement device is displayed in Appendix H.

Finally, in order to describe our sample and ensure that it was not skewed, an instrument was developed to collect data on the personal background of each interviewee on a broad array of factors typically found to influence social behavior (Mitchell, 1981). This instrument, the 'Personal Data Form', is shown in Appendix I.

The Sample

Sampling occurred at both of the analytical levels: the states' and the individuals'.

Selecting the states The six sample states were selected to get variation, in the range of possible states, on the following variables:

1 political culture (described in detail in chapter 6), which is related to both geographic region and degree of centralization of state policy control. Two states representing each of the three political culture types ('Moralistic', 'Individualistic', and 'Traditionalistic') were chosen, using Elazar's (1972) calculations of the culture of each state.
2 urbanization (as measured by the 1978 US Census), since the proportion of the population living in urban areas was viewed as an important mediating role in policy-making. Additionally, it was viewed as important to select states with a range of balances of population size and density.
3 degree of fiscal stress, which was viewed as an important constraining role on policy options. Adams' (1982) analysis of states' fiscal status was used to select states with high, medium, and relatively low fiscal stress.

Also states were chosen to meet the pragmatic criterion of low-cost data collection. Therefore, the home states of the three researchers (California, Illinois, and Pennsylvania) were natural choices. The other three states, Wisconsin, West Virginia, and Arizona, were chosen to maximize the range of variables as much as possible.

Round one sample In Round One the sample of interviewees (a minimum of twelve in each state) was selected to represent the following types:

1 governor's key education advisor;
2 legislative education policy committee chairs;
3 legislative fiscal (finance and appropriations) committee chairs;
4 key staff members to education and finance committees;
5 chief state school officer, top staff;
6 top officials in the States School Boards' Association;
7 top officials in the school administrators' association;
8 top officials in the teachers' associations;

9   key informants who were long-time observers of education policy-making, e.g., education reporters, educational administration professors, and people who were in policy positions in the past; and

10   state board officials.

This sampling was based on assumptions about who was 'obviously' involved and had important insights regarding education policy-making. The response rate (agreeing to be interviewed) was 95 per cent.

Round Two sample During Round One interviewees were asked to identify key actors who were involved and knowledgeable in education policy-making. Round Two's sample in each state was drawn from this insider-based list. Approximately 70 per cent of Round Two interviewees were the same individuals as the Round One sample since they were in 'obvious' positions *and* they were identified by insiders as being knowledgeable and involved in policy-making for education. The remaining 30 per cent of the Round Two sample were large city schools' lobbyists, additional special interest group lobbyists, legislative staff, and SDE staff.

Content Analysis of the Education Codes

The analysis of codes was viewed as another way of testing the viability of the taxonomy. The taxonomy was used to organize units in the codes according to the State Policy Mechanism in which they fit, to the approaches they exemplified, and the *dominant value* evidenced. Common operational definitions of units of analysis, State Policy Mechanisms, approaches, and values were developed to conduct the content analysis of the codes. The form created for this content analysis is shown in Appendix J.

Data Reduction and Analysis Procedures

The data, both qualitative and quantitative, were analyzed according to the original logic of using as the unit of analysis individual policy actors, whose perceptions were sensors of policy-making in their states. The data were aggregated within and among states to describe the unique characteristics of states, to identify differences by comparing states, and to identify national trends as evidenced by the six states. This section recounts the methods of analysis.

Transcription of audiotapes Selected tapes were transcribed verbatim. These transcriptions were used as aids to making cross-state comparisons and as data sources for discovering differences and similarities in language and stories in the six states.

Document analysis Documents collected during field work were filed and were treated as data sources, as checks for accuracy, meaning, and validity in interpreting other data. They were particularly useful in the construction of the case studies.

Case studies As an aid in cross-case analysis and as a display of the various data regarding the background, processes and context of policy-making, case studies of each state were compiled following a common outline. The recounting, in rich description, of the background conditions, structures, and current education policy-making showed ways in which our states were importantly different.

Quantitative data analysis techniques There were seven sets of data analyzed by statistical methods appropriate to the research questions. In addition to descriptive statistics on all of the relevant variables, L-tests of group differences, discriminant analysis of state differences, analysis of variance and correlation analysis were utilized where appropriate to illuminate the level of significance and substantiate meaning of the data collected. Details of each analytic technique employed are described in the chapters and in the study's final report (Mitchell, Wirt, and Marshall, 1986).

Analysis of qualitative data One state's qualitative data (Pennsylvania) were analyzed and filed by computer according to informant, date, position, and major theoretical categories. These data were examined, using a focus on words, a social interaction framework, and the constant comparative method of analysis of qualitative data (Glaser and Strauss, 1967) to identify patterns and to generate domains of assumptive worlds, as reported in chapter 2.

Validity Checking

The essential design validity question was whether the sampling strategy was confirmed by the data. This section displays data regarding the two levels of analysis: the individual and the state.

The validity of the sample of individuals The characteristics of the respondents showed a distribution of background and orientations that reflect the general characteristics of education policy-makers among the states, as shown in table A.1. There is no indication that the sample of individuals was skewed or non-representative of state education policy actors. In addition there was no significant difference among the states in the patterns of individuals' self-reported knowledge of the seven SPMs.

The distribution of respondents across the six sample states, classified according to their formal roles within the policy system, is shown in figure A.1. As indicated by the modest variation in cell values within the table, and the non-significant chi-square value shown below the table, our respondents were well distributed. The largest number (31.9 per cent) were representatives of various state-wide interest groups (primarily professional educator groups, but a sprinkling of taxpayer groups and other non-educator groups were included). A similar number (30.4 per cent) were drawn from the ranks of the executive branch of government. Legislators were the third largest group (21.5 per cent) and legislative staff consultants the smallest group (16.3 per cent).

Within the sample the full range of the seven SPMs was represented in respondents' self-reported knowledge, although self-reported knowledge in finance (the most reported) far outweighed self-reported knowledge in curriculum materials and buildings in the sample.

As can be seen, there was no significant difference in roles in the samples. One hundred and twelve unweighted cases were usable for the statistical analysis.

Summary

A complex but coordinated research design allowed comparative analysis of six states' processes of embodiment of values. It allowed us to explore the viability of a taxonomy for organizing policy/values enactments and to examine the explanatory power of several paths to understanding how values are incorporated into policy.

Table A.1   Average Background Characteristics of Respondents from Six States

	The Average Respondent
Tenure in present position	4–5 years
Age	40–49 years
Sex	80 per cent male
Ethnicity	94 per cent white
Occupation	30 per cent were educators
Highest degree earned	Masters
BA field	Education, science and math, social sciences
MA field	Education, science and math, social sciences
PhD field (N=35)	Education, science and math
Possesses teacher certification	51 per cent of sample
Possesses administrator's certification	35 per cent of sample
Possesses law license	6 per cent of sample
Family income	$50,000
Political orientation	Moderate
Political party affiliation	Slightly more Democrat than Republican

Figure A.1   Cross-tabulation of Respondent Role and State of Residence

ROLE	**STATE** AZ	CA	IL	PA	WV	WI	Total
Executive Branch	10	5	8	5	7	7	42 (30.0%)
Legislative Staff	4	5	5	4	1	5	24 (17.1%)
Legislators	6	4	2	8	4	6	30 (21.4%)
Interest Group Representatives	10	3	8	10	7	6	44 (31.9%)
TOTAL	30	17	23	24	17	24	135

Appendix B: Interview Protocol

Initial Interviews with Key Policy Actors

Introductory Statement

It's good of you to take the time to meet with me . . .

As you may recall from my letter, I am part of a research team being supported by the National Institute of Education to review state-level education policies. We will be taking a detailed look at six states — trying to develop a comprehensive picture of each state's overall policy framework. We will be looking at education statutes and regulations in each state, but will need help from knowledgeable people like yourself in order to get a feel for how written policies are working out in actual practice.

This is the first of several visits which I and (name), my research associate will be making to (the state capital). This week I'll be interviewing about a dozen key people here in (the state capital) — some elected officials, a small group of senior staff people, and a few representatives of the major education interest groups. While I'm doing these interviews, (name) will be spending time in the state library collecting various documents and reports which will help to clarify the educational policy picture for us.

Before we begin, I would like to record our conversation, if I may — that way I won't have to slow down to take notes. The recording will be for research purposes only — no one except members of our research team will have access to the tape, and we won't be quoting people by name in our final report. If in the course of our conversation anything comes up which you would rather not have on tape, just shut the machine off with the switch here on the microphone (indicate how to work the switch).

(After the recorder is working) . . . There are three matters I'd like to ask you about:

1 key actors in (name of state's) education policy-making that you feel we should be sure to talk with,

2   any reports or other documents you think would be helpful to us in getting a clearer picture of education policy in this state, and

3   I'd like you to give me a little background on???? policies in this state. (Indicate one of the seven SPMs.)

Perhaps you have some questions about the project before we begin? (Remember that *review* and *analysis* of *overall* policy *frameworks* and basic education policy *goals* are the key terms in our explanation of the project.)

OK, let's talk about the key education policy people in this state. If we could only do eight or ten interviews on education policy issues in this state, who would you suggest that we talk to? (Ask about knowledgeable people in each of the seven policy areas: governance, revenue generation, resource allocation, program definition, personnel certification, student assessment, and curriculum materials development).

Let's talk a bit about printed material which might help us get a handle on policy and practice in this state. Can you put me onto any good reports or summaries of education policy in this state? (Probe for help regarding each of the seven policy areas, as well as general information about issues and practices.)

Could we turn now to a bit of background in the area of (particular policy area). I know this state has ???? and ???? (name a couple of policy elements) in this area. How would you describe the overall framework of (particular policy area) policy?

What do you feel are the most important goals or objectives of policy in this area?

Have there been major changes in this area in the last few years? (What brought those changes about?)

Are you personally happy with the way these policies are working?

Closing Statement

Thank you for your time (this morning) — you have been extremely helpful. We would like to come back to talk with you again at a later date, after we've had a chance to review the available written material and talked to some of the other key people. By that time, I hope we'll have a pretty good idea about how our six states differ, and you could help me check on our interpretation of the major education issues and goals in this state. At that point, we'd be happy to provide you with some information about our overall analysis, if you'd be interested.

Appendix C: Alternative State Education Policy Mechanisms Project Interview Protocol

Introductory Statement

To those interviewed previously: Since we last talked I have met with the other team members on our state-level education policy research project. We had a chance to compare notes on the different approaches to K-12 education policy being used in our six-state sample.

Now we would like to ask you, along with the others we have previously interviewed, to respond to a common set of questions so that we can compare policies and programs across the states.

To those not previously interviewed: As I mentioned in our letter, I am part of a team funded by the National Institute of Education to take a look at state-level education policy in six states. Preliminary interviews were held in each state a few months ago. The people interviewed in this state identified you as a person we should be sure to talk with in order to get a full understanding of K-12 education policy in this state.

Since doing our preliminary interviews, the research team met to discuss the various approaches to K-12 education policy being taken in our six sample states. We have developed a common set of questions to be used in each state so that we can more fully understand the similarities and differences in approach across the sample states.

If you don't mind, I would like to tape record our interview.
[Turn on tape recorder.]
Although the specifics differ from state to state, our preliminary work indicates that similar basic issues are being worked on in most states. I would like to go over some of these issues with you — they are described on the pages of this notebook.
[Give respondent the notebook.]

1   On the first page of the notebook, you will see a list of seven of br educational policy issues areas that we have found to be important in the states we have been studying. Which of these seven policy areas would ¹ say has been getting the most attention in your state over the last two three years?

Which has been receiving the least amount of attention?

Could you rank order the others?

2   How do you feel about the relative amount of attention being giver each of these policy domains? Do you feel that some areas should be gett more attention? Are some getting too much attention? Which ones?

3   Would you look at the list of seven policy domains once again and p the three areas in which you feel most knowledgeable — I would like to h you look somewhat more closely at state policy in each of these areas.

[For the three SPMs for which each respondent is most knowledgeable as

4   If you would turn to the next (next) page in the notebook you will that our preliminary work identified:

Five .... basic approaches .... School Finance
Four .... to policy-making .... School Personnel Policy
Five .... in the area of............... Student Testing and Assessment
Four... School Program Definition
Eight... School Governance
Three .... Curriculum Materials Development
Four... School Buildings and Facilities

5   Would you look at the alternative approaches to SPM.

Which of these No. approaches has been receiving the most attention recent SPM policy decisions in this state?

6   Which would you personally view as the least promising?

[If more than three] How would you personally rank the others?

7   Could you give me an example of how you would like to see this st incorporate Approach given as #1 into SPM policy?

8   On a scale of 1 to 10, how likely is it that this state will follow yc preferences on SPM policy in the near future?

[Go back to Question 4 until all SPMs are covered. After all of the SP₁ have been covered, go to next page.]

9   Please turn to the next page in the notebook. This page asks you indicate whether state has responded directly to the report of the Presider 'Commission on Excellence'. Five recommendations from the Commissi report are present in a sort of 'box-score' format. Would you mark direc on the form provided whether any of these recommendations have be receiving attention? Mark the appropriate column for each recommendati that has gotten attention.

10   The next two pages ask you to record your own personal judgme regarding the relative importance of various educational policy problems a the relative influence of various participants in the state policy-making syste Would you take five minutes or so to record your views on these two pag

11   Around the country, there are different ways that people view government and politics. This may well affect education policy in each of our six
states. Would you please give me your perceptions of how people in this state
feel?

12   The last two pages in the notebook ask for a little information about
your personal background and training. If you would complete them now, I
will be finished with my questions — then I'll be glad to answer any questions
you may have about any aspect of our project.

[Thank each participant for their cooperation]

Appendix D: Seven Major Policy Domains for K-12 Education Policy

1 *School finance*: controlling who pays for education, how those costs are distributed, and how human and fiscal resources are allocated to the schools.
2 *School personnel training and certification*: controlling the conditions for getting or keeping various jobs in the school system.
3 *Student testing and assessment*: fixing the timing and consequences of testing, including subjects covered and the distribution of test data.
4 *School program definition*: controlling, program planning and accreditation, or otherwise specifying what schools must teach and how long they must teach it.
5 *School organization and governance*: the assignment of authority and responsibility to various groups and individuals.
6 *Curriculum materials*: controlling the development and/or selection of textbooks and other instructional materials.
7 *School buildings and facilities*: determination of architecture, placement, and maintenance for buildings and other school facilities.

Alternative Approaches to School Finance Policy

A *Equalizing* the amount of money spent to educate each child in the state (perhaps under court order).
B *Limiting or increasing* the total amount of money spent on schooling.
C *Targeting* funds on children with special needs — non-English speakers, disadvantaged minorities, low achievers, handicapped, gifted, etc.
D *Financing* particular school services or functions — textbooks, staff training, program planning, minimum salaries, building maintenance, etc.
E *Offsetting* burdensome costs incurred by school districts with specific problems — declining enrollment, extensive pupil transportation, high cost urban environments, building construction, etc.

Alternative Approaches to School Personnel Policy

A *Pre-service training and certification improvement*: credentialing reform, basic skills testing, increasing minimum salaries, etc.

B *Professional development programs*: in-service training requirements, teacher centers, principal academies, summer institutes, etc.

C *Accountability systems*: linking compensation or job security with performance assessments, merit pay, special compensation for outstanding work, new evaluation or employee discipline requirements, etc.

D *Changing teacher job definition*: mentor teacher programs, development of career ladders, differentiated staffing plans, etc.

Alternative Approaches to School Organization and Governance Policy

A *Redistributing authority among state-level agencies*: creating new commissions, giving new powers to the chief state school officer, expanding oversight by the legislature, etc.

B *Strengthening state agencies at the expense of local districts*: moving personnel, curricular, fiscal, or other policies into the hands of state-level decision-makers.

C *Strengthening site-level governance*: advisory committees, school site councils, or other mechanisms for broadening participation at this level.

D *Strengthening teacher influence*: appointment of teachers to policy committees, giving them meet-and-confer or collective bargaining rights, etc.

E *Clarifying student rights and responsibilities*: defining due process requirements, mandating discipline programs, modifying suspension or expulsion regulations, etc.

F *Strengthening administrative control*: more discretionary authority over program or personnel, reorganizing school districts, mandating evaluation and employee discipline programs, etc.

G *Expanding parent/citizen influence*: more parental rights in student assignment or transfer, requiring citizen involvement in decisions, perhaps even tuition tax credits or educational vouchers.

H *Altering local district roles and responsibilities*: reorganization and consolidation of districts, granting new powers to local boards, changing election or appointment procedures for board members, etc.

Alternative Approaches to Student Testing and Assessment Policy

A *Specifying the format or content of tests*: adopting new tests, shifting from norm-referenced to criterion-referenced tests, adding new subjects, new grades, or new student groups, etc.

B   *Testing students for special program placement*: certification of handicapped or gifted students, requiring tests for graduation or promotion, etc.

C   *Using tests to evaluate program or teacher performance*: linking salaries or program funding to test scores, etc.

D   *Measuring non-academic student outcomes*: assessment of physical skills, attitudes, interests, or other personal and social characteristics.

E   *Requiring local districts to develop their own tests*: local promotion or proficiency testing for students, requiring local tests for program evaluation, etc.

Alternative Approaches to School Building and Facilities Policy

A   *Technical architectural review* of local school district building plans to insure they are cost efficient, meet safety standards, etc.

B   *Long range planning for school construction*: demographic studies, allocation of state construction funds, etc.

C   *Remediation of existing building problems*: asbestos, earthquake safety, energy conservation, access for handicapped students, etc.

E   *Providing new instructional capacities*: science and language laboratories, libraries, media centers, etc.

Alternative Approaches to Curriculum Materials Policy

A   *Mandating local use of materials* selected or developed by state agencies: textbook review and approval procedures, tight control over curriculum materials budgets, etc.

B   *Specification of the scope and sequence* of materials to be used in local districts: identification of topics to be covered in various courses or grades.

C   *Development of specialized instructional materials* for particular purposes: new technologies, computer literacy, materials for gifted or handicapped children, bilingual materials, etc.

Alternative Approaches to School Program Definition Policy

A   *Changing time requirements*: modifying the school day, school year, or specifying the number of minutes or hours for particular subjects, etc.

B   *Mandating specific subjects*: physical education, alcohol/drug abuse, creationism, driver education, American economic or political system, etc.

C   *Setting higher program standards*: new graduation requirements, promotion/-retention policies, etc.

D   *Developing programs for special groups*: remedial courses, special education, bilingual, alternative schools, etc.

Appendix E: Alternative State Education Policy Mechanisms Project Data Recording Form for Final Interviews

RESPONDENT:_____

STATE: _____

POSITION: _____

DATE: _____

TIME: _____

CODE: _____

On the seven policy domains:

                  1. Attention.   2. Needs + or -   3. Knowledge

    I. School finance

   II. Personnel

  III. Test assessment

  IV. Program definition

   V. Governance

  VI. Curriculum materials

 VII. Plant and facilities

I. School Finance

   1. State's rank order of approaches:

   —A. Equalizing   —B. Limiting/Increasing

   —C. Targeting   —D. Financing

   —E. Offsetting

   2. Example of a specific policy incorporating the approach getting the most attention:

   3. *Personal* ranking of approaches:

   —A. Equalizing   —B. Limiting/Increasing

   —C. Targeting   —D. Financing

   —E. Offsetting

   4. *Personal* example of how state should incorporate approach ranked #1:

5. Estimate of likelihood that state will follow *personal* preferences: 1–2–3–4–5–6–7–8–9–10.

II. School Personnel Policy
   1. State's rank order of approaches:
—A. Pre-Service/Certification   —B. Professional Development
—C. Accountability   —D. Changing Teacher Job
                                  Definitions

2. Example of a specific policy incorporating the approach getting the most attention:

3. *Personal* ranking of approaches:
—A. Pre-Service/Certification   —B. Professional Development
—C. Accountability   —D. Changing Teacher Job
                                  Definitions

4. *Personal* example of how state should incorporate approach ranked #1:

5. Estimate of likelihood: 1–2–3–4–5–6–7–8–9–10.

III. Testing and Assessment
   1. State's rank order of approaches:
—A. Format or Content   —B. Special Program Placement
—C. Evaluate Teachers/Programs   —D. Measure Non-academic
—E. Require Locals to Develop   Outcomes
     Own Tests

2. Example of a specific policy incorporating the approach getting the most attention:

3. *Personal* ranking of approaches:
—A. Format or Content   —B. Special Program Placement
—C. Evaluate Teachers/Programs —D. Measure Non-academic
—E. Require Locals to Develop   Outcomes
     Own Tests

4. *Personal* example of how state should incorporate approach ranked #1:

5. Estimate of likelihood: 1–2–3–4–5–6–7–8–9–10.

IV. Program Definition Policy
   1. State's rank order of approaches:
—A. Changing Time Requirements —B. Mandating Specific Subjects
—C. Setting Higher Standards   —D. Developing Programs for Spe-
                                    cial Groups

2. Example of a specific policy incorporating the approach getting the most attention:

3. *Personal* ranking of approaches:
—A. Changing Time Requirements —B. Mandating Specific Subjects
—C. Setting Higher Standards   —D. Developing Programs for Special Groups

4. *Personal* example of how state should incorporate approach ranked #1:

5. Estimate of likelihood: 1–2–3–4–5–6–7–8–9–10.

V. School Governance Policy
   1. State's rank order of approaches:
   —A. State Level Redist.   —B. State at Expense of Locals
   —C. Strengthen Site Level   —D. Strengthen Teachers
   —E. Student Rights   —F. Administrative Control
   —G. Citizen Influence   —H. Alter Local District Role

   2. Example of a specific policy incorporating the approach getting the most attention:

   3. *Personal* ranking of approaches:
   —A. State Level Redist.   —B. State at Expense of Locals
   —C. Strengthen Site Level   —D. Strengthen Teachers
   —E. Student Rights   —F. Administrative Control
   —G. Citizen Influence   —H. Alter Local District Role

   4. *Personal* example of how state should incorporate approach ranked #1:

   5. Estimate of likelihood: 1–2–3–4–5–6–7–8–9–10.

VI. Curriculum Materials Policy
   1. State's rank order of approaches:
   —A. Mandating Local Use   —B. Specifying Scope and Sequence
   —C. Develop Specialized Materials

   2. Example of a specific policy incorporating the approach getting the most attention:

   3. *Personal* ranking of approaches:
   —A. Mandating Local Use   —B. Specifying Scope and Sequence
   —C. Develop Specialized Materials

   4. *Personal* example of how state should incorporate approach ranked #1:

   5. Estimate of likelihood: 1–2–3–4–5–6–7–8–9–10.

VII. Building and Facilities
   1. State's rank order of approaches:
   —A. Technical/Architectural   —B. Long-Range Planning
       Review
   —C. Remediation of Problems   —D. New Instructional Capacities

   2. Example of a specific policy incorporating the approach getting the most attention:

3. *Personal* ranking of approaches:

—A. Technical/Architectural   —B. Long-Range Planning
    Review

—C. Remediation of Problems   —D. New Instructional Capacities

4. *Personal* example of how state should incorporate approach ranked #1:

5. Estimate of likelihood: 1–2–3–4–5–6–7–8–9–10.

Appendix F: Individual Value Systems and Education Policy-making. What do You Feel Are The Important Education Policy Problems In Your State?

Indicate your views by placing an 'x' on the line nearer to the phrase in each pair that you feel is more important. Mark the space closest to the end of the line if that item is *much* more important than the other; mark the next space if it is *somewhat* more important; and mark the space close to the center of the line if it is only a *little* more important.

INCREASING PROGRAM FLEXIBILITY	—: —: —:: —: —: —	MAKING PROGRAMS MORE COST-EFFECTIVE
IMPROVING THE USE OF EDUCATION TAX DOLLARS	—: —: —:: —: —: —	GREATER EQUALIZATION OF RESOURCES
MORE EFFICIENT SCHOOL MANAGEMENT	—: —: —:: —: —: —	PROVIDING MORE CHOICES FOR FAMILIES AND CHILDREN
MAKING PROGRAMS MORE COST-EFFECTIVE	—: —: —:: —: —: —	SETTING HIGHER ACADEMIC STANDARDS
REDUCING RESTRICTIONS ON LOCAL EXPENDITURES	—: —: —:: —: —: —	IMPROVING THE USE OF EDUCATION TAX DOLLARS

INCREASING PROGRAM FLEXIBILITY —: —: —:: —: —: — GIVING MORE ATTENTION TO CHILDREN WITH SPECIAL NEEDS

INCREASING THE LEVEL OF FUNDING FOR SCHOOLS —: —: —:: —: —: — GREATER EQUALIZATION OF RESOURCES

BROADER PARTICIPATION IN DECISION-MAKING —: —: —:: —: —: — MORE EFFICIENT SCHOOL MANAGEMENT

GIVING MORE ATTENTION TO CHILDREN WITH SPECIAL NEEDS —: —: —:: —: —: — SETTING HIGHER ACADEMIC STANDARDS

REDUCING RESTRICTIONS ON LOCAL EXPENDITURES SCHOOLS —: —: —:: —: —: — INCREASING THE LEVEL OF FUNDING FOR SCHOOLS

DEVELOPING QUALITY CONSCIOUS LEADERSHIP —: —: —:: —: —: — PROVIDING MORE CHOICES FOR FAMILIES AND CHILDREN

SETTING HIGHER ACADEMIC STANDARDS —: —: —:: —: —: — INCREASING PROGRAM FLEXIBILITY

GREATER EQUALIZATION OF RESOURCES —: —: —:: —: —: — REDUCING RESTRICTIONS ON LOCAL EXPENDITURES

PROVIDING MORE CHOICES —: —: —:: —: —: — BROADER PARTICIPATION IN DECISION-MAKING

MORE EFFICIENT SCHOOL MANAGEMENT	—: —: —:: —: —: —	DEVELOPING QUALITY CONSCIOUS LEADERSHIP
GIVING MORE ATTENTION TO CHILDREN WITH SPECIAL NEEDS	—: —: —:: —: —: —	MAKING PROGRAMS MORE COST-EFFECTIVE
IMPROVING THE USE OF EDUCATION TAX DOLLARS	—: —: —:: —: —: —	INCREASING THE LEVEL OF FUNDING FOR SCHOOLS
DEVELOPING QUALITY CONSCIOUS LEADERSHIP	—: —: —:: —: —: —	BROADER PARTICIPATION IN DECISION-MAKING

Appendix G: Perceptions of Influences in State Policy-making

PLEASE CIRCLE A NUMBER FROM 1 TO 7 TO INDICATE THE LEVEL OF INFLUENCE OVER EDUCATION POLICY EXERCISED DURING THE LAST FEW YEARS BY EACH OF THE FOLLOWING IN YOUR STATE:

		Very Low	Very High
a.	The Governor and the Executive Staff	1–2–3–4–5–6–7	
b.	The Chief State School Officer and Senior Staff in the State Department of Education	1–2–3–4–5–6–7	
c.	The State Board of Education	1–2–3–4–5–6–7	
d.	The State Legislature	1–2–3–4–5–6–7	
	1. Leading Members of Legislative Committees	1–2–3–4–5–6–7	
	2. Key Legislative Staff Consultants	1–2–3–4–5–6–7	
e.	All the Education Interest Groups Combined	1–2–3–4–5–6–7	
	1. The Teacher Organization(s)	1–2–3–4–5–6–7	
	2. The State Administrator Organization(s)	1–2–3–4–5–6–7	
	3. The State Association of Local School Boards	1–2–3–4–5–6–7	
	4. Lay Groups (PTA, advisory councils, etc.)	1–2–3–4–5–6–7	
f.	Non-Educator Interest Groups (business leaders, tax-payer groups, etc.)	1–2–3–4–5–6–7	
g.	Producers of Education Related Products (textbook manufacturers, test producers, etc.)	1–2–3–4–5–6–7	
h.	Direct Referenda Initiated by Citizens	1–2–3–4–5–6–7	
i.	The Courts (State or Federal)	1–2–3–4–5–6–7	
j.	Federal Policy Mandates to the States	1–2–3–4–5–6–7	
k.	Education Research Organizations	1–2–3–4–5–6–7	
l.	Any Others: _____	1–2–3–4–5–6–7	

Appendix H: Perceptions of Political Culture

HOW DO PEOPLE IN YOUR STATE VIEW GOVERNMENT?

Around the country people view government and politics in different ways. These differences may affect education policy. Would you please give us your perceptions of how people in your state feel. Please place a '1' beside the phrase that *best* completes each of the following statements. Place a '2' beside the second best phrase, and a '3' beside the least descriptive phrase. Remember, we are seeking your perception of how people in your state generally feel about these matters.

1. *Generally speaking, government is viewed as . . .*
   —something like a marketplace, where policy demands and political resources are exchanged.
   —a means for achieving a good community through goal-setting and program development.
   —a means of maintaining the existing social order through laws and regulations.

2. *The most appropriate sphere of government activity is seen as . . .*
   —economic — support for private initiative, guaranteeing contracts, economic development, etc.
   —community enhancement — public services, community development, social and economic regulation, etc.
   —maintenance of traditional social patterns and norms — setting social standards, enforcing separation of private and public sector activity, etc.

3. *Governmental programs are generally initiated when . . .*
   —public demand is strong and direct.
   —political leaders identify community needs.
   —they serve the interests of those in power.

4. *Governmental bureaucracies are viewed . . .*
   —ambivalently — they are efficient but interfere with direct political control over public services.

—positively — they insure political neutrality and effectiveness in the delivery of public services.

—negatively — they depersonalize government and reduce overall program performance.

5. *Civil service or merit systems for government employees are . . .*
   —accepted in principle, but poorly implemented.
   —broadly supported and well implemented.
   —rejected as interfering with needed political control.

6. *Generally, the public views politics as . . .*
   —a distasteful or dirty business — left to those who are willing to engage in that sort of thing.
   —an important healthy part of every citizen's civic duty.
   —an activity for special groups of people with unique qualifications.

7. *Politics is viewed as an activity for . . .*
   —political party professionals.
   —all citizens.
   —members of civic, economic, family, or other élite groups.

8. *Political parties are seen as . . .*
   —business organizations — organizing political interest groups; providing rewards and assigning responsibilities.
   —issue oriented groups — articulating goals and mobilizing support for programs.

9. *Membership in the political parties is . . .*
   —pragmatic but loyal — the parties are coalitions of interest groups.
   —subordinate to principles and issues — creating tenuous loyalty to the parties.
   —based on historic family, ethnic, social, economic ties — creating strong traditional loyalties to the party.

10. *Competition among the parties is . . .*
    —active, but not over issues or ideological principles.
    —focused on issues, philosophy, or basic principles.
    —primarily between élite-dominated factions within the party.

11. *The dominant aim of party competition appears to be . . .*
    —winning offices and other tangible rewards.
    —gaining broad support for a program or policy.
    —extending the control of particular élite groups.

Appendix I: Personal Data Form

PERSONAL DATA
Please check the appropriate response to each of the following questions about yourself:

1.   How long have you held your present position?
     —Less than 2 years.   —8 to 10 years.
     —2 to 4 years.   —11 or more years.
     —5 to 7 years.

2.   How old are you?
     —Less than 30.   —50 to 59.
     —30 to 39.   —60 or older.
     —40 to 49.

3.   What do you consider to be your regular occupation?—

4.   Which of the following degrees do you hold? (Indicate all degrees held).
     —BA or BS —— Major:—
     —MA or MS —— Field:—
     —PhD or EdD —— Field:—
     —Law Degree

5.   Are you professionally licensed in any of the following fields?
     —Teaching   —School Administration   —Nursing
     —Law   —Engineer/Architecture   —Medicine/Dentistry
     —Psychology   —Other:—

6.   What is your political party affiliation?
     —Democrat   —Republican   —Independent   —Other   —None

7.   How would you describe your overall political orientation?
               —Strongly conservative
               —Moderately conservative
               —Moderate

—Moderately liberal
—Strongly liberal

8.   What is the range of your current family income?

—$25,000 or less   —$55,001 to $65,000
—$25,001 to $35,000   —$65,001 to $75,000
—$35,001 to $45,000   —$75,001 to $85,000
—$45,001 to $55,000   —More than $85,000

Appendix J: Content Analysis of Education Codes

STATE CODE INDEX BY SPMs

Code: _____   State: _____

Section	Description	SPM	Public Value EF — EQ — QU — CH

Index